D0221454

PUERTO RICAN CHICAGO

PUERTO RICAN CHICAGO

Felix M. Padilla

UNIVERSITY OF NOTRE DAME PRESS
NOTRE DAME, INDIANA

Library of Congress Cataloging-in-Publication Data

Padilla, Felix M.
    Puerto Rican Chicago.

    Bibliography: p.
    Includes index.
    1. Puerto Ricans—Illinois—Chicago—History.
2. Chicago (Ill.)—Ethnic relations.   I. Title.
F548.9.P85P33   1987   977.3'11004687295   86-40244
ISBN 0-268-01564-3

This book is dedicated, properly so,
to my two daughters, Star and April.
At a time of despair
for Puerto Rican ethnic and cultural traditions,
they continue to renew my faith in the future.

Contents

Acknowledgments   ix

Introduction   1

1. The Beginnings of Marginalization: The Migration Experience   23

   The Hacienda Economy   23
   American Agricultural Capitalism   29
   American Industrialism   45

2. Growth of the Puerto Rican Barrio and Intensification of
   Ethnic Subordination   56

   Racial Minority Stereotype   56
   Nostalgia and Disenchantment: Considerations
      on Returning to the Island   66
   The Puerto Rican Family and Friendship Network   72
   First Barrios   78
   The Division Street Area   83

3. Organizational Response to Ethnic Oppression   99

   Chicago's Social and Economic Conditions   99
   The Puerto Rican Working Class   110
   Racial Friction Flareups   117
      Housing Discrimination   117
      Police Injustice   123
   Organizational Response among Puerto Ricans,
      1950–1965   125
      Los Caballeros de San Juan   126
      The Migrant Press   137

4. **Evolution and Resolution of Conflict**   144

Riots on Division Street   144
Rise of a Politicized Ethnic Consciousness   155
  Staff Activism   162
  Advisory Council Activism   165
The Repression of Protest   168

5. **Institutionalization of the Ethnic Minority Classification**   180

The Growth of an Educated Elite   180
The Professionalization of Community Organization   190
Strategies for Overcoming Inequality   194
  Machine Politics   194
  Clientele Politics   200
  The Emergence of Latino Solidarity   204
The Salience of Puerto Rican Ethnicity   208
  The Problem of the "Dropout"   209
  "They're Burning El Barrio" and the Problem of
    Gentrification   214

Conclusion   222
Prospects for the Future   225

Notes   241

References   253

Index   269

Acknowledgments

I am deeply indebted to hundreds of individuals from the Puerto Rican community in Chicago who shared with me their lifetime of experience in this city. They really wanted to assure the preparation and completion of this book. My hope is that the study will re-pay, in part, their commitment and generosity. They are all wonderful people. To thank them all would require a chapter of its own. Some, however, to whom I owe the greatest debt, must be thanked here.

The book would not have been written were it not for the unpublished collection of papers, files, and records of several individuals and organizations. Mr. Gabino Moyet, a former member of Los Caballeros de San Juan, the first major community organization established to service Puerto Ricans in Chicago, invited me to examine the records of this organization. He also spent many hours sharing with me his recollections of the days when Los Caballeros were indeed the voice of the Puerto Rican community in Chicago. To Mr. Moyet, *un millón de gracias*.

Mrs. Janice Nolan also shared her own collection of interviews (over 3,000 written pages of field notes) which she collected during the summer and fall of 1966 while directing and working for a research project for the University of Notre Dame. I owe a great deal to Mrs. Nolan.

I owe much to Mr. Alfredo Torres de Jesus for allowing me to use his collection of one of the first Puerto Rican newspapers published in Chicago.

I wish to express my special thanks to Mr. Juan Díaz, a leader in the Puerto Rican community for over thirty years, for his graciousness in giving me time to talk to him for endless hours. Mr Juan Díaz acted as a "volunteer research associate," supplying countless anecdotes and insights into the Puerto Rican experience in Chicago which were a continuing source of instruction and help.

Patricia Villareal and Melissa Arndt, two of my former graduate assistants at the Center for Latino and Latin American Studies, Northern Illinois University, enhanced this study through their enduring commitment to find some of its most important facts. I also appreciate their dedication, friendship, good conversations, and ideas. Special thanks go to both.

I also want to thank some of my friends and colleagues, like Alfredo Mirandé, Jim Pitts, Howard Becker, and Joan Moore, who read parts of the manuscript. They made me aware of some very important points.

To José Hernández Álvarez, a senior scholar and student of the Puerto Rican experience: *Muchas gracias* for reading the entire book; your comments contributed immensely in making this study a truly fine sociological story.

These individuals, and many others, were all my teachers in this project. I should like, however, to pay special tribute to my wife, Beatrice A. Padilla, the most influential teacher I have had. In fourteen years of sharing life together, there has hardly been a day when I have not learned from her—lessons about how to love and how to give of oneself, which is to say, how to live as a sensitive and caring human being. Drawing upon her experience of growing up in Chicago as a second-generation Puerto Rican woman and her expertise as a classroom teacher, she profoundly influenced the content and tone of the book. Beatrice took valuable time from her own demanding academic activities to give me detailed criticisms. This is her book as well as mine.

Introduction

The Spanish-speaking in the United States today are one of this country's fastest-growing populations. As a group, Mexicans in the Southwest, Puerto Ricans in the Northeast, Cubans in the Southeast, together with Spanish-speaking communities in other areas represent the nation's second-largest minority. There has been increasing speculation that they will surpass blacks as the most numerous minority group in the country in the not too distant future. During the 1970s this group came to occupy a prominent place in the national consciousness—an awareness directly reflected in an upsurge of literature, conferences, symposia, and even new university departments and/or centers dealing with the experiences of Spanish-speaking populations in urban America.

The news media contributed enormously in alerting the American public to the "coming of these new Americans." *Time* magazine's lead article in the fall of 1978 is a classic example. Suggesting that the 1980s would represent the "Decade of the Hispanics," this article predicted that "Hispanics' very number guarantee that they will play an increasingly important role in shaping the nation's politics and policies . . . [and] just as black power was a reality in the 1960s, so the quest for Latino power may well become a political watchword of the decade ahead" (1978:48). Four years earlier, *U.S. News and World Report* carried a story noting that at a "rate of more than half a million a year, Latin immigrants [were] spreading across the U.S. — with increasing impact on the nation's life and culture" (1974:19).[1]

Despite the emergence of this so-called Latin American or Latino "Awakening," the story of some of the groups comprising

1

this wider scale unit or category remains untold. Puerto Ricans in Chicago are part of this "forgotten minority," to borrow the phrase popularized by Mexican American scholars in the 1970s. Although Puerto Ricans have lived in this midwest metropolis for almost five decades, a systematic study of their way of life is still lacking today. It is surprising to find that in the city of Chicago—the leading "laboratory of community studies," pioneered by Robert Park and Ernest Burgess—there is such a paucity of scholarly research on the Puerto Rican population. The few scattered first-hand observations touch only sporadically and casually on particular aspects of their lives.[2] Yet their cultural survival and vigorous resistance to complete assimilation, long after ethnic affiliation had been written off by social scientists as a viable entity in modern industrial societies, is another reason for wanting to learn more about the Spanish-speaking group. The salience and persistence of Puerto Rican ethnicity in urban America holds untold lessons for social scientists working in the field of race and ethnic relations.

The present study is an attempt to fill this void. The story of Puerto Ricans in Chicago is, above all, a case study of a conquered, colonized, economically marginal people and their efforts to achieve equality, respectability, recognition, and legitimacy amid difficult conditions. Their struggle against racial/ethnic oppression and their quest for self-determination began after the military conquest and colonial subjugation of their homeland in 1898, and continues today, not only in Puerto Rico, but in a number of major American urban areas like Chicago and New York.

The methodology employed in this examination provided a context in which first- and second-generation respondents could reveal their way of life as Puerto Ricans in Chicago without the constraint of specific questions.[3] The interviews were as unstructured and spontaneous as possible in hopes that this method would increase the possibility for establishing normal, routine conversations as well as promoting exchange of ideas with the respondents. All of the study participants presented autobiographical accounts of their individual and social lives (oral histories), organized around experiences with major institutions: family, school, work, police, politics, etc. Several of the respondents who were or had been affiliated with different community organizations permitted me to examine certain organization records and documents. Other sources of information, such as personal letters, poems, music, films, and local newspaper stories—all of which are part of a people's way of expressing their life—were also used.

I met many of the respondents during twelve months of field work which I spent collecting data for another research project on the emergence and growth of Latino ethnic identity and mobilization in Chicago (Padilla, 1985). Other participants were acquaintances, neighbors, and co-workers from the Puerto Rican community. I have lived in *el barrio* (the name given to a Puerto Rican ethnic enclave or neighborhood) for most of my adult life. After coming from Puerto Rico at the age of thirteen I attended high school in el barrio; I worked for a community organization and served as advisor, consultant, and member of the board of directors of other organizations there; I taught high school in one of the schools of the neighborhood. While many statements in the text are thus based on my familiarity with the development of the Puerto Rican community in Chicago, most are the result of extensive consultation with a wide variety of information sources. In all cases, reports of the ideological sentiments of the participants are based on either written or oral evidence obtained from many actors speaking from various perspectives.

Not only did my firsthand experience with the life problems and needs of the community help provide better understanding of the relevant techniques of analysis for this study, it strongly recommended that these hardships be the starting points for both the theoretical perspective and the research design of this study. The needs, wants, ideas, and goals of the Puerto Rican community could not be ignored. I knew of the urgency to provide an alternative picture: one that could really be called a Puerto Rican perspective. I also knew that such a perspective could not be established simply by using the study participants as objects or as means to my own ends. Their stories, the way they perceive themselves and others, their relationships with family members, neighbors, co-workers, and other individuals outside their primary groups—this was the information I would use. In a real sense, then, this book represents the collaboration between a Puerto Rican sociologist and the Puerto Rican people of the city of Chicago.

In general, this study examines the evolution of the Puerto Rican ethnic consciousness in Chicago. More specifically I will trace and analyze the changes in Puerto Rican ethnic-conscious behavior from the emerging sense of "nationality" at the time of the American takeover to the conversion of a stigmatized status as a racial minority into a positive sense of ethnic consciousness.[4] This growth in ethnic consciousness and behavior will be related to two major conditions. The first condition is the Puerto Ricans' status as a colonized people, while the second is related to what I perceive to be internal organizational responses among Puerto Ricans to structural factors and conditions emanating primarily from social, political, and community-related issues, disputes, or conflicts with members of the dominant American society. Correspondingly, I will combine two complementary theoretical models to form a general conceptual scheme. First, it will be argued that the experience of Puerto Ricans in Chicago is a clear case of internal colonialism. And, the oppressive conditions of the Puerto Rican community resulting from its status as an internal colony have given rise to continuing ethnic-conscious efforts toward "decolonization" — toward winning self-determination, reestablishing self-pride, self-dignity, and self-worth, and gaining greater control over their community while maintaining their collective identity.

Generally, internal colonialism has been used as an analog to classic colonialism (Moore, 1970; Barrera, 1979). According to Robert Blauner, "classical colonialism traditionally refers to the establishment of domination over a geographically external political unit, most often inhabited by people of a different race and culture, where this domination is political and economic, and the colony exists subordinated to and dependent upon the mother country" (1969:395). Internal colonialism, on the other hand, will refer to a relationship of socioeconomic exploitation, subordination, and inequality within the borders of the imperialistic power, which enhances the position of the dominant group. In the words of Gonzalez-Casanova, a Mexican social scientist, "internal colonialism corresponds to a structure of social relations based on domination and exploitation among culturally heterogenous, distinct groups" (1965:33). Similarly, in his elaborate description of internal colonialism, Hechter stresses (1975:9):

The spatially uneven wave of modernization over state territory creates relatively advanced and less advanced groups. As a consequence of this initial fortuitous advantage, there is a crystallization of the unequal distribution of resources and power between the two groups. . . . This stratification system, which may be termed a cultural division of labor, contributes to the development of distinctive ethnic identification in the two groups.

The classic colonialism of the American conquest of the Puerto Rican nation resulted from the United States' involvement and subsequent victory in the Spanish American War. The dying Spanish empire, which had colonized and ruled Puerto Rico for nearly 400 years, was no competition for the more technologically advanced American military forces. Although Spain had granted Puerto Rico an "autonomous" status in 1897 after much pressure from the Puerto Rican people, this newly won standing was simply ignored by the United States. The peace treaty which ended the war awarded Puerto Rico and several other colonial possessions once controlled by Spain to the United States. In effect, after 1898 Puerto Rico reverted to the status of colony. The only difference was that now the colonial "master" was the United States.

The American colonization of the Puerto Rican people was a multifaceted process—political, economic, social, racial, cultural, ideological psychological, etc. The political and technological superiority of the colonial metropolis was at once established. "This objective supremacy," writes Robert Blauner in reference to non-Western and non-white people in general, "buttressed the West's sense of cultural superiority, laying the basis for racist ideologies that were elaborated to justify control and exploitation of non-white people" (1969:84). Although there may have been a very limited settlement of Anglo Americans in Puerto Rico, there was indeed a formal recognition of differing powers. To this day, most of Puerto Rico's political and economic decisions are made by Washington's politicians and bureaucrats, who tend to view their subjects as inherently alien, culturally degenerate, and biologically inferior. Thus, despite the absence of a wide-scale Anglo settlement in Puerto Rico, the control and exploitation of Puerto Ricans still continues today.

American colonialism, like all other forms of colonialism, was not a system of control and subordination which was simply imposed on the Puerto Rican people as an end in itself. Driven by an intense desire for territorial and economic expansion, the United States wasted little time in adding Puerto Rican land, raw materials, and labor to its growing empire. Puerto Rican *jibaros* and *campesinos* (peasants) were paid low wages for producing export crops. American imperialists secured a source of extra profits through investments as well as by establishing a monopoly-controlled market for the import of their manufactured goods.[5] To further enhance and secure control of the colony, the United States extended American citizenship and imposed an educational system centered around the learning of the English language and acquisition of the American culture.

The shift from "classical colonialism" to "internal colonialism" occurred with emigration and the establishment of Puerto Rican barrios in different American mainland cities. After the takeover of Puerto Rico, the new "colonial masters" transformed Puerto Rico's multi-crop agricultural economy into a technologically based, single cash-crop industry; several decades later it was changed again and built around a factory system which was capital- and not people-oriented. Because of their nature, these economic changes failed to provide jobs for an ever-increasing population, resulting, in turn, in a large-scale uprooting and forced exile of hundreds of thousands of people from their native land because of urgent economic needs. In a very real sense, then, in addition to creating a colony in the Puerto Rican national territory, American imperialist expansion resulted in the transplantation of that colonial system into various mainland cities.

The definition of Puerto Ricans as an internal colony can be specified on at least two levels. At the institutional or interpersonal level, internal colonialism means that Puerto Ricans exist in an exploited condition which is maintained by their lack of control over those decisive factors in the institutions which affect their lives. These institutions as a rule are administrated by outsiders, or at best, those who serve the interests of outsiders. For example, the schools in el barrio are administered by whites; whites teach in the classroom and design the curriculum — not to meet the needs of Puerto Ricans but to Americanize them. The major businesses and industries located in el barrio are not only owned by whites, but more importantly, the capital that could be used to improve the economic situation within el barrio is taken into white sectors in much the same way that capital is drained from Puerto Rico by American industrial imperialists. Further, el barrio represents a very important supply of cheap labor. In short, these conditions of exploitation have resulted in the Puerto Rican community finding itself locked into low incomes, poor housing, inadequate health care, and low educational levels.[6] In a comparative light, Reich's summary of black ghetto exploitation seems equivalent to the case of Puerto Ricans:

> Blacks pay higher rent for inferior housing, higher prices in ghetto stores, higher insurance premiums, higher interest rates in banks and lending companies, travel longer distances at greater expense to their jobs, suffer from inferior garbage collection and less access to public recreational facilities, and are assessed at higher property tax rates when they own housing. (1977:57)

At the individual level, American colonial subjugation results in the dehumanization or cultural exploitation of the Puerto Rican. Puerto Rican individuals find themselves under constant psychological assault. Take the case of Puerto Rican school children for example. They are reminded daily of the inferiority of their culture; they are scorned for speaking Spanish in school; they are placed in bilingual classes to learn the language and values of the dominant American society as fast as possible. These children are made to feel ashamed of their Puerto Rican cultural traditions; they are consistently belittled, diminishing their sense of personal worth and dignity. A similar argument as to cultural exploitation is presented by Cabral in his *National Liberation and Culture* (1970). He views culture as an essential element in the history of a people: it is simultaneously the fruit of a people's history and the determinant of that history. Imperialist domination violently usurps the free operation of the process of development of the productive forces. It thereby negates the historical process of the dominated people, as well as their cultural development.

These and other features of the internal colonial status have fostered a Puerto Rican consciousness and solidarity. Puerto Ricans have had to defend their ethnic/cultural personality and integrity and they have responded by proclaiming the validity of their own culture as the basis of distinctive identity and as resistance to domination. Puerto Rican ethnicity has served as the leading medium for overcoming the attacks directed against their ethnic/cultural foundation. A sense of Puerto Rican ethnic/cultural identity and behavior (*El Puertorriqueñismo*) has come to affirm the values of the Puerto Rican way of life positively and in their own right. El Puertorriqueñismo expresses the distinctive qualities of what are assumed to be the common elements in the Puerto Rican culture and traditional way of life. The contents of El Puertorriqueñismo may be developed independent of the characterizations of white racism, or with keen awareness of, and in reaction to, these characterizations.

The second major theoretical component of my conceptual scheme asserts that the sense and accelerated growth of Puerto Rican ethnic conscious identity and behavior have developed from conditions of both first contact and continuous interaction between this Spanish-speaking group and the dominant society. In other words, Puerto Rican ethnicity results, in part, from interactions and not isolation, as Fredrik Barth (1969) and others have long argued about the salience of ethnic behavior and action the world over. My approach is analagous to Blumer's theory of racial prejudice:[7]

> An analysis of how the sense of group position [in my case group identity] is formed should start with a clear recognition that it is an historical product. It is set originally by conditions of initial contact. Prestige, power, possession of skill, numbers, original self-conceptions, aims, designs and opportunities are a few of the factors that may fashion the original sense of group position. Subsequent experience in the relations of the racial groups, especially in the areas of claims, opportunities and advantages may mold the sense of group position in many diverse ways. (1958:5)

More importantly, the interactions and/or conflicts between Puerto Ricans and whites revolve around socio-political issues, as in housing discrimination, access to educational opportunities, police injustice and brutality, and the like. The approach I am following in this study differs from that which dominates contemporary scholarly thought on the topic of inter-group relations in the United States in regard to the effect of the economic order in the shaping of group relations. It is the general assumption of prevailing theoretical and conceptual orientations that inter-group competition in the labor market is responsible for shaping and expanding the scope of ethnic identities and increasing their intensity. Professor William Wilson provides a concise summary of this perspective:

> Students of race relations have paid considerable attention to the economic basis of racial antagonism in recent years, particularly to the theme that racial problems in historical situations are related to the more general problems of economic class conflict. A common assumption of this theme is that racial conflict is merely a special manifestation of class conflict. Accordingly, ideologies of racism, racial prejudices, institutional discrimination, segregation, and other factors that reinforce or embody racial stratifications are seen as simply part of a super-structure determined and shaped by the particular arrangement of the class structure. (1980:4)

An examination of Bonacich's (1972 and 1976) "split labor market" theory of ethnic antagonism, a popular and leading component of this wider framework, provides a more detailed insight into this argument. A basic thesis advanced by Bonacich is that "ethnic antagonism first germinates in a labor market split along ethnic lines" (1972:549). Under this circumstance, "high-priced labor" takes protective action to prevent scabbing and wage cutting by "low-priced, other-ethnic labor." Victory for more expensive labor takes the form of exclusion of low-priced, other-ethnic labor from the territory, or caste exclusion of low-priced workers from high-priced sectors. Victory for cheap labor displaces high-wage workers from their industries or occupations (Bonacich, 1976:41). In sum, Bonacich argues that the new conflict-ridden situation is likely to resemble a "split labor market" in which newcomer ethnics form a cheap labor threat to incumbent old-ethnics.

The case of Puerto Ricans in Chicago suggests that despite forming part of a "split labor market" as another pool of cheap labor, their racial conflicts with whites have originated outside the economic order and have had little connection with labor-market strife.[8] Having migrated to Chicago already stigmatized as economically marginal people Puerto Ricans secured primarily the low-paying and dead-end jobs of the rapidly declining blue-collar economic sector — non-corporate, non-technological jobs which were not in high demand and which therefore did not generate racial or ethnic competition or strife. In other words, Puerto Rican arrival in Chicago coincided with the growth and expansion of industrial technology, a period which, in the view of Professor Wilson (1980:97), was primarily responsible for increasing the number of workers victimized by technological unemployment. The expansion of industrial technology began to sharply decrease the need for semiskilled or unskilled labor in the factory. In the face of this decreasing demand, Puerto Ricans entering the labor market for the first time found it increasingly difficult to obtain employment in the expanding industrial-technological sector. Thus the Puerto Rican entry point into Chicago's economic order was primarily in specific occupations and industries abandoned and/or not desired by "old-ethnic labor." Puerto Rican workers came to do the dirty work of this and other American cities — the work no other group was willing to perform. Puerto Rican workers were not used by employers or management to undercut wages of other ethnic labor. Unlike black and Mexican labor before them, to cite two analogous cases, Puerto Ricans were not even considered as strike-breakers during times of management and labor disputes. Puerto Ricans in Chicago serve as a "non-competing group." Their economic status has been characteristic of a reserve labor pool, to be used when all other workers are employed and there still remains a labor shortage. In other words, many Puerto Ricans are permanently jobless, and correctly perceive their chances of working as contingent only on everyone else having a job. For this reason, in addition to the officially "unemployed," thousands of Puerto Ricans are out of the labor force, or economically inactive. Thus they are separate from members of other working classes, producing very little racial/ethnic tension in the workplace.

Throughout the years in Chicago and in other cities of settlement, Puerto Ricans have been denied access to the skilled and higher-paying jobs of corporate industries and of the expanding government sector by cultural and racial discrimination and segregation.[9] Thus, racial problems between Puerto Ricans and whites have not been related to group struggles over economic resources but, rather, to the exploitation of Puerto Rican labor. The development of a Puerto Rican middle class in the second generation, and the legal pressure put on by Affirmative Action programs and other similar policies contributed significantly to overcoming some of the barriers during the 1970s, but only for a very small and select group of educated individuals. However, because the rise of this emerging middle class of teachers, businessmen, social service workers, and organizers resulted primarily from the expansion of institutions and organizations created to serve the needs of a growing Puerto Rican population, many of these professionals remained segregated in the barrios or within particular occupations in certain firms and industries. Even if there were cases where these developments can be said to have caused labor market strifes between the more privileged Puerto Ricans and whites, the Puerto Rican underclass is a different matter. The Puerto Rican poor, including the growing number of younger Puerto Ricans emerging from inferior barrio schools, find themselves locked in the low wage sector of the labor market (i.e. in operative, laborer, and service-worker categories) with little opportunity for advancement and a high rate of job turnover.

This study advances the argument that the acceleration of industrial-technological growth and expansion, which coincided with the mass arrival of Puerto Ricans in Chicago did not give rise to manifestations of racial antagonism between Puerto Ricans and whites in the work place. It is true that increasing numbers of Puerto Ricans did in fact confront whites in new relationships, sometimes as a consequence of economic change, but more often this intergroup relation occurred in non-economic contexts. The vast majority of Puerto Ricans were hardly affected by the rapidly expanding technological order or any other major change process, and consequently their confrontations with whites came in the socio-political arena. In a manner similar to Castell (1976a and 1976b), Lojkine (1977), and Harvey (1978), this study emphasizes that a key element of the capital-vs.-labor struggle occurs outside the work site, over the reproduction of labor power (through biological and socialization processes) and provision of collective consumption (e.g. housing, transportation, and education). Thus, the class struggle originating in the work process is "displaced" into community living space and institutions. As Harvey states (1978:117–118): "The conditions of life in the community are of great import to the working class and they can therefore become a focus of struggle which can assume a certain relative automony from that waged in the factory. The institutions of community can be captured and put to work for working class ends. . . . The principle of community can then become a springboard for class actions rather than an antidote to class struggle."

From this point of view, Puerto Ricans, unlike their European predecessors, entered an American economic context not suited for the creation of class-conscious workers' movement on the factory floor—the place where the primary contradiction of capitalism is seen to be most intense. Instead, Puerto Ricans have had to rely on the strength of ethnic identity and solidarity to establish a movement based primarily on community interests. The concentration of Puerto Ricans in certain jobs of the city's economic order frustrated their efforts to create class unity across racial/ethnic lines. As a result of having been cut off from the mainstream of the working class movement, a continuous intra-ethnic unity and solidarity development between the emerging Puerto Rican middle class and the Puerto Rican working labor force, and both groups expressed their class interests in explicitly ethnic terms.

It is important to elaborate two major points related to the conceptual scheme used in this study. The present use of the colonial analogy (that is, internal colonialism) will undoubtedly be resisted by mainstream American social scientists. These scholars may very well conclude that the internal colonial model has outlived its usefulness and that it is now time to turn to newer and broader formulations.

While the conditions in which Puerto Ricans find themselves in the United States can not be precisely defined in classical colonial terms, they are similar enough that the internal colonial model is useful in assessing some of these conditions. Previous research on Puerto Ricans in the United States (particularly those living in the barrios of the Northeast), conducted primarily by Anglo social scientists, has failed to answer the most compelling questions about the incorporation, or non-corporation, of Puerto Ricans into the mainland society. To suggest that this process of incorporation merely involves the emigration of Puerto Ricans from the Island-nation to the United States ignores the fact of colonial domination. If, for example, Puerto Ricans represent a typical group of emigrants, then why do they remain at the bottom of society's economic and political structures seven decades after entering American society? Why are Puerto Ricans not fully integrated in the institutional life of the society? What are the reasons for the unequal participation among Puerto Ricans in those systems and structures which we are told are integrative by nature?

The most common explanation given is that Puerto Rican deprivation is the function of flaws in the Puerto Rican culture. Built around the culture of poverty thesis, such explanations claim that the pathology found in the behavior patterns of Puerto Ricans is not only an inherent element of their cultural tradition, but more importantly, it tends to prevent them from taking advantage of opportunity structures (i.e. achieving high levels of education, using the electoral political process, etc.). In other words, this explanation suggests that by their own culture Puerto Ricans generate their own problems, and this impedes their material advancement. Thus economic determinism has been equated with cultural determinism, as suggested by Oscar Lewis (1965) and other scholars. Such distorted answers suggest that conventional theories and concepts have proven woefully inadequate in explaining the manner of participation of a segment of the Puerto Rican working class in the institutional life of the colonial metropolis.

The inadequacies of these and similar explanations of Puerto Rican life stem from the fact that the colonization of Puerto Rico and its direct consequences on Puerto Ricans in the Island and mainland, for the most part, have remained unexamined. While social scientists must agree that Puerto Ricans were conquered militarily, some would also conclude that as American citizens they simply represent another volunteer group of migrants. Thus, Puerto Ricans have been expected to follow the same assimilation path of earlier immigrants, who came to the United States voluntarily in search of economic opportunities and/or political freedom, and subsequently, became fully integrated in mainstream America (see Fitzpatrick, 1971).

In contrast, I argue that a deep understanding of the Puerto Rican experience must take into account the multifaceted impact colonization has had and continues to have on the lives of this Spanish-speaking population. For example, the mass wave of the Puerto Rican working class that of necessity traveled to the colonial metropolis for economic survival must be viewed, first and foremost, as a mobile labor force displaced from its homeland by American colonialism and capitalism. In general, for Puerto Ricans, colonization has been responsible for the way they've organized their lives, that is, for their way of existing and survival. As in the case of Mexicans, I concur with Mirandé's view that "colonization is not a theory but rather a historical fact and a way of life" (1985:193). I also find Mirandé's rationale for integrating the legacy of colonization into theory of Chicano sociology applicable to the Puerto Rican experience:[10]

> Its inclusion is called for not because it is a more adequate theory but because it is consonant with our historical experience . . . it is one of the broadest units that differentiates Chicano from mainstream sociology. I contend that any theory of Chicanos, whether on a macro or micro level, Marxist or culturalist, must take into account the colonization of the Chicano. To do otherwise is to ignore history. In the same way that any theory of black oppression must consider the legacy of slavery, so must we consider our legacy of conquest. (1982:499)

When it is recognized that Puerto Rican life in American society is filled with common features of internal colonialism, one can begin to understand why Puerto Ricans have adapted a set of political survival strategies very different from those employed by European ethnics. In the main, Puerto Rican survival has revolved around a Puerto Rican struggle of liberation.[11] which again stands in sharp contrast to the strategy of assimilation. The desire to be fully incorporated into the mainstream of American life or the idea of becoming just ordinary Americans, often pursued by European immigrants and their descendents, has never been the strong suit of the Puerto Rican people. Instead this Spanish-speaking population has stressed consistently a reevaluation of the Puerto Rican cultural tradition and social institutions and a commitment to their continuation and development both within el barrio and the mainstream.

Since their first arrival in Chicago, an impressive cultural ferment has been taking place between Puerto Rican cultural tradition and identity and the individual's relationship to American society, a ferment that has informed public and private discourse, political and personal action, and art and literature. A particularly characteristic expression of this trend has been the bilingual education and Puerto Rican Studies movements, a struggle within education for the recognition of the Puerto Rican experience (see chapter five). Yet another illustration can be inferred from the behavior pattern of the Puerto Rican youth of today. Even though they are second-generation, and in other instances third-generation, the Puerto Rican youth in the 1980s are expressing an almost mystical faith in the dignity of the Puerto Rican people. As will be shown in the conclusion of this book, complete assimilation has become unacceptable for this new generation of Puerto Ricans. They are expressing very clearly an unwillingness to assimilate into an American culture they believe stands for the "dehumanization" of the individual person. Further, they are very conscious, perhaps more so than the emigrant generation, of the continuous negative results experienced by non-white groups who have come up against the system of American racism. The Puerto Rican of today wishes to "make it" in America, but to still retain the dignity and pride of Puerto Rican cultural life.

Absorbed within the sphere of the United States mainland life for many years, Puerto Ricans in Chicago, New York, and elsewhere have experienced a particular form of racial, ethnic/cultural oppression. Unlike voluntary immigrants from Europe, Puerto Ricans have been prevented and/or have chosen not to melt into the "American pot" nor accept the tenets of total assimilation. Experiences of severe race and cultural discrimination have led Puerto Ricans to reaffirm their ethnic/cultural distinctiveness, and from the commonality of oppression they have forged their own ethnic movements of liberation.

In this light, the ethnic/cultural base of the Puerto Rican struggle of liberation becomes understandable. When an oppressed people becomes aware of its oppression, yet sees no secular or "normal" means of redress, then a cultural revitalization movement poses a radical alternative. This point is made clear by Robert Allen (1969: 102), a black sociologist, in his interpretation of the black experience in the United States:

> Human beings usually are able to make some suitable adaptation to the hard realities of life which are imposed by nature. They find it more difficult, in the long run impossible, to adapt when they know the burden is unfairly imposed by other men. But history and circumstance do not always offer the best conditions for open rebellion against tyranny. There are situations where one must look in unexpected places for the embryonic signs of revolt. This is especially true in cases where the oppressed group believes that the normal channels for change are closed, or when it is not even aware that such channels exist. Seeing no way out, the oppressed group looks for some other means of change, and if none exists, it is created out of cultural fabric which is the only thing the oppressed can call their own.

In effect, Puerto Ricans have relied on and converted their cultural traditions into weapons, however impractical, of social change. It will be shown throughout this book how these traditional cultural forms have been used as powerful mechanisms of communal integration, solidarity, and political cohesion and subsequently have been combined with other factors for the purpose of mobilization.

It is very important to recognize that the position of Puerto Ricans in society, like that of other oppressed non-white groups, results in part from their position as a colonized and marginal working class. It is true that under American capitalism someone has always played this role. European immigrants first served as the structural equivalent of the Puerto Ricans, blacks, and Mexicans. However, institutionalized or structural discrimination has contributed directly to the exploitation and subordination of the racial minority populations. In other words, discrimination has played the special historical role of perpetuating Puerto Rican, black, Chicano, and Native American poverty and exploitation.

The important distinction to be made here is that discrimination and racism have not been the cause of marginality as much as they have served as the justification for exploitation and racial domination. Although racism and notions of racial superiority have developed independent characteristics of their own, they have served basically as the rationale for the exploitation of non-white workers. It is within this structural framework that the place of Puerto Ricans as a colonized marginal working class becomes clear. Puerto Ricans were not only the latest arrivals and were often found standing at the end of the hiring line, but also, to some extent, they were standing in a different line.

The second point I want to stress concerns certain limitations of the internal colonial model when used for explaining the Puerto Rican experience. In and by itself, the internal colonial model may be inadequate or too narrow for describing and explaining the Puerto Rican way of life. I share the views advanced by Blauner regarding the prevailing difference that exists between classical colonial and internal colonial relations:

> Though there are many parallels in the cultural and political developments between colonialized nations and the "internally" colonized groups within America, the differences in land, economy, population composition, and power relations make it impossible to transport wholesale sociopolitical analyses or strategies of liberation from one context to another. (1972:246)

Thus just stating that the only factor which differentiates classical colonialism and internal colonialism is the Puerto Ricans' close proximity to the dominant Anglo American society obscures the complexity of their situation in urban America. In the main the internal colonial model is useful for explaining the institutional and structural dimensions of Puerto Rican subordination and inequality. My usage of an "internal organizational approach," a microlevel theory, allows for the explanation of processes involved in detailing the day-to-day realities of Puerto Rican urban life. If we are to answer Professor José Hernández's call for the development of a "social science by Puerto Ricans and for the community" (1980: 11) which would enable us to achieve a comprehensive understanding of sociohistorical reality of the Puerto Rican urban experience, we must recognize the need to adopt or combine several theoretical approaches. Certain existing models have elements that are useful in the development of a Puerto Rican social science, but it is only by combining elements of these theories that we can develop a Puerto Rican social science perspective.

To illustrate the point of specific terms, this would mean that instead of perceiving a mutual isolation between the Puerto Rican community and the larger American society, this community must be viewed as actually having been integrated into society's major institutions. This integration, however, has occurred on a very unequal basis—that is, it is restricted to the lowest segments of these structures. Puerto Ricans came to the United States and formed part of what Hechter calls "a cultural division of labor"—a system of stratification that assigns individuals "to specific types of occupations and other social roles on the basis of observable cultural traits, or markers" (1975:316)—or formed part of labor market segmentation, a concept used by Barrera to explain the economic causes and contexts in which Mexican subordination operates: "Chicanos have been incorporated into the United States' political economy as subordinate ascriptive class segments and . . . they have historically been found occupying such a structural position at all class levels" (1979:77).

Indeed, this form of integration (in direct contrast to the "pure" cases of group or community isolation advanced in the internal colonial model) resembles cases of classical colonialism as Puerto Ricans and other ethnic minorities are found concentrated in the most unskilled jobs, the least advanced and stagnant sectors of the economy. And, in common with the experiences of other oppressed groups, Puerto Ricans have been frozen for long periods of time in these least favorable levels of the American economic order. This form of institutional integration must be recognized as it can lead to the development of questions more consistent with the lifeways of Puerto Ricans than those developed within a context of isolation.

The persistent practice of identifying the Puerto Rican culture as the primary determinant of the behavior patterns and actions of this Spanish-speaking population, a leading normative explanation of the internal colonial model, has limitations in its explanatory ability. This approach can benefit considerably by the incorporation of the study of specific and practical circumstances of the everyday life of Puerto Ricans. The Puerto Rican way of life exists at different levels including, of course, familiar cultural aspects as well as "common sense interpretations" of social structure. By way of illustration it is appropriate to note how Puerto Ricans have learned to use society's expanding opportunities and resources to better themselves. They, like other ethnic minorities, were quick to cleverly understand the usefulness of War on Poverty programs and fundings for politicizing and subsequently mobilizing community residents to obtain desired wants and needs. Thus, from this point of view, Puerto Rican ethnic-conscious behavior and action has a great deal to do with the expansions of government-sponsored programs and policies.

A similar limitation of the internal colonial model is inherently found in its emphasis on the negative results of racial oppression. While it is important to see Puerto Rican life in the context of systematic racial oppression, there is also a need to understand that within these conditions Puerto Rican people have developed particular ways of coping with the hardships. For some Puerto Ricans, the innovation of special everyday skills has come to represent an important part of their survival. The observation of contemporary New York made by Rodríguez and her colleagues illustrates this point: "The strong spectre of drugs in the Puerto Rican neighborhoods and the expanding welfare sector combined with extreme economic contraction in the New York metropolitan region, influenced the nature and style of the hustle to survive in the Puerto Rican ghettoes" (1980:5).

One must also recognize that, to some extent, Puerto Rican inequality results from lack of meaningful and permanent job opportunities in the American economic order. The traditional blue-collar employment opportunities which enabled European immigrants to get a foot inside the institutional door of society are no longer part of the economy of America's leading urban centers. After World War II, nation-wide socioeconomic changes and technological developments began to influence investment in manufacturing and industrial production in other, more profitable locations outside Chicago, New York, and other major urban areas. The chances of securing worthwhile employment for Puerto Ricans and other ethnic minorities have been severely complicated and frustrated by this development.

These and other similar factors, which I feel fall outside the realm of the internal colonial explanation, reaffirm the need for incorporating macro-level theories of social structure and micro-level theories of interaction in the development of a Puerto Rican social science perspective to significantly revise our understanding of Puerto

Ricans. Major emphasis must be given to the interaction between the lives of this Spanish-speaking population as they emerge as social and historical actors and the operation of society or the force of the social structure on Puerto Ricans. The study of the life experiences of Puerto Ricans in the United States will remain incomplete until they are informed by such a wide-ranging perspective or imagination.

This book is an initial ground-breaking effort and is not intended to be a definitive statement. In a volume of this sort, certain dimensions of Puerto Rican life simply cannot be examined. For instance, the gang problem, which has existed since the early days of the Puerto Rican community but which has captured national attention only recently, is minimally described. Another important topic is the participation of some barrio residents in the national Puerto Rican independence movement and how this movement has and perhaps continues to affect the lives of Puerto Ricans living in Chicago. A worthwhile and sound examination of these and other similar topics will require the preparation of separate treatises. It is my hope that these and other topics not covered in this analysis will motivate further research on the urban life of Puerto Ricans.

It is also my hope that by describing and explaining the origins, nature, structure, and dynamics of Puerto Rican life in Chicago, this study will contribute in defining the emergence of a Puerto Rican social science and will suggest basic premises for a clear understanding of Puerto Rican life in the United States. A Puerto Rican social science, like Chicano and black sociologies before it, is developing as a reaction to the biases of mainstream social science and as a positive step toward setting forth basic definitions, concepts, and theory-building that utilize the actual experiences of Puerto Ricans. In other words, a Puerto Rican social science is arising out of the need to study the Puerto Rican life and culture as an internal social system while understanding the external constraints on Puerto Rican lives and institutions.

This study is divided into five major chapters and a conclusion. Chapter one provides a socio-historical overview of the leading social, economic, and political colonial conditions forced upon the Puerto Rican people during the first fifty years of American control and how these conditions increasingly influenced a mass movement of Puerto Rican migrants to the United States. During the fifty-year period examined in the chapter we observe that the various colonial elements imposed upon the Puerto Ricans combined to give shape to a clear underclass identity—that is, Puerto Ricans were rendered marginal before emigration.

The examination presented in chapter two focuses on the various barrios formed by Puerto Rican migrants in Chicago. Special attention is given to the process by which the dominant or primary Puerto Rican barrio was formed and how its emergence sets the ground work for the kinds of group relationships that developed between Puerto Ricans and the white population. In brief, the discussion stresses that the formation of the leading Puerto Rican community in Chicago led to particular conflicts and frictions regarding community issues and problems. It is during this period that a clear Puerto Rican underclass identity or inferior minority status begins to take shape.

In chapter three, major attention is given to the analysis of the leading factors and conditions which served to influence the accelerated growth of Puerto Rican consciousness in Chicago between 1950 and 1965, a period of the first massive immigration of Puerto Ricans to the city. Primarily through the work of Los Caballeros de San Juan, the first major Puerto Rican community organization in the city, an attempt was made to "cleanse" the stigma of an oppressed minority status. Los Caballeros hoped to accomplish this by relying on the assimilationist approach, which in the long run, resulted in very little success and a great deal of frustration for the Puerto Rican masses.

The first urban riot among Puerto Ricans in the United States provided the major framework for the discussion presented in chapter four. We will show how the Division Street Riot, as this outburst was called, signaled that the will to resist had broken the mold of assimilation or accommodation. The riot represented a "nascent movement" toward community identity. It also stimulated the growth of a new politicized and activist response to the Puerto Rican condition in Chicago. Finally the chapter will also demonstrate how this political agenda ended in defeat and how a system of social control for the Puerto Rican oppressed ethnic minority was reestablished.

Chapter five focuses on the factors that generated a relative wide-scale diversity of status and leadership among Puerto Ricans during the 1970s. We will show that during this decade the old elite was either displaced or joined by a new emerging middle class — college-trained leadership of Puerto Rican professionals — with new and different tactical approaches for overcoming the oppressive elements of colonial domination in el barrio.

The conclusion of the book provides certain guidelines that can be used for the uplifting of the Puerto Rican community. Of special importance, it stresses the need to establish a Latino/black coalition in the city. In the conclusion, I also examine the mass of despair among Puerto Ricans today and how they are turning more and more to their cultural pride for overcoming this condition.

1

The Beginnings of Marginalization: The Migration Experience

The study of Puerto Ricans in Chicago begins in the Island nation. One of the Greater Antilles, a chain of tropical Caribbean islands including Jamaica, Haiti, the Dominican Republic, and Cuba, Puerto Rico is the smallest but the most densely populated. It is here that the process of social and economic change created the conditions that led to the migration of thousands of Islanders to the United States mainland.[1]

This study will follow López and Petras' thesis that the Puerto Rican migration experience needs to be analyzed from a theoretical framework that focuses "on the socio-economic forces that transform societies (and allocate labor), and dictate the term and place of individual existence" (1974:313). This transformation, and its effect on the initial movement of Puerto Ricans from rural to urban areas within the Island and later to different places in the United States, began to gather impetus with the American takeover of the Island nation in 1889. It was in the decades of the 1940s and 1950s, however, when the exodus from Puerto Rico reached massive proportions.

THE HACIENDA ECONOMY

For four centuries preceding the North American invasion and takeover of the Island in 1898, Puerto Rico was part of Spain's colonial empire.[3] As was the case in the other colonial possessions

23

in Central and South America, the original or indigenous native society in the Island was reshaped and transformed to fit Spain's imperialistic needs. But while the Spanish colonizers extracted economic wealth from other New World colonies, such was not the case in Puerto Rico. López (1974:9) notes that the Island's economy was closely tied to the production of "foodstuffs and materials and to the defense needs of the Spanish colonial metropolis, [and it was] administratively and militarily top-heavy at the cost of internal economic development." Similarly, in his very comprehensive study on Puerto Rico, Professor Gordon Lewis writes (1963:47):

> The main genius of Hispanic colonization tended to bypass Borinquen [indigenous name for Puerto Rico]. Wealth-hungry adventurers from Spain found little attraction in an island that could not satisfy their lust for gold, and official attempts to maintain the island's Spanish population by prohibiting emigration to the burgeoning societies of the Central and South American mainland were ineffective in the face of the exotic legends that rapidly developed about Mexico and Peru.[3]

During most of the period of Spanish domination, the colonial economy of Puerto Rico developed very slowly with most of the economic production in the Island basically for subsistence. On the eve of its colonial demise in the Americas in the mid- and late- nineteenth century, however, Spain was determined to maintain some remnant of a once great empire. This meant that the colonial metropolis would use its few remaining possessions such as Puerto Rico and Cuba to obtain the financial tribute that no longer came from the former colonial territories in Central and South America. As a result of this policy, major steps were undertaken to transform Puerto Rico's subsistence economy into a producer of commercial goods, particularly sugar.

> The Haitian revolution had reduced the most advanced sugar-producing area in the world to a largely self-contained peasant economy; the sugar-producing British West Indies had fallen upon hard times; the revolutions in South America had restricted the scope of Spanish colonial rule so that Spain's antillean possessions increased proportionately in importance; royalist emigres from South America were in need of a place

to settle; and Spain was eager to secure and to develop her remaining holdings in the New World. (Mintz, 1953:225)

In Puerto Rico this change led to a social and economic movement toward establishing capitalist relations of production within agriculture.[4] This goal, however, was not fully realized. Several factors prevented capitalism from unfolding and shaping Puerto Rico's labor relations. One of these conditions is clearly described in a thought-provoking analysis of Puerto Rican migration by El Centro de Estudios Puertorriqueños (The Center for Puerto Rican Studies) of the City University of New York:

> During the last third of the nineteenth century, . . . the hold of the Spanish metropolis on Puerto Rico became increasingly tenuous. Throughout most of Europe, the system of capitalist production was consolidating. . . . The Spanish metropolis was unable to adjust its relations of production so as to enter fully into this process, and the result was the obstruction to the emergence of capitalism in one of its colonies, Puerto Rico, and the channeling of Puerto Rico's external commerce to other expanding nations. (1979:67–68)

Attempts to establish a system of agrarian capitalism were severely hindered by two other interrelated factors. First, Puerto Rican sugar producers, who controlled the means of production and ownership of the land, lacked the economic power and solvency to finance large-scale projects that would lead to the transition. The Puerto Rican sugar producers found it nearly impossible to acquire sufficient credit to finance these projects. The Spanish government had withdrawn its grants of credit to the producers in 1865, and on those occasions when the producers did secure credit the interest on these loans was astronomically high.

Second, the Spanish merchants, who controlled the means of exchange in Puerto Rico, tried everything in their power to thwart the development of capitalist modes of production since "agricultural progress tended in the long run to undermine their dominant role" (El Centro, 1979:77). These merchants were, in a sense, anti-capitalist. It was as if they glorified self-sufficiency, establishing what Merrill (1965) calls the "household mode of production." They feared all aspects of capitalist development and clung tenaciously to a rough egalitarianism, knowing that the wealth of the few would lead to impoverishment and loss of autonomy for the many. The merchants were essentially a backward-looking class, hoping to escape proletarianization by avoiding capitalist development. One practice common among the merchant class was to provide credit at exorbitant rates to the sugar producers for their commercial production while controlling the marketing of commercial crops. Obviously, this structural situation favored the merchants who tried to exploit the state of dependency in which the producers found themselves.

These various factors combined to prevent a system of agrarian capitalist relations, leading instead to the development of a family-type *hacienda* engaged in pre-capitalist forms of production. The *hacienda* was primarily a family-operated plantation enterprise system.[5] The social structure of the hacienda economy was comparatively simple. Unlike present day capitalists, the *hacendados* (the sugar producers) were actively involved in the daily social and economic activities of the Puerto Rican workers and their families. In the words of Quintero-Rivera, "the *hacendado* was an ever-present element, as a person, in the life of the laborers and the small producers, just as they were, in turn, present in the life of the *hacendado*. To a large extent, [hacendados and workers] shared a common life, although with different roles and from a different social position" (1974:98). In short, social relations within the family-type hacienda were primarily based on deference and paternalism.

If the hacendado or a member of the owning family did not live on the hacienda, then a *mayordomo* (manager) was employed by the family to take up residence in the hacienda house, and assume the responsibilities of the operations in the hacienda. Immediately below the hacendados and the mayordomos in status and income were the artisans — barrel makers, carpenters, and the blacksmiths and assistants. This group was closely followed by the *paleros*, or ditchers. Mintz (1953:242) defines the *paleros* as field laborers with special skills who earned more than the common field laborers and were respected by all in the hacienda.

Puerto Rican women were also an important part of the hacienda's labor force. Many female workers were employed in various occupations in the sugar industry. For instance, women workers "fed cane into the grinders, loaded it on the hammocks which carried onto the mills, spread manure, cleaned seeds, weeded, and cleaned the fields after harvesting" (Mintz, 1953: 240).

Most of the work in the hacienda, however, was carried out by the *agregados*—tenant workers who cultivated the land for their immediate subsistence needs while contributing to the commercial production of the hacendados. In other words, the agregados were free plantation laborers, who received some wages, housing, and other perquisites for their work. In his analysis of hacienda life on the south coast of Puerto Rico, Mintz (1953:243) points to the scarce use of cash payments under this system: "On many *haciendas, agregados* were paid half their wages in *vales* or scrip, redeemable at the *hacienda* store." Quintero-Rivera provides further insight into the system of cash payments within the hacienda plantation:

> Since land was the most abundant factor in the economy, this situation fostered a system where landowners graciously allowed peasants the use of land under their dominion in exchange for work by the peasants in the hacienda or in the owner's demesne. The peasant was given opportunity to cultivate land for his immediate subsistence needs while contributing to the commercial production of the *hacendado*. (1974:95)

Near most haciendas were the subsistence plots of the workers, where agregados could, on their own time, raise minor crops for their home use without cost to themselves. The agregados concentrated on the production of subsistence crops such as plantains, bananas, yams, and yucca, and on the raising of a few domestic animals such as chickens and pigs. In his study, Mintz indicates that some of the haciendas maintained *la pieza de los pobres* (the plot of the poor). This plot of land, according to Mintz, "was ground about Christmas time every year and the molasses, sugar, and rum produced from it were given to the poor of the neighborhood" (1953:239).

The way of life in Puerto Rico's hacienda society differed considerably from that which was operative in agrarian capitalist societies such as the British West Indies where the introduction of centralized grinding mills revolutionized the sugar industry. The relations of production within the hacienda's agricultural system placed the Island's sugar producers at a competitive disadvantage compared to producers from countries with technically superior sugar industries. This relative disadvantage subsequently led to the cultivation and processing of commercial crops that required less labor and capital investment. By the latter part of the nineteenth century, certain crops began to challenge the export dominance of the sugar industry. The cultivation of coffee was taken in such earnest that by the late 1880s it had replaced sugar as the chief export product and source of revenue in the colonial economy. In the 1890s, coffee acreage made up some 40 percent of the total land under cultivation on the Island, and, by the middle of the decade, over 57,000 pounds of Puerto Rican coffee were being exported to Europe (Crist, 1948:321).

Tobacco cultivation and processing came to represent another major commercial enterprise during this period. Although of secondary importance, by 1895 the value of tobacco exports was 4.4 percent of the total colonial economy (Quintero-Rivera, 1974:103). López summarizes the increasing significance of the growth in the production of tobacco in Puerto Rico: "Tobacco exports, however, never reached the importance of sugar and coffee during that century. Unlike sugar and coffee, however, tobacco production stimulated the development of some important manufacturing activities in the urban centers" (1974:57).

In the fall of 1898 the United States took over an island that was, economically, a mixture of mountain-slope subsistence farming and a system of hacienda plantation agriculture producing sugar, coffee, and tobacco, with almost a non-existent domestic market. When the U.S. invasion occurred, the Island's population was close to one million people, with 85 percent of the population in the rural areas. The Puerto Rican society was essentially divided into two classes: a divided hegemonic class of hacendados and merchants and the working class of agregados. In addition, there were thousands of subsistence farmers who periodically worked on the sugar, coffee, and tobacco haciendas to supplement their incomes. In short, since the attempts to establish agrarian capitalism in Puerto Rico had not reached the level of capitalist relations of production in the traditional sense, the Island's economic system was based on familial or servile relations of production.

AMERICAN AGRICULTURAL CAPITALISM

In the late nineteenth century, as a consequence of capitalist development, western Europe and the United States found themselves unable to use the excess productive capacity they had built. They sought foreign markets (often with the use of military force) and excluded foreign products from their own markets through protective tariffs (Dillard, 1979). To win a competitive edge against each other, they looked for ways to gain supplies of raw materials and labor. The United States expressed interest in Puerto Rico and in other Latin American and Asian territories as early as 1867. Maldonado-Denis (1972) uses the comments of two American officials as evidence of this desire for control of Puerto Rico, Cuba, and other Third World counties. One official is quoted as saying in that year: "the United States has constantly cherished the belief that someday she can acquire these islands by just and legal means and with the consent of Spain." In 1876, another American official declared, "I believe there are three non-continental places of enough value to be taken by the United States. One is Hawaii; the others are Cuba and Puerto Rico" (1972:55).

This interest became a reality just before the close of the century. The involvement of the United States in the Spanish-American War and her subsequent victory resulted in the wresting of Puerto Rico, Cuba, Guam, and the Philippines from the dying Spanish empire. Over the protest of some Puerto Ricans who desired independence for their national territory, Puerto Rico was given to the Americans as a prize of the war and became in the "purest form" a colony of the United States.

The addition of Puerto Rico to the American capitalist empire as a colonial territory meant that all facets of the Island's social and cultural life were to be penetrated and reshaped as instruments of control. "The U.S. colonial officials . . . made little or no effort to maintain and manipulate traditional institutions as vehicles of indirect control. The U.S. imperialist experience in Puerto Rico was shaped by a totalitarian vision in the literal sense of the word" (López and Petras, 1974:121). In general, American imperialism in Puerto Rico took the form of direct colonial domination and the imposition of foreign political rule as well as economic penetration through

American investments and an unequal trade agreement. Thus, the forces unleashed by the American penetration were primarily auxiliary agents of American corporate capitalism.

The total institutional transformation of Puerto Rico began shortly after the American takeover. After two long and humiliating years of a military form of government, the U.S. Congress passed the Foraker Act in 1900 instituting civilian rule in Puerto Rico. The Foraker Act created the office of Governor, who was nominated and appointed by the President of the United States to serve one or more four year terms. This political-constitutional framework of American colonialism lasted until 1948 when it was replaced with a new contractual relationship that granted the Island self-government and culminated in 1952 with a new status of "commonwealth association" with the federal union.

There was no local participation in the appointment of Puerto Rico's governor and no significant local influence upon the duration or the direction of his policy.[6] In a hard-hitting, anti-American analysis, one Puerto Rican scholar provides a general description of the large majority of American officials named to govern the Island during the first four decades of American rule:

> The criterion used by the President of the United States to choose the colonial governor and his cabinet was, with very few exceptions, one of compensation for political favors received. Many of these men came to Puerto Rico without knowing the language or, at times, even the location of the island. . . . The same can be said of many of the bureaucrats sent to Puerto Rico in the colonial free-for-all: they were ignorant and prejudiced, with the feeling of superiority common to all colonizers. (Maldonado-Denis, 1972:77)

Assisting the governor was an Executive Council composed of eleven members, with a majority of six American-appointed officials and the remaining five going to local or native inhabitants of the Island. The Jones Act of 1917, which also extended American citizenship to Puerto Ricans, changed the colonial executive branch to a council of eight members—five named by the governor and the remaining three by the President of the United States. There was a legislative branch—Senate and House of Representatives—elected by universal suffrage, and the judicial branch consisting of an insular Supreme Court appointed by the President with the advice and consent of the Federal Senate. Under the provisions of the Jones Act, local political parties could compete electorally for the bicameral legislature of nineteen Senate seats, and thirty-nine House seats, in addition to the post of Resident Commissioner in Washington. Although the Resident Commissioner was only allowed to speak on the floor of the United States House of Representatives and not vote, the political group that commanded a majority in the insular legislature selected one of its own members to this post.

Under American influence, Puerto Rico became a "constitutional democracy," a political transition that Americans felt was necessary to further the development of the Puerto Rican economy along capitalist lines. The political framework created in Puerto Rico should not be mistaken for a true local governing democracy; rather, it was no more than a structure of imperial supervision which ensured the continuing control of the Island by the Washington politicians and bureaucrats. The relationship between Puerto Rico and the United States in reality was/is a servant-master relationship. In the words of Gordon Lewis, one of the leading scholars in the sociology of the Puerto Rican experience, "The government of Puerto Rico, in effect, governs practically nothing" (1974:14).

The Island's educational system, too, was dramatically altered to mirror that of the colonial metropolis. The most important change replaced Spanish with English as the language of instruction and set the priority of English acquisition above other more legitimate educational goals. Congruent with this aim, the American system of education demanded acceptance of core American norms and allegiance to its symbols. This change in educational systems amounted in reality to the inculcation of Americanism — an important dimension of cultural imperialism and colonial domination.[7] Puerto Ricans were expected to display their loyalty by subordinating the language of their culture to English. The emphasis on English instruction and Americanization deprived Puerto Rican youth of information that could increase their welfare and strengthen their ties to their own national culture. The impact of an American education program on the Puerto Rican society is nowhere better defined than in Gordon Lewis' discussion of the effect of this system on Puerto Rican students in the colonial metropolis:

Historically, it is a cardinal feature of colonialism everywhere that it generates in its subject-peoples not only economic and political dependency, but also a secondary intellectual and ideological dependency. The colonial educated class, trained in the respective metropolitan centers of learning, absorbs the metropolitan culture bias and thought-patterns. The metropolitan scholarship thus becomes, in Maunier's phrase, the *instituteur social* of the colonial person, trapping him within a framework of reference that only too often is comically inappropriate to the problems of the colonial or neo-colonial society. The colonial thus becomes converted into his own executioner; first, in the struggle for national independence and, after that, in the struggle to build up a viable cultural identity, his capacity to interpret and understand his world is gravely compromised by his instinctive temptation to see it all in terms of metropolitan values, norms, and priorities. (1973:147)

Thus, the cultural assimilation policy, buttressed by English language instruction, represented a major instrument of American colonial dominance and control. Although it was resisted by the Puerto Rican population, the American education program distorted the entire educational process for over a period of thirty years.[8]

The change which most severely affected the Island's population occurred, however, when American individuals and corporations established control over all aspects of the colonial economy, including obviously and foremost, the means of production and ownership of land. From the early years of the twentieth century until the 1940s, Puerto Rico underwent an economic metamorphosis. In this relatively short period of time, a market economy devoted to the production and exportation of a single agricultural commodity, sugar, supplanted the native Puerto Rican subsistence economy. The process toward capitalist relations of production rudimentarily present in the Island's hacienda system of agriculture was accelerated by the appropriation of the means of production and ownership of land. The Island's traditional family-type hacienda was transformed very quickly into a system of agriculture capitalism which led to Puerto Rico's total economic dependence on the United States.

Shortly after the American takeover, the essential features of the sugar plantation system were firmly established. The first trend was that of sugar production, creating the "sugar way of life" in the Island, and making sugar the leading commercial crop and leading industry of the colonial economy. Sugar, a much needed commodity in the United States, offered the most favorable terms of trade. The cultivation and production of sugar was undertaken with such intensity that by 1920 it already represented 66 percent of the total value of exports in comparison to less than 30 percent in 1896 (Perloff, 1950:130). Christopulos describes the increase of commercial sugar in monetary terms by showing that while the value of exports rose quickly from $8.5 million in 1901 to $103.5 million in 1928, sugar consistently accounted for over half of the total (1974:130). The profitability of the sugar industry is also suggested in the exorbitant types of investments made by American corporations in the industry: "in 1909, there were three enterprises (all of them established after 1898) with capital investments of $500,000 to more than $1,000,000; in 1919 there were thirty-two" (Mintz, 1953:229–30).

While Puerto Rican sugar producers did not possess the financial ability to modernize the sugar industry, American investors controlled or had access to the necessary capital for making this transition. During the first decade following the American invasion, corporate *centrales* (sugar mills) that controlled raw sugar production were established in the Island. Large sums of money were needed to build these centrales, an investment outside the financial reach of the Puerto Rican sugar producer (in 1899 a mill rendering 5,000 tons of sugar annually required an investment of $500,000). Thus it is not surprising that by 1910 large American sugar corporations had taken over the bulk of cane production in Puerto Rico, and by 1935 nearly 50 percent of all lands operated by sugar companies in Puerto Rico were under the control of four large American-owned corporations. The inability of the Puerto Rican hegemonic class to compete against American individuals and corporations is clearly reflected in Quintero-Rivera's assertion that the Puerto Rican hacendados were in their infancy and "had not matured as a bourgeoisie [capable] of presenting a common front against the North American capitalist companies" (1974:110).

In addition to the advantage of American capital, various

measures taken by the new colonial metropolis helped foster the growth of agrarian capitalism in Puerto Rico within the sugar industry. The first of these measures was the inclusion of Puerto Rico within the United States protective tariff system. With this change, "all local production was brought under U.S. tariff, thus reducing access to European markets for local production" (El Centro, 1979: 95). This development led to an immediate reduction of commercial crops (in particular coffee) sold in Europe, the major market for these products.

Another important measure was the change in currency decreed in January, 1899. "The Puerto Rican monetary unit, whose real value at the time of the invasion was estimated at .90 of a U.S. dollar," writes Quintero-Rivera, "was changed to dollars at a rate of exchange of .60, which in real terms constituted a forced devaluation" (1974:108). With this change the diminutive amount of liquid capital in the Island during this period was grossly reduced. In addition there was a freeze or restriction on local credit operations. The restraint on credit eliminated the basis of the hacendados' commercial production, thus, further weakening their position of dominance in the Island.

These measures, along with the importance of sugarcane production combined to suppress the development and growth of other important industrial enterprises. The coffee industry which had become the leading export crop of the colonial economy was abandoned in the closing years of the nineteenth century. Christopulos explains the fate of the coffee industry:

> The United States failed to duplicate Spain's protective tariff on coffee. Sugar, tobacco, and textiles received protection from foreign competition, but coffee did not. The high quality Puerto Rican bean cost nearly twice as much as its Brazilian and Colombian rivals, and Congress would not consider doubling the price of coffee merely to insure that Americans would wake up to a better taste in the morning. (1974:130)

Control of the sugar industry by American capitalists gave impetus to the entry of U.S. capital into other areas of the Puerto Rican economy. "The profitability of sugar . . . ", writes Gordon Lewis, "stifled the continuing growth of production of rice and corn, both of which had been industries of considerable importance before

1898" (1963:90). Morley makes similar observations regarding other industries:

> U.S. corporations played a prominent role in the tobacco and fruit industries, were the major source of investments in public utilities (telephone, gas, light and power) and, together with Canadian interests, owned over half of all Puerto Rican bank resources in 1929. Increased U.S. demand for Puerto Rican needlework products encouraged U.S. entrepreneurs to import the necessary raw materials and establish a low quality, low cost operation carried mainly in private homes. By the late 1920s this industry was employing approximately 50,000 women and children under the most exploitative sweatshop conditions. The great majority of these workers received wages of from 15 to 25 cents a day. (1974:217)

The transition to a "monoculture" commercial sugar industry proved to have far-reaching social and economic effects on the Puerto Rican society. First, during the period of the hacienda system capital investment was mainly restricted to machinery which was usually an inexpensive expenditure. The cost of land was relatively low and in some cases the Spanish crown granted parcels of land as gifts. Similarly, cultivation was very simple and unscientific; investment was speculative. The introduction of American agriculture capitalism changed this economic structure very quickly and dramatically. Under agrarian capitalism, the investment of capital went into machinery, land, and labor; agriculture became intensive and scientific—the application of technology and machinery, primarily to the cultivation and milling of sugar, was very intensive. These capital investments, beginning with the mills, created an internal stimulus for the continued expansion of production. All these improvements required tremendous amounts of money and demanded the growers' constant vigilance over the entire production process. Unable to raise or mobilize the capital needed to shift to large scale production, the Puerto Rican hacendado was often obliged to yield to one of two courses, according to Lewis; "either to continue borrowing until his capital expired or to sell his property outright to the larger concerns" (1963:90). "The statistics of land sales," he adds, "indicate that [the hacendado] was driven, more often than not, to do the latter" (1963:90). The decline of the hacendado was inevitable; he was working against impossible odds. This decline meant the gradual absorption of the "small man" into the larger American holdings with all the social and cultural effects that land concentration always brings.

Indeed, the effect of this transition was also strongly felt by the owners of the small and medium-sized farms. For both small planters and hacendados, the lack of grinding facilities prevented the grinding of their own cane. (These centrales, which in 1910 numbered up to 500, were reduced to 46 large corporations by 1930.) Both small planters and hacendados alike were left with no alternative grinding facilities; as a result, they were obliged to pay the high prices charged for the grinding of cane by the American owners of centrales. In order to obtain the necessary capital to continue production, these landowners found themselves compelled to sell some of their holdings. After repeating this process several times, the planters were ultimately left without any land; that is, the sale of their land did not generate sufficient capital to remain in business.

Second, the Puerto Rican economy increasingly developed away from subsistence farming as the aggressive promotion of commercial crops required most of the arable land for sugar cultivation. For instance, while in 1898 food crops accounted for 32 percent of the cultivated acreage, this number was reduced, to approximately 13 percent by 1930 (Christopulos, 1974:129). The steady decline in the production of subsistence crops meant that the Island became increasingly dependent on imports of certain foodstuffs and manufactured goods from the colonial metropolis. The Puerto Rican consumer was forced to buy imported foods, including his indispensable foodstuffs, from the American market at tariff-inflated prices. Thus, while the cost of living on the Island sky-rocketed, life for the landless, often wageless, worker became precarious in the extreme.

As noted by Mintz, "the local subsistence pattern of home-grown vegetables, livestock, free sugar, molasses, and rum, and occasional gifts of fresh meat by the hacendados was largely upset in this transitional period" (1953:245). Thus, Puerto Rican workers became increasing "proletarianized" and decreasingly able to provide any of the means of subsistence for themselves and their families. Wage earnings had to be gradually increased simply for labor to reproduce itself. However, during this transitional phase of American agricultural capitalism and incomplete labor absorption, the brunt of the cost of subsistence and reproduction of the work force was sustained by the worker and his/her family.

Third, under American agriculture capitalism, the agregado's economic activity was the sale of his labor rather than his produce. The economic life of the worker became centered on money. Once they sold their labor power, they were left with nothing but wages, and the wages earned by the Puerto Rican agregado were very low and had very little purchasing power. The quality of life of Puerto Rican wage earners under American agrarian capitalism is concisely summarized by Christopulos (1974:132):

> Puerto Rican wages improved, but they still averaged less than one-half the average for other tropical countries producing the same goods. The sugar worker could buy more rice with one hour's labor in 1930 than in 1897, but he bought rather than grew much more of his food by 1930. Also he had to work 104 days to pay for his family food in 1930, a task that had required only 70 days of work in 1897. At the end of the 1920s, the Puerto Rican sugar worker spent 94 percent of his income for food, a proportion matched only in Asia.

And last, the characteristic social type of the hacienda economy—the individual and independent hacendado working his family farm—gave way to the managerial hierarchy of the corporate *central* (sugar mill) factory based on value patterns traditionally associated with the "King Sugar" ideology. This change struck a severe blow to the Puerto Rican folkways as delineated by Professor Gordon Lewis (1963:94):

> A semi-feudal paternalism, protecting the workers from the worst of the onslaughts of rural life, gave way to an impersonal wage system. The local resident landowner who cared for his employees and who gained, in many cases, the reward of their affectionate respect, was replaced by the American manager whose attitude, on the contrary, was shaped by the fact that he was an outsider likely in the future to be posted elsewhere by his distant head office in the States. The old face-to-face relationship . . . yielded to a more formalized and bureaucratized dependency upon the manager, the store boss and the labor foreman. . . . The older social types of the Puerto

Rican small town and country-side were followed by types more adjusted to the new production relations.

Overall, what took place in Puerto Rico during the first four decades of American rule was the addition of the Island to the production-means of American agrarian capitalism. This meant that the exploitation of the Island's resources became at once more systematic and more routinized. But while continuously expropriating the population's means of producing its own livelihood, capitalist relations of production did not absorb larger numbers of workers into its productive apparatus. American agrarian capitalism, in fact, led to the creation of an expanding population of available wage earners. Forty years after the American occupation of the Island, both urban and rural landless workers grew in number and in economic vulnerability: the Island's population grew from 953,243 to 1,869,255 during this period (López, 1974:317), while the adult male unemployment rose from 17 percent to 30 percent from 1899 to 1930 (Christopulos, 1974:131). The Puerto Rican economy at the end of the first four decades of American rule was underdeveloped and stagnant. An extreme dependence on sugar, chronic unemployment and underemployment, absentee monopoly land ownership, and a steady decapitalization in the form of external profit remittances were features of the society.

The colonial situation of the Island by 1931 had become so notoriously bad that American observers referred to it as a "broken pledge" (Diffie, 1931). By 1935, the Puerto Rican tragedy had deepened and become so severe, both in quantitative measurement and in qualitative character, that it was finally recognized by politicians in Washington. "Puerto Rico," wrote Secretary of State Ickes to Senator Duncan Fletcher in 1935, "has been the victim of the *laissez faire* economy which has developed the rapid growth of great absentee-owned sugar corporations, which have absorbed much land formerly belonging to small independent growers and who in consequence have been reduced to virtual economic serfdom" (quoted in Lewis, 1963:97).

From a different point of view, it's reasonable to suggest that up to this period American imperialist powers had used their political and economic advantages to subvert industrial development in the Puerto Rican society. Through selected tariff and other policies,

Puerto Rico was forced to concentrate in raw material production and was prevented from producing manufactured goods that could compete with the more advanced American capitalism. More and more, Puerto Rico became dependent on American investment and loans, with profits and interests being drained from the colonized society. In addition, investment decisions were made in relation to the requirements of American imperialist capital and were not necessarily oriented toward internal development. Puerto Rico's national development, which could have presumably progressed if left to its own devices, was subverted and altered, with the not so uncommon consequence of it becoming "underdeveloped."

In the meantime, the Island's relative surplus population became a major and disturbing problem — a problem requiring immediate action. The publication of several reports and studies during this period gave support to the alleged view that the Island's economic ills were a consequence of population pressure. The Brookings Institution Report of 1930 observed, for instance, that "population has outrun the capacity of the present economic resources and organization to furnish full employment and satisfactory living conditions" (Clark, 1930:xxv). Similarly, the Zimmermann Report flatly stated that "the people of Puerto Rico had reached an impasse — overpopulation" (Zimmermann, 1940:32). This doctrine of overpopulation quickly became the rationale used by government officials to explain and deal with Puerto Rico's economic problems. The immediate solution was mass migration. These officials assumed that exporting a large number of Puerto Rico's surplus population would reduce competition for jobs among those who remained in the Island and thus, would reduce the high unemployment conditions. Migration, then, became a way of life for thousands of Puerto Rican workers.

Puerto Rican migration started with an initial movement toward the burgeoning centers of the Island where tobacco manufacturing and needlework trades were rapidly becoming the leading economic activities of the urban labor force. Highland farmers and sharecroppers moved to the Island's major cities in search of work in several small industrial enterprises. "This process," explains Gordon Lewis in another thought-provoking essay on post–World War II Puerto Rico, "gave new impetus to rural depopulation and the massive drift to the cities, replacing the traditional rural barrio, so often portrayed in Puerto Rican romantic literature, with new shanty-town barrios (1974:61). The overall geographic dispersion of the Puerto Rican population during this period is clearly described by Sánchez-Korrol (1983:23):

> Between 1899 and 1940 the traditional coffee-producing central western mountain region extending from Morovis to Mayaguez . . . experienced a relative depopulation, but the northeastern non-coffee-producing mountain region increased in population. Cane-growing municipalities on the coast also grew along with the urban San Juan-Rio Piedras region, emerging in time as the main urban concentrations in Puerto Rico.

The underdevelopment associated with American imperialism, thus, laid the groundwork for labor emigration from Puerto Rico. Puerto Rican *campesinos* or *jibaros* (peasants) either were forced off their land or retained an increasingly tenuous hold on it. These peasant families supplemented their meager livelihood by sending members to work at least part-time or seasonally in urban capitalist-run enterprises. Thus, as a result of imperialism, a population was created that desperately needed employment in order to survive.

The migration of Puerto Ricans from rural areas to urban centers within the Island was closely followed by external or outward emigration. The initial external shift in the Puerto Rican population began in 1900, when groups of former landowners and landless peasants were recruited as contract laborers to work for Hawaiian plantations. This early movement resulted in the transfer to Hawaii of over 5,000 Puerto Ricans, followed several years later by a few smaller parties of recruits. In the autumn of 1926 arrangements were made to transport some 1,500 Puerto Rican cotton pickers to Arizona under an agreement between the Arizona Pima Cotton Growers Association and the Insular Bureau of Labor. The first group consisted of families and were accompanied by representatives of both the employers' association and the Insular government. The results of this experiment were so unsatisfactory that the sailing of the last of the three shiploads was cancelled.

It was primarily to New York, however, that external emigration from Puerto Rico was directed during this period. Clark indicates that "various proposals [were] made to facilitate an exodus of such labor by subsidizing steamships to enable them to carry steerage passengers at low fares and by using Army transports for this purpose" (1930:519). In her excellent historical analysis of New York's pre–World War II Puerto Rican community life, Virginia Sánchez-Korrol shows that by 1920 an estimated 7,364 migrants from the Island were already residents of that city. By 1930 the Puerto Rican population in New York, according to Sánchez-Korrol, increased to 44,908 and ten years later it surpassed 60,000 (1983:28).

Despite attempts to export part of the Island's surplus population, the economic problems of Puerto Rico remained unresolved. When it became convincingly clear during the worst period of the economic depression of the 1930s that emigration could not solve the overall conditions in Puerto Rico, a new method was devised to deal with this tragedy. The new approach was the extension to Puerto Rico of all New Deal's federal aid programs originally designed for the states. The New Deal, like the emigration strategy, was disappointing. Capital investment and growth in Puerto Rico's New Deal was directed toward government programs in the form of relief and public works projects rather than toward investment in genuine business enterprises. For example, between 1934 and 1939 federal appropriations for the Puerto Rican Reconstruction Administration (PRRA)—the major office established in the Island under the New Deal program—equalled 57 million dollars, with 50 percent being spent on labor or personnel services. Further, relief cases aided by the agency increased from 126,000 to a total of 222,000 over a five year period. Not one of PRRA's projects ever really managed to become an enduring or important part of the Puerto Rican economic scene. This point is further elaborated by Gordon Lewis (1963:125):

> The program, however, was not much more than an expanded public works (for all of the social idealism of its local officials) treating the problem as a depression emergency instead of the chronic maladjustment of land-hungry and sugar-dominated economy that it was in reality; it was estimated that at the height of its activities the agency was giving direct or indirect relief to 35 percent of the island population.

One direct result of New Deal programs in Puerto Rico was the involvement of insular communal efforts in dealing with the social and economic problems of the Island. Subsequently, it was assumed or expected that if Puerto Rico was ever to be revived, it would have to be through an indigenous leadership determined to solve the local problems by local means and on local terms. In other words, the colonial metropolis came to the conclusion that the Island's social and economic crisis should be met primarily by the efforts of a new insular machinery of government—intermediary leaders or a "national bourgeoisie" was created to consolidate a program that could address these ills.

The creation of this group of intermediaries is a typical practice of colonial rule. Robert Allen makes the point that such alliances are often "made in order to minimize the chances that the colonial power would have to resort to brute force in preserving its domination" (1969:10). It's in this context that one begins to understand the social significance of the awakening in the Puerto Rican consciousness during this time. This Puerto Rican national consciousness and identification, which began to manifest itself in several political-conscious activities primarily among residents of the Island's major urban centers, was directly responsible for forcing a change in the whole colonial climate. Throughout the first few decades of American rule, Puerto Ricans responded more and more consciously to the process of colonization or Americanization; that is, they began to express resentment and opposition to the American colonial domination in the Island. But it was the "crisis of the thirties [which] helped to bring to the fore all those problems that had hitherto been submerged in the consciousness of Puerto Ricans: the colonial problem, the cultural problem, the economic problem, and others" (Maldonado-Denis, 1972:309).

One of the earliest examples of political-conscious behavior among Puerto Ricans was expressed by sugarcane workers who took the initiative and tried to unionize the cane fields. During the early years of the 1930 decade they struck against some of the major American-owned sugar industries in the Island. "The most dramatic examples of popular militancy," writes Christopulos, "occurred in the sugar industry, which controlled half of the cultivated land and over one-third of the agricultural work force. Cane workers at the South Porto Rico Company went on strike late in 1933. In early 1934, they were joined by employees of the Fajardo Sugar Company and Central Aguirre Associates, so that the entire eastern section of the industry came to a standstill" (1974:136).

In the early 1930s, the insular intelligentsia also began to reflect a positive search for cultural autonomy and a sense of peoplehood, epitomized in Antonio Pedreira's well-known essay on *Insularismo*. Pedreira's intellectual concerns regarding this search for national identity and peoplehood are clearly expressed early in the essay when he asks: What are we? And where are we going? Influenced by Pedreira's work, Tomas Blanco's *Prontuario Histórico de Puerto Rico* is another clear denunciation of American colonialism in the Island. Tomas Blanco analyzes the problem of the Island in economic and political terms and suggests an appropriate program of national reconstruction which would "liberate ourselves from domination, foreign interference and compromise" (1935:27).

The most militant challenge to American dominance in Puerto Rico was presented by the anti-colonial movement of the "Nationalist Party." The Nationalist Party was headed by Pedro Albizu Campos, who trained at Harvard Law School and who, because of his charisma and compelling eloquence, quickly rose to the leadership of the party in 1930, a few years after he joined it. Pedro Albizu Campos had encountered racial discrimination when he enlisted in the United States Army during World War I, an experience over which he harbored bitter thoughts and which allegedly expressed itself in the party's anti-American stance. The party was predicated upon the theory that, legally as well as morally, the American authority had no right to be in the Island except by the fiat of conquest.[9]

The Nationalist Party's first direct expression of anti-colonialism in the Island occurred in February 1936 when two Nationalists shot and killed Colonel Francis Riggs, Puerto Rico's chief of police. A year later, the Island's police force revenged the Riggs murder by firing upon an unarmed demonstration of the Nationalist Party in the southern town of Ponce. The "massacre of Ponce," as this affair came to be called, and its aftermath of violent emotionalism had the immediate effect of widening relations between Washington and the Island. All Puerto Ricans were blamed for the murder of Colonel Riggs and they came to be perceived as cowards with little gratitude for "all that America" had done for the Island. In another revengeful act, Senator Millar E. Tydings of Maryland, Democratic chairman of the Senate Committee on Territories and Insular Affairs, introduced the Tydings Bill of 1936 calling for an insular plebiscite on the question of independence as a means of ridding the American nation of an embarrassing encumbrance. The Tydings Bill, which was introduced and withdrawn in the course of four to five weeks, brought out issues that had hitherto remained in the background. In particular, the events of the Island's own political history during these years played directly into the hands of federal reaction and contributed to a further disintegration of relations between the Island and the colonial metropolis.

This was the overall colonial climate that the newly created Puerto Rican national bourgeoisie was asked to change: the Island was experiencing its most depressing economic conditions coupled with nationalist-conscious sentiments and political mobilization challenging American colonialism. The intermediary leadership that rose to the occasion was *El Partido Popular Democrático* (The Democratic Popular Party), which successfully seized legislative power during the insular political elections of 1940.[10] Under the leadership of Luis Muñoz Marín, El Partido Popular proceeded to implement a far-reaching program of economic and social development with the help of newly appointed Governor Rexford B. Tugwell—the latter "is considered without doubt the ablest of all American governors in the insular history" (Lewis, 1963:152). Both Governor Tugwell and the Populares leader Muñoz Marín were New Deal enthusiasts who broadly agreed on the manner in which the Island's problems should be corrected. They both agreed that the more compelling need was economic rehabilitation. The Populares' commitment to improve economic, social, and health conditions was based on a belief that living conditions were of greater concern for the Puerto Rican people than the issue of political status espoused by the Nationalist Party and other groups. In other words, although the Puerto Rican national bourgeoisie shared an interest in ridding Puerto Rico of the American imperialist control and domination which undermined their own development and exploited their national resources, they did not choose to join in a movement of national liberation. Instead, they embarked on a program to transform the Island's agricultural economy into an industrial one. For the local leadership of El Partido Popular, which was comprised of descendants of those hacendados who had lost their economic and political control in Puerto Rico to American corporations, the establishment of a successful industrial society represented, according to one Puerto Rican scholar, the best and easiest way to regain superficial political domination in the Island: "the social structure of the *hacienda* being destroyed, this group, as a class, needed to find a new economic basis to establish its social hegemony" (Quintero-Rivera, 1974:204).

AMERICAN INDUSTRIALISM

The Populares' economic development program of the 1940s, which initiated the transformation of the Island's economy from agricultural capitalism to industrial modes of production, represents the second major economic change intimately related to Puerto Rican emigration. The industrialization of the Island was undertaken to reduce unemployment and increase the workers' wage scale. In general, it was anticipated that industrialization could provide new employment opportunities and a solid base for economic development and advancement.

The initial industrialization program of the Tugwell-Muñoz Marín alliance was undertaken when the Economic Development Administration established a program by the name of *Fomento* in 1942. The Fomento program, which was a form of state capitalism, organized insular companies to produce rum bottles, cardboard boxes, structured tile, bricks, cement, sewer pipes, and other similar goods. In an effort to promote tourism, the Island's first large hotel, the Caribe Hilton, was built under the sponsorship of the Fomento program. In its first four years of operation, Fomento organized four major subsidiary corporations: the Puerto Rican Glass Corporation, the Puerto Rican Cement Corporation, the Puerto Rican Clay Products Corporation and the Puerto Rican Shoe and Leather Corporation. By June, 1946, government-owned properties were estimated at $11,743,456, giving employment to 1,379 persons (Lugo-Silva, 1955:90).

It became quite clear by the mid-1940s that the industrial base established by Fomento was too limited to move the Island's economy ahead. Perhaps the biggest problem with the Fomento enterprises was that they failed to live up to their expectations. By 1945, manufacturing as a whole contributed 12 percent of the Puerto Rican GNP and employed 56,000 workers, or about 11 percent of the labor force. More than a third, however, were employed in grinding cane in the sugar mills. Another third were employed in garment production, primarily hand sewing by women at very low levels of output and earnings. Most of the remainder were in tobacco plants, rum distilleries, and breweries (Reynolds and Gregory, 1965: 12). The employment openings or job opportunities offered by Fomento fell far short of its anticipated goal of 10,000. By 1947 the number of employees in Fomento enterprises reached a mere 1,500 (Ross, 1969:83). Further, Fomento's economic development program was unable to generate the necessary capital for uplifting the colonial economy. Wells (1969:101) shows that while the Island's economy required over a billion dollars yearly, Fomento was producing only four million dollars. Finally, when the difficulties experienced by these business initiatives were widely covered in the insular press, this economic program failed to attract local private capital as was originally intended (Ross, 1969:82).

In sum, despite the establishment of government-owned industrial enterprises, Puerto Rico continued to function as a labor-surplus economy at a low level of industrial development. At this pace, Puerto Rico simply could not achieve a level of employment commensurate with an acceptable rate of unemployment, nor could it balance employment between agricultural and industrial sectors. In effect, the problems that beset the insular industrialization program suggested a need for reorientation.

Subsequently, in the last years of the 1940s, El Partido Popular followed this initial attempt by opening the Island's market to American investors in light factory industries. The underlying purpose behind this shift in program was to promote and encourage private investment in the industrialization of the Island. It was anticipated that private investment would broaden the industrial base of the colonial economy and create more jobs. The new direction of the policy meant that now the Puerto Rican government would serve as the major agency responsible for the supervision and management of Fomento-sponsored industrial projects. Through Fomento, government resources were used to construct factory buildings for lease to prospective users, conduct market surveys, give preemployment training to workers, provide other advisory and technical services, and make loans or even assume a minority interest in the firms. The government's initial attempts to encourage private investment in the Puerto Rican economy started via a program known as "Operation Bootstrap"—an extensive mainland advertising campaign which alerted American owners of firms and industries to the advantages of doing business in Puerto Rico. As a foreign market, Puerto Rico provided American capitalists an opportunity for making especially advantageous exchanges. One of the chief attractions was the access it gave American industrialists to cheaper labor, enabling them to reap larger profits than they would in the colonial metropolis.

The dominant consideration of Puerto Rico's new economic development policy was its tax inducements. This provision, outlined in the Industrial Incentives Act of 1947, rendered eligible for tax exemption an individual, partnership, or corporation which manufactured a product not produced in the Island before January 2, 1947; or which manufactured any of 34 major categories of products listed in the act; or which operated a commercial or tourist hotel. The period of tax exemption ranged from 10 years for plants located in San Juan and other areas designated as the "High Industrial Development Zone" to 17 years for plants located in areas designated by the governor as the "Underdeveloped Industrial Zone"—the intent was to encourage more balanced geographical distribution of industrial activity throughout Puerto Rico. The exemption applied to taxes on real property as well as to income taxes.

The rate of the Fomento-promoted plant openings accelerated over the years. From 30 or 40 new plants a year in the late 1940s, the number rose to 70 or 80 by the mid-1950s, and well above 100 in the early years of the 1960s (see Table 1). The great majority of the new manufacturing plants were branch plants of mainland manufacturing companies. Reynolds and Gregory show that at the end of 1961, only one-sixth of the Fomento-promoted plants in operation were local concerns. They also indicate that the local concerns were on the average only about half as large as the mainland branch plants, so that they had less than 10 percent of the total employment (1965:22).

Manufacturing plants established in Puerto Rico during this period were typically small, about 80 employees per establishment for the Fomento group as a whole. Further, the distribution of employment in these industries was overwhelmingly in the direction of garment manufacturing and other light consumer goods industries. The metal products, machinery, and instrument groups consisted of radios and parts, electronic apparatus, and other products requiring relatively low-skilled assembly work (see Table 2).

TABLE 1

Government Sponsored Manufacturing Plants and Employment, 1942–1962

		NUMBER OF PLANTS			EMPLOYMENT IN REPORTING PLANTS AT YEAR END (IN THOUSANDS)
YEAR	Opened	Closed	In Existence at Year End	In Operation and Reporting	
1942-47	19	—	19	13	2.0
1948	16	—	35	24	2.1
1949	31	2	64	45	4.1
1950	38	6	96	84	7.1
1951	37	5	128	122	9.0
1952	72	12	188	180	14.8
1953	84	14	258	250	21.8
1954	58	36	280	267	23.0
1955	69	21	328	317	28.5
1956	90	30	388	369	33.1
1957	98	32	454	439	35.8
1958	101	49	506	469	36.4
1959	99	45	560	536	45.0
1960	133	37	656	607	46.5
1961	131	44	728	701	55.1
1962	130	46	812	761	58.9*

Source: Puerto Rican Planning Board, "Annual Statistical Report of the Economic Development Administration Manufacturing Plants, 1960–61," pp. 30-34.

*Data for end of June 1962.

TABLE 2

Distribution of Employment in Fomento Plants by Industry Groups

INDUSTRY	JUNE 1954	DECEMBER 1961
Food & kindred products	2.4%	4.0%
Tobacco manufacturers	2.6	7.1
Textile mill products	10.7	8.0
Apparel & other fabricated products	40.4	35.4
Furniture & fixtures & misc. wood products	.7	2.1
Paper products, printing & publishing	1.3	1.9
Chemical, petroleum refining & allied products	.6	4.0
Rubber, leather, & plastic products	9.4	10.8
Stone, clay, & glass products	6.7	4.3
Metal products, machinery & instruments	16.6	15.9
Misc. manufacturing	8.7	6.7
TOTAL*	100.0	100.0

Source: Puerto Rican Planning Board, "Annual Statistical Report of the Economic Development Administration Manufacturing Plants," June, 1962.

*Totals exceed 100% because percentages were rounded to nearest tenth.

This light, relatively unskilled, character of the production operations accounts for the fact that about 60 percent of the workers in the new enterprises were women. The new industries tended to draw additional female workers into the labor force, leaving most of the males unaffected. What Puerto Rico received was not modern industrial forms and modern technology, but forms of factory organization and types of machinery perhaps long obsolete in the United States. Or, it received industries that were too costly to maintain in the colonial metropolis.

Another characteristic of Fomento-promoted firms is that most of them were oriented toward the mainland economy, receiving their raw materials or component parts from the mainland and shipping their finished products back to the mainland. Few plants were established that produced either intermediate or final products for local industries and consumers, or were based on local availability of raw materials. The "*Fomento* sector," according to Reynolds and Gregory, "[was] largely an economic enclave or extension of the mainland economy" (1965:23). In many cases when the processing operations performed by these plants became unprofitable, they simply closed down. Workers were dismissed and the rental factory building was turned back to Fomento.

The low wage levels and high unemployment rates prevailing in the 1940s were the two major reasons for wishing to accelerate manufacturing development in Puerto Rico. The assertion was that the transfer of labor to more productive employment in manufacturing would permit a rise in income levels as well as a reduction of unemployment. And, indeed, the rate of wage increase since the early 1950s, in comparison to the preceding decade, was significant. Between 1950 and 1963 average hourly earnings in Fomento-promoted plants almost tripled, rising from $0.41 to $1.16 per hour (see Table 3). But while one may interpret this progress in real wage rates as a substantial rise, it is also important to note that average hourly earnings in Puerto Rican manufacturing in 1950 were only 27 percent of the average for the mainland United States and in 1963 the figure was only 47 percent. Further, the increase in wage rates did not reduce the unemployment problem in the Island during this period. According to official reports, the overall rate of full-time unemployment remained in the high teens throughout the 1950s (see Table 4). This applied to both male and female workers as il-

TABLE 3

Average Hourly Earnings of Production Workers in Fomento Plants and in All Manufacturing Industries, Puerto Rico and the United States, October 1950–63

Year	Fomento Plants	All Manufacturing Puerto Rico	All Manufacturing United States	Ratio of Earnings in Fomento Plants to U.S. Manufacturing
1950	$0.41	$0.42	$1.50	.27
1951	.44	.45	1.61	.27
1952	.45	.44	1.70	.26
1953	.47	.47	1.79	.26
1954	.50	.50	1.81	.27
1955	.60	.55	1.91	.31
1956	.72	.66	2.02	.35
1957	.83	.77	2.09	.39
1958	.88	.82	2.14	.41
1959	.93	.86	2.21	.42
1960	.98	.94	2.30	.42
1961	1.03	1.00	2.34	.42
1962	1.09	1.07	2.39	.45
1963	1.15	1.13	2.47	.47

Source: Puerto Rican Planning Board, "Annual Statistical Report of the Economic Development Administration, 1961–1962," pp. 27-31.

TABLE 4

Labor Force, Employment, and Unemployment in Puerto Rico: Quarterly and Annual Averages, 1950s

	1950	1951	1952	1953	1954	1955	1956	1957	1958
Labor force annual average	705	705	659	634	631	643	640	632	539
Employment									
January	557	575	541	520	522	525	547	546	555
April	638	632	586	573	559	578	584	567	579
July	615	594	572	547	536	555	554	543	543
October	594	564	535	531	591	544	543	543	523
Annual Average	601	591	559	543	534	551	557	550	550
Unemployment									
January	120	142	128	123	117	124	97	101	97
April	83	84	76	64	72	67	66	63	68
July	96	111	90	77	90	88	81	80	86
October	116	117	106	100	109	90	89	82	104
Annual Average	104	114	100	91	97	92	83	82	89
Unemployment Rate	14.8	16.2	15.2	14.4	15.4	14.3	13.0	13.0	13.9

Source: Puerto Rican Department of Labor, Bureau of Labor Statistics, "Employment and Unemployment in Puerto Rico, Quarterly Reports, 1950–1959."

lustrated in Table 5. Table 5 also shows the enormously high rates of underemployment (workers employed less than 35 hours a week) for both men and women.

The crisis of unemployment and underemployment in the newly established industrial order was compounded by a decline in the number of workers in agriculture during this period. Employment in agriculture dropped from 214,000 to 124,000 between 1950 and 1960. The agricultural totals conceal complicated cross-currents for particular commodities: a stagnation of output in sugar and most other export crops during the fifties and sixties and a decline in production of such traditional low-income foods as yucca, corn, beans, etc. Total agricultural output seems to have risen slightly in real terms between 1950 and 1962, but the 1962 output was produced with only two-thirds of the industry's working force. Part of this doubtlessly represents productivity increase, arising from improved cultivation methods, equipment, and fertilizer, but it also suggests that the 1950 agricultural labor force was substantially underutilized.

Despite the change from agricultural labor relations to indus-

TABLE 5

Employment, Underemployment, and Unemployment of Puerto Rican Labor Force, 1951–1955

	1951		1953		1955	
	Number	Percent	Number	Percent	Number	Percent
MEN						
Labor force (thousands)	508	100.0	472	100.0	468	100.0
Employed	431	84.8	402	85.2	395	84.4
35 hours or more	255	50.2	250	53.0	235	50
Less than 35 hours	162	31.8	134	28.4	138	29
Employed but not working	14	2.8	17	3.6	20	4
Unemployed	78	15.3	70	14.8	73	15.6
WOMEN						
Labor force	205	100.0	174	100.0	169	100.0
Employed	173	84.4	148	85.1	144	85.2
35 hours or more	71	34.6	73	42.0	71	42
Less than 35 hours	93	45.4	67	38.5	64	37
Employed but not working	9	4.4	8	4.6	11	6
Unemployed	32	15.6	26	14.9	25	14.8

Source: Puerto Rico Department of Labor, Bureau of Labor Statistics, "Employment and Unemployment in Puerto Rico, Quarterly Reports, 1950–1959."

trial modes of production, the Island's economic ills persisted. Industrialization was not able to relieve significantly the high rates of unemployment, underemployment, and low wages in Puerto Rico. As in previous decades, an increasing mass of surplus labor constituted part of the way of life in Puerto Rico. And, as in earlier periods, the immediate solution to this problem was mass emigration. The overpopulation thesis once again, and not surprisingly, was used to explain the economic problem plaguing the Island. It is important to note here that the thesis that economic problems are a direct consequence of population pressure has been proven to be an inadequate explanation for the Island's economic ills. El Centro's critique of this perspective is one example:

> Between 1898 and 1940 the Island population did in fact nearly double, but the annual rate of increase only rose slightly. Death rates declined very slowly until 1940, migration played only a small role in keeping numbers down. . . . Since the proportion of gainfully occupied individuals remained roughly the same during these years . . . the work force approximately doubled in size. There was no really impressive surge in natural increase until well into the 1940s, and it was not until then that a significant extension of sanitary and health services into rural areas began, despite easy assertions about great strides in this connection during the early decades of U.S. occupation. As late as 1947 life expectancy at birth stood at forty-six years.
>
> The compelling and persuasive facts were the sizeable and growing population, the miserable wage scales of those fortunate enough to have any employment, however intermittent or precarious, and the substantial mass of people outside the labor force. How this situation had come about and continued to deteriorate was taken as self-evident: an unfortunate ratio of people to resources, inefficient agriculture, and the absence of industry. The solution to population pressure was a new and different pressure, the pressure on the people to leave or to curb their numbers. (1979:120–21)

Unable to provide jobs for its population the government of El Partido Popular shifted the responsibility for employment to the poor by urging them to leave Puerto Rico. The colonial relationship between Puerto Rico and the United States—Puerto Ricans are natural-born American citizens who can move without restrictions anywhere in the continental U.S.—enabled Puerto Ricans to travel to the mainland without a pass or special papers. At the same time travel to the mainland was enhanced by low rates of air transportation permitted by the Federal Aviation Administration at the request of the Puerto Rican government. The establishment of a migration division social service agency or office in American cities by the Puerto Rican Department of Labor also substantially encouraged external movement and aided migrants in the United States. In the words of Christopulos (1974:152), "the head of the migration division served as an unofficial ambassador in New York City."

The population shift experienced in Puerto Rico represents a classic form of international migration resulting from the logic of capitalist development. American capitalist development in the Island led to imperialism, which in turn distorted the development of the Puerto Rican society. As a result, many people were displaced from their traditional economic pursuits, becoming available for emigration. The emigration of Puerto Rican workers to the United States took place within the context of an ever-increasing capitalist penetration of the Island and its concomitant absorption into the world capitalist economy. Puerto Rican migration can not be viewed simply as discrete and unconnected factors in the sending and receiving societies but of the historical connections between the two countries.

Puerto Rico's economic conditions were such that thousands could not survive locally. Given Puerto Rico's level of industrial development relative to available numbers of workers, the Island's urban centers could not absorb all the surplus labor from the countryside. The overflowing surplus in the Island, unable to find jobs in the cities or to survive in the countryside, was thus drawn to the United States to seek employment. After this process was set in motion, the comparative economic advantage of working in the United States, created by the unequal relationship between the colonial metropolis and the colony, induced a pattern of migration which still continues today.

The Puerto Rican worker became attracted to the idea of migration primarily by its promise of an immediate improvement in his material life. Tens of thousands of Puerto Ricans migrated to American cities after World War II. Their uprooting was "involuntary" insofar as it was not a matter of choice but of necessity that they find new or better jobs elsewhere. Or, as stated by Professor Gordon Lewis, "Puerto Ricans have become involuntary actors in one of the most dramatic migratory episodes of modern times" (1974:18). Puerto Rican migrants were not workers in colonial industries who had lost their jobs because of foreign competition; instead, they came from a stratum of underemployed or unemployed workers from the countryside who had not been able to find a place in urban industries. In this sense, they might be termed "semiproletarian," for it appears that they would have accepted work for wages had it been available.

Following the pattern of the 1920s and 1930s, the majority of post–World War II Puerto Rican newcomers settled in New York. Beginning in the late 1940s, but more so in the early 1950s, Puerto Ricans began to establish communities of settlement in other American cities. Chicago was one of those urban metropolises, and what follows is the account of the lives of Puerto Ricans in this midwestern city.

The historical notes presented in this chapter are of great importance for several reasons. They provide an explanation of the colonial system established in Puerto Rico and the difficult circumstances encountered by Puerto Ricans in pursuit of their self-determination and liberation. The colonial administration in the Island advanced the designs of the Anglo Americans, enabling them to deny the Puerto Rican people any semblence of political or economic power. American colonialism robbed Puerto Ricans of their land and culture. However, from the beginning of the conquest, Puerto Ricans organized against the oppressors, showing a great deal of resistance against American colonial domination. This behavior helps to refute myths of Puerto Rican docility, for Puerto Ricans throughout their history have fought to retain their culture and language even during periods of intense repression. Of course, many times their efforts have been rewarded by even greater measures of suppression, as in the case of the Nationalist Movement. Nonetheless, this overview demonstrates that the Puerto Rican struggle toward liberation has been an ongoing historical process continued in the mainland in different forms.

Another significant element of this overview is that it points to the mode of entry of Puerto Ricans into the American society.

The mode of entry most often sets the pattern of the treatment received by the emigrating group in the receiving society. While it is true that a large number of Puerto Ricans will claim to have come to the United States "voluntarily," once in the country they have found themselves in a situation that had been structured through exploitation. So while each individual may not have found himself/herself involuntarily included in the system, the group as a whole did, and, this has determined, in part, how Puerto Ricans have fared in the mainland. It will be illustrated in subsequent chapters how involuntary incorporation into the American system has come to mean perpetual subordination in the lowest reaches of the institutional life of the society for Puerto Ricans, as has been the case with Chicanos, blacks, and Native Americans.

Further, these historical notes reveal that Puerto Rican migrants were not only terribly poor — that, once in America, they had to offer their labor power for meager wages — but then these were people who, before coming to Chicago, New York, and elsewhere, had already been placed in an inferior and subordinate status. The attitudes formed during the early colonial period gave Puerto Ricans the stigma of inferiority. And this stigmatization, of course, severely intensified in Chicago, becoming, to a considerable extent, a major factor in the shaping of the Puerto Rican way of life in this midwestern city.

2

Growth of the Puerto Rican Barrio and Intensification of Ethnic Subordination

RACIAL MINORITY STEREOTYPE

Before the mass exodus of Puerto Rican workers from their homeland to the American mainland in the 1940s, the size of Chicago's Puerto Rican population was very small. According to Clarence Senior's findings in *Puerto Rican Emigration*, only 15 Puerto Ricans were reported by the Census Bureau as living in Illinois' largest city in the year 1910. Ten years later this number had increased to 110, and by 1940 it had doubled to a total of 240 (1947:45).

The large-scale movement of Puerto Ricans to Chicago after World War II formed part of the second great shift of surplus labor from the Island to the United States. The first large movement of the Island's underclass surged to the Northeast, particularly to New York. From 1946 through 1950 an average of 30,000 Puerto Ricans a year came to the United States. The recession of 1953 reduced the flow to 21,000 in 1954. The net flow rose again to over 27,000 each year until 1960, when it dropped to 16,000 (Table 6). And it was to New York that the overwhelming majority of Puerto Ricans migrated. According to a report by the U.S. Commission on Civil Rights, the New York metropolitan area was the home of 61,000 Puerto Ricans in 1940; by 1950 the number had increased by 400 percent to 245,080; and by 1960 it surpassed the half-million mark with 612,574 (1976:21–23). The allure of New York began to decrease in the 1950s and particularly during the 1960s. The re-

56

TABLE 6

Net Migration Between Puerto Rico and the United States, 1944–1965

Year	Net Migration	Year	Net Migration
1944	11,000	1955	45,464
1945	13,000	1956	52,315
1946	39,911	1957	37,704
1947	24,551	1958	27,690
1948	32,775	1959	29,989
1949	25,698	1960	16,298
1950	34,703	1961	-1,754*
1951	52,899	1962	11,664
1952	59,103	1963	-5,479*
1953	69,124	1964	1,370
1954	21,531	1965	16,678

Source: Clarence Senior and Donald O. Watkins. 1966. "Toward a Balance Sheet of Puerto Rican Migration," in *Status of Puerto Rico, U.S.-Puerto Rico Commission on the Status of Puerto Rico*. Senate Document No. 108, p. 703.

*The minus figure indicates a net outflow from the United States to Puerto Rico.

TABLE 7

Puerto Ricans in the United States in 1960, Within Regions by States

Regions and States of Residence	Total Puerto Rican Origin		Born in Puerto Rico		Puerto Rican Parentage	
	Number	Percent	Number	Percent	Number	Percent
Total U.S.	892,513	100.0	617,056	100.0	275,457	100.0
Northeast	740,813	83.0	518,403	84.0	222,402	80.7
New York	642,622	72.0	448,585	72.7	194,037	70.4
New Jersey	55,351	6.2	39,778	6.4	15,572	5.7
Pennsylvania	21,206	2.4	14,659	2.4	6,547	2.4
Connecticut	15,247	1.7	11,172	1.8	4,075	1.5
Massachusetts	5,217	.6	3,454	.6	1,763	.6
North Central	67,833	7.6	46,611	7.6	21,222	7.7
Illinois	36,833	4.0	25,843	4.2	10,238	3.7
Ohio	13,940	1.6	9,227	1.5	4,713	1.7
Indiana	7,218	.8	4,781	.8	2,437	.9
South	45,876	5.1	31,904	5.2	13,972	5.1
Florida	19,535	2.2	14,245	2.3	5,290	1.9
Texas	6,050	.7	3,869	.6	2,181	.8
West	38,030	4.3	20,138	3.3	17,892	6.5
California	28,108	3.1	15,479	2.5	12,692	4.6
Hawaii	4,289	.5	1,197	.2	3,092	1.1

Source: *U.S. Bureau of the Census, U.S. Census of Populations: 1960*. Subject Reports. Puerto Ricans in the United States, Final Report PC (2)-1D, Table 15

sulting change in the geographic pattern of Puerto Rican migration led to the establishment of Puerto Rican communities in such areas as Chicago-Gary, Cleveland and Lorain, Ohio, and Milwaukee, Wisconsin (Hernández-Álvarez, 1968:41). (Table 7 shows the distribution of Puerto Rican communities in the United States in 1960.)

The migration of Puerto Ricans to Chicago was the result of two major factors. The first group of Puerto Rican migrants to Chicago (less than 1,000 in actual numbers) arrived as contract laborers. According to Elena Padilla (1947), in 1946, Castle, Barton, and Associates, a private employment agency from Chicago, established an office on the Island in agreement with the Insular Department of Labor of the Puerto Rican government for the purpose of recruiting migrant workers for the Chicago area. This initial group of Puerto Rican workers were contracted for employment in domestic and foundry work.

The testimonies of this study's participants provide the second explanation: migration to Chicago was spurred by news from relatives and friends that manufacturing employment opportunities in New York's economy were in rapid decline. They were convinced that there were more Puerto Rican workers than available jobs in New York and, that Chicago and other cities could offer more favorable circumstances.

Puerto Rican migration to Chicago coincided with the massive arrival of black migrants from rural areas of the American South, an expanding black urban population, and large numbers of Mexican immigrants/migrants from Mexico and the Southwest, respectively. Very large numbers of both blacks and Mexicans had been residents of the city for many decades. The increasing job opportunities created by the outbreak of World War II attracted thousands more into Chicago's industrial economy in search of jobs.

Puerto Ricans came to share with these two populations the "status or stereotype of a racial minority group." Stereotypes assigned to society's subordinate groups provide a framework or series of cues for thinking about, and behaving towards, members of these various populations. These stereotypic images or myths offer convenient explanations for political and economic discrimination, social exclusion and denigration, overcrowding and other manifestations of poverty. They help to justify the inferior status to which Puerto Rican people have been relegated—that of a conquered people.[1]

In specific terms, the striking feature of a racial minority stereotype is the way it portrays a people in an image so totally the reverse of what the larger American society considers worthy of emulation and recognition. It is believed that the major and traditional American values are all absent from the Puerto Rican, as well as from the black, Mexican, and Native American. These groups are conceived of as lazy in an ambitious culture, improvident and sensuous in a moralistic society, happy in a sober world, and poor in a nation that offers riches to all who care to take them. In its ultimate form, members of these oppressed groups are equated with objects, with things. This stereotypic perception resembles the "animal characterization" reserved for the very lowest strata in American society:

> Well, while they're fixing supper for us I just want to mention one more class. Now, this one is really a lulu. These are the families that are just not worth a goddam. Now, they're not immoral—they're unmoral—they're just plain amoral. They just simply don't have any morals. I'll tell you they just have animal urges, and they just respond to them. They're just like a bunch of rats or rabbits. (Warner, 1949:51–2)

Many of the stereotypes and myths assigned to Puerto Ricans have their foundation in the early years of the twentieth century when white Americans began to establish their imperialist and colonial domination of Puerto Rico. The views were nurtured by the accounts whites gave of Puerto Ricans: "The natives are lazy and dirty, but are very sharp and cunning, and the introduction of American ideas disturbs them little" (quoted in Bonilla, 1974:439).

Puerto Ricans who came to live in Chicago were given a reception based on the racial prejudices of the city's white population. This is evident from the accounts of some of my study's participants. For instance, a respondent who lived in Westtown/Humboldt Park, a near northside community, provides one example. When discussing one of his experiences in a white tavern in this area of the city during the mid-1950s, he says: "We were always considered black. I remember this one time, I went to a tavern with a friend and the owner of the bar refused to serve us. I said to the guy, 'We want two beers,' and he said, 'We don't serve niggers here.' I replied that we were Puerto Ricans and he just said, 'That's the same shit.' "[2]

Another respondent's account of his exhaustive and futile efforts in finding an apartment serves as further evidence of how the racial minority stigma has been used against Puerto Ricans in Chicago. The respondent, a dark-skinned Puerto Rican man, commented:

> The first apartment that we found for the entire family was actually the work or doing of my wife. I tried getting an apartment for several weeks and each time I would answer a newspaper ad or a sign posted on a building, I was not rented the facilities. This went on for a long time. One day I told a friend about it and he told me to have my wife go the next time. "After all," my friend said, "she looks more white than you." And do you know that the first time she went out to look for an apartment, she found one?

Another major source of prejudice against Puerto Ricans was the stereotypes of the group presented in newspapers. During the formative years when they comprised a small number of the city's total population, Puerto Ricans were often described as "gentle" and "loving people." The common theme of most newspapers and magazine articles was that Puerto Ricans were the most docile of all immigrants to a city known for its aggressiveness. Donald Janson, a correspondent for the *New York Times*, in an article entitled: "Chicago Good City to Puerto Ricans," described this group as well behaved and rapidly integrated into Chicago's society. Despite housing discrimination and problems with the police, he concluded, "Puerto Ricans have adjusted to the new environment without strife" (*New York Times*, 1961).

Similar statements were made by Sam S. King, a reporter for the *Chicago Daily News* (1959). The major emphasis of his article was to show that Puerto Rican migrants were "quite eager to work hard and did not want any handouts." This is clearly shown in the reporter's description of one Puerto Rican family:

> La Boy [father's last name] recently became a CTA bus driver, a status job among his people. He is a happy man, he smiles easily as he talks. He is part of a new migration wave into the city. And like the migration waves of the past—those that brought the Poles, Italians, and Irish—he is a hard-working family man whose main goal in life is a better life for his children.

With the growth of the Puerto Rican population, the reported accounts changed quite radically.[3] Correspondents began to describe the social behavior of the Puerto Rican migrants and their children in lurid terms. A classic example is provided by the *Saturday Evening Post* in 1960 in an account of a physical fight between Puerto Ricans and Italians. The report depicted Chicago's Puerto Ricans as senseless killers: "The two Puerto Ricans had never met Guido Garro; they murdered him only because he happened to be an Italian" (1960:19). In his story, the correspondent added to the stereotypical image of the Puerto Rican by highlighting, what he considered, salient features of the group's urban life:

> In warm weather they live on the streets and sidewalks, not indoors. They are noisy. Young Puerto Rican males stand on street corners and make loud admiring remarks about girls passing by. They drive fast and nervously with much horn blowing.

> Their groceries are stocked with yams, garlic, tropical roots, tortillas and, above all, rice and beans. Their restaurants serve fried bananas, pork-and-rice, chicken-and-rice and rice-and-beans. Their night clubs are dimly lighted, with a hint of danger. They have almost no social clubs or civic groups. Their clubs are the taverns (1960:44).

The printing of this account brought forth a vehement protest from Puerto Ricans. People from the Puerto Rican community were deeply enraged with this damaging picture of barrio life. One leader wrote a letter to the editor of the newspaper denouncing the article:[4]

> The article, plus the yellow tag, "Racial Violence in Chicago," attached to newsstand copies, badly clouds the remarkable achievement of Puerto Ricans in Chicago. . . . Puerto Ricans are scattered throughout the city, considerable segments live in at least 23 of Chicago's 50 wards. There is no Puerto Rican ghetto. This integration is a unique achievement of Chicago's Puerto Ricans.

The attitudes of this correspondent were perhaps typical of those held by many other newspaper reporters. His treatment of the Puerto Rican urban life illustrates the antipathy that whites felt toward this Spanish-speaking population. As the newspapers continued to regale their readers with vignettes of Puerto Rican low-life as well as chilling tales of their sinister and deviant behavior, the Chicagoan was predisposed to view the Puerto Rican with distaste and suspicion as a boastful, uncouth, undesirable, perhaps even *sick*, person.

As with most stereotypical thinking, assumptions about characteristics of racial and ethnic groups tend to be self-confirming. That is to say, by taking the premises as true, people tend to respond to the members of the racial and ethnic groups in terms of these assumed characteristics, and they thereby help to make these characteristics come into being.[5] Elena Padilla captures this point in her discussion of the daily life experience of Puerto Ricans in New York City as they come into direct contact with white America. She writes (1970:558–9):

> Individual achievements by Puerto Ricans are seldom recognized as such. Many of their relationships with white society seem humiliatingly tainted with patronizing behavior. Stereotypes mar friendships, professional relationships, and opportunities. Even sophisticated educated New Yorkers feel that they must confess to us how much they are doing for "your people." In turn, all educated persons of Puerto Rican origins are expected to know the best and cheapest tourist hotels or abortion mills in San Juan, and to be able to provide social services for other Puerto Ricans, from scholarships for medical school to child placement. These kinds of stereotypes — degrading as they are — stimulate defensive group identity, resentment and discontent.

Stereotypic images can be infinitely more effective instruments of domination if they are accepted by members of the subordinate population. It's very likely that some Puerto Ricans have accepted the negation of their culture and of themselves. This behavior pattern is not very difficult to understand in light of Memmi's (1967) discussion in *The Colonizers and the Colonized*. He comments how the colonized often have been brought to admit that their misfortunes result directly from their racial and cultural characteristics. They try to escape the guilt and inferiority they experience by proclaiming total and unconditional adoption of the new cultural models and by irreversible condemnation of their own (1967:38–9).

However, despite everything, Puerto Ricans have resisted the total foundering of their social being. *Despierta Boricua defiende lo tuyo* (Awaken Puerto Ricans, defend that which belongs to you) has been a theme consistently heard in el barrio. The message conveyed in 'Children of the Damned," a poem by Jaime Rivera, a second-generation Puerto Rican from Chicago, illustrates this consciousness. In the final stanzas of the poem, Mr. Rivera stresses in a very powerful form the dire need to become acutely aware of the conditions of Puerto Ricans (1974:61–62):

> Awaken children of the damned!
> Awaken! Stop your crying!
> The teacher called you stupid,
> and the class began to laugh at you—
> Soon you all dropped out of school.

> Despierta! Ramon, Carmen, Maria.
> Awaken! Stop your crying! You lost your jobs
> To Carols, Teds, Alices, and Bobs—
> they have what you haven't got!

> Awaken children of the damned!
> Awaken! Get off the street!
> Put your clothes back on and stop selling!
> You need money for your dying mother,
> for your brother Ramon who's in jail
> for selling dope—the church still says to pray for hope.

> Despierta! Ramon, Carmen, Maria.
> Awaken! Before it's too late—
> Before you meet the same fate
> As your 'queridos' in wonderland.
> Despierta! Despierta! Or you'll miss
> your train—the revolution is here in town.

Large sections of the Puerto Rican people were never culturally alienated and did not share in the denigration of their culture, but continued to live their customary way of life, adapting to changed circumstances. Thus, side by side with the alienation of a section of the Puerto Rican community, there was also the persistence of traditional culture and values.

However, these stereotypes facilitated the control of the Puerto Rican by politicians, social welfare workers, mental health experts, and others, under the guise of therapeutic and welfare programs, based on the assumption that he/she is a sick and deviant person. If taken for granted, this stereotypic image can lead to dangerously pessimistic conclusions. In a thought-provoking paper, David Hernández and Pedro Valez (1973) have pointed to a reification process in which the Puerto Rican is seen as trapped within a veritable crab's nest of chaotic and senseless violence: "It is significant to indicate that these characteristics are the result of a sociological preoccupation which conceives the Puerto Rican's psychological characteristics as the result of static macro-social power relations. This perception conceives of the Puerto Rican in terms of the spontaneity, aggressiveness, self-assurance and positive self-image by the social actor. In fact, he is never seen as a free agent in social interaction." A similar view is shared by Professor Frank Bonilla, Director of the Center for Puerto Rican Studies, Hunter College in New York City. In a perceptive essay he points out: "The dialectic of impotence and stubborn resistence, however covert and diffuse, is perceived as a grinding friction shredding individuals and social ties, but is denied any prospect of political resolution. We are, perhaps, developing a dangerous virtuosity in documenting the prostration, insecurity, ambivalence, and ideological bafflement within our ranks and assigning too little value to the contrary signs that point to a remarkable capacity for survival in a context of prolonged and radical ambiguity" (1974:442).

This discussion does not mean to suggest that "white perceptions" of Puerto Ricans, and the historical inculcation of these perceptions in the minds of Puerto Ricans themselves, are solely at the root of the "Puerto Rican problem." Unquestionably individual racism, with its dehumanizing effects on Puerto Ricans, is important. It is individual racists who perpetuate the institutions which deny equal opportunity to Puerto Ricans and other non-white ethnics. It is individual racists who use racism and discrimination to justify the lowly position of Puerto Ricans and others in society. The point that needs to be stressed is that the circumstances of inequality and oppression experienced by Puerto Ricans in most major cities have always been compounded by their low position in both the economic order (the average economic class position of Puerto Ricans as a group) and the social order (the social prestige accorded individual Puerto Ricans because of their socially assigned racial minority status).

The Puerto Rican struggle for liberation promotes numerous attempts to overcome their assigned, stereotyped racial minority status. Frank Bonilla is correct in pointing out that "Whether on the Island or in New York [in my case Chicago], breaking out of this confining encirclement is a first step toward that space in which we may take a liberating breath" (1974:440). One very important step taken by Puerto Ricans is their development of their own ideology, aimed primarily toward dehumanizing the dominant racial group. The process of ethnic growth and pride, that is, decolonization, has greatly stimulated the development of a Puerto Rican ideology of cultural difference. An essential feature of this ideology is the rejection of "white definitions" and myths of subordination, and their replacement by Puerto Rican definitions. It has become common for this ideology to define Puerto Ricans as possessing precisely those human qualities in which dominant white America is so morally deficient, and some of the very qualities by which white America defines this subordinate group are transformed from denigration to approbation. Directed by the reawakening of social values and ethnic pride, persistent cultural differences have been associated with Puerto Rican ethnicity and ideology and these, in turn, have proceeded directly to the reassertion (albeit in modified forms) of the traditional Puerto Rican culture. I will show in the conclusion how particular elements of the Puerto Rican culture, expressed in activities such as music, have come to symbolize Puerto Rican ethnic consciousness and values and resistance to American racial oppression and domination.

An important part of the Puerto Rican struggle for liberation has been a continuing challenge to those stereotypes and myths assigned to them by the larger American society — not only for the sake of historical accuracy, but for another, and even more crucial, reason. Both in the Island and on the mainland, Puerto Ricans are an oppressed group. They are exploited and manipulated by those with more power. Although some Puerto Ricans have come to believe that the way to get along in white America is by becoming

"Americanized," a much larger group has used their awareness of history—of the Puerto Rican struggles—to restore pride and a sense of heritage to a people who have been oppressed for so long.

NOSTALGIA AND DISENCHANTMENT: CONSIDERATIONS ON RETURNING TO THE ISLAND

Unlike other immigrant groups in urban America, the Puerto Ricans who formed the first wave of emigrants did not come to stay, to settle, and to become "Americanized." The form of population shift of this Spanish-speaking population differed dramatically from the international migration of the last century, which was largely a one-way movement with major streams of immigrants leaving Europe and Asia for North America. It was generally assumed that those who left the Old World would not return. In direct contrast, most Puerto Ricans came to Chicago as "sojourners," expecting to work a few years to amass sufficient capital or acquire a new skill in order to return to a better future life in their homeland. In particular they planned to buy *un terrenito* (a piece of land) which was to assure them of a better way of life from the one they had left behind. In this regard, Puerto Rican emigration was largely a "temporary migration" in the sense that most migrants intended to return to their families after a few years in Chicago.

Among Puerto Rican people expectations of return became part of their migrant ethos and tradition. This return ideology consists of a set of beliefs and values forming one part of the cognitive model which the migrant holds as to the nature and goals of his migration. The return sentiment as an aspect of the migration experience includes, among other things, ideas about the proposed length of the migration period, especially that it will be less than lifelong. It was not that Puerto Rican migrants suffered from a severe longing for the good old days or developed a myth of "lost paradise." Rather, most Puerto Ricans tended to anticipate returning to the Island for the purpose of resettlement. As stated by Manuel Maldonado-Denis, who has written extensively on the Puerto Rican experience (1980:19):

> The Puerto Ricans who, pushed by economic necessity, have suffered and continue to suffer painful exile in the United States,

have never lost the hope of returning to the national territory in order to put an end to their condition as exiles.

The temporary nature of Puerto Rican labor migration was completely rational from the point of view of the emigrant and his family. The purpose which these migrants pursued with single-minded tenacity was to save enough money to be able to purchase land to sustain their families upon their return. In other words, the typical Puerto Rican emigrant was a family representative, forced to work in the colonial metropolis for a limited period of time in order to supplement the family's declining subsistence base. It was hoped that his savings would enable the family to reestablish itself, perhaps by paying off debts or repurchasing lost land, at which time he would return. It was as if Puerto Ricans were seeking a temporary form of economic relief by traveling to the U.S. mainland.

All of my study's respondents, their relatives and friends, in one way or another, were part of this nostalgic yet disenchanting process. The case of one emigrant who arrived in the city in 1953 is a classic example:

> I came to Chicago to work. I came from a *campo* in the small town of Manati. There I had been unemployed for about two years. I would work now and then but never permanently. So the intentions were to come and work in Chicago for several years, make some money and return to Manati. But things, as you can see, did not work out that way. My first three or four years were spent working as a dishwasher in different hotels downtown. I was never paid enough to even consider returning home.

The myth or ideology of return was no better expressed than in the remarks of one respondent who was nearing his retirement from the company for which he had worked almost thirty years. After living all these years in Chicago, he had accomplished his dream:

> I was just in Puerto Rico where I bought a house. My wife is already living in it. This was my lifetime present to her, a present I promised her many years ago. I've always known that I would go back, that I would buy her a house in Puerto Rico. I've been saying this for a very long time and now even my two daughters are planning to come with us as well.

Of course, there were some emigrants who were able to save some of their earnings and return to the Island, and there were others who gave up chasing the dream and saved or secured just enough money to purchase a return airline ticket to Puerto Rico. Members from the latter category perhaps refused to accept the way of life in American society (American racism and discrimination as well as the strangeness of its language, people, and customs), or could not bear the psychic costs of being separated from close friends and the familiar environment of home. Unfavorable economic conditions in the United States, such as layoffs and unemployment within a single industry, may have resulted in return migration for other Puerto Ricans. This explanation is supported by data collected by Hernández-Álvarez (1967) on Puerto Ricans returning to the Island during the 1960s. He reports that many Puerto Rican migrants in the United States returned to Puerto Rico during this period as a result of being displaced from their jobs by automation and mechanization.

But the large majority of Puerto Rican migrants decided to settle in Chicago. There can be two possible explanations for this phenomenon. One is that these emigrants found it extremely profitable to work in Chicago. They were able to send money back to their families, and from the point of view of their own futures as well as the fortunes of their families in Puerto Rico, it was better to settle permanently in Chicago. An examination of those jobs secured by Puerto Rican workers during the 1950s and ensuing decades offers clues to the contrary. Emigrants who had originally intended to return to Puerto Rico found that it was more difficult to save money in Chicago than they had expected. They became trapped in a vicious cycle of poverty, marginal employment, chronic unemployment, and welfare. The fate of Puerto Rican migrants in Chicago is reflected in the poetry of Richard García. In one stanza of his "America You Lied to Us," written over a decade ago about Puerto Ricans in New York where he was born and raised, Richard García describes in lucid terms the many deceptions experienced by this Spanish-speaking population after arriving in New York, Chicago, and other American cities in search of the "promised land" (1974:15):

> To my Father
> You promised him a job,

Where eight hours a day is enough.
Where a union would protect his rights.
Where his taxes from his pay would
supply good books for his children.
A protected neighborhood
The garbage collected five a days a week.
A house that was well built.
A place for his children to play
Television to entertain poor mother,
After the house cleaning, the cooking and
washing clothes was done.
You promised my father Social Security, Pension Plan, Union
Benefits, Life Insurance
BUT INSTEAD YOU GAVE HIM
A list of unemployment agencies
an apartment held up by matches
enough credit cards for a lifetime
plenty of rats and roaches
schools where human beings are dissected,
injected and infected instead of frogs
a tv and newspaper which controls and fools him
everyday before going to work
AMERICA YOU LIED TO US

The large majority of Puerto Ricans had very little choice but to become permanent residents of Illinois' largest city. There was no way out of their entrapment. But even after many years away, most Puerto Ricans, no matter how settled they were in Chicago, no matter how difficult their conditions, kept open the possibility that they would one day go home to the Island. For the large majority of the first generation of Puerto Rican migrants, life in Puerto Rico continued to form a very vital part of their existence and struggle in Chicago. Moreover, as American citizens, Puerto Ricans were not affected by political restrictions which would prevent free movement between the Island and the mainland. In fact, the relative ease with which this Spanish-speaking population could return to their homeland has led to the adaptation of a migratory pattern involving a continuous movement from the mainland to the Island and back again. Referred to as the *van y ven* (back-and-forth) phenomenon by some students of the Puerto Rican experience, this practice "reinforces many links to Puerto Rico, although it also reflects repeated ruptures and renewal of ties, dismantlings and reconstructions of familial and communal networks in old and new settings" (Rodriguez et al., 1980:2).

The ideology of return, combined with the *van y ven* phenomenon, provided the Puerto Rican migrant with a scale of values and preferences which differed substantially from those of other immigrants and from those of the larger American society. Puerto Rican migrants had little inclination to learn anything but the most rudimentary American ways, for they had little interest in settling permenently in America. To perceive of the movement of the Puerto Rican working class to the United States as simply another in a series of "immigrations," as Handlin (1959) and Fitzpatrick (1971) have suggested, can set up interpretations in which the group behavior can be seen as non-participatory or apathetic. For example Forni (1971:1) proclaims "They [Puerto Ricans] are one of the least capable of all minority groups of rapid life-style improvement. And, in spite of the occurrence of . . . [some] spontaneous outburst . . . they are not as active in the political and civil rights field as some other minorities." When examining group behavior and action among Puerto Ricans, the question should not be whether the Puerto Rican migrant and his children are passive, but instead to examine the priorities of the newcomers and how these are geared to improving their condition, and that of their families, in the society of origin.

It is true that among the great mass of working-class Puerto Ricans, and among many of the middle class as well, apathy exists side by side with a growing, festering resentment of their lot. These Puerto Rican city residents are more and more convinced that they should have a better life, they are less and less convinced that they themselves can do anything about it—despair and apathy, of course, are basic ingredients of any underclass community. Puerto Ricans in Chicago do share in middle-class values and aspirations: they, too, value financial success, want their children to be educated, are ashamed of illegitimacy. To be sure, the Puerto Rican underclass does not always act accordingly; Puerto Ricans do drop out of schools and they do have more illegitimate children than members of the middle class. But the reason, in many cases, is their poverty— intellectual as well as financial. Some Puerto Ricans know what they want (according to middle-class standards) but do not know how to achieve these goals. Others know both, but their daily struggle for existence drains them of the energy they need to achieve their aspirations. Some of these Puerto Ricans are simply frustrated victims of middle-class values. Precisely because they have been acculturated into middle-class values, their inability to climb out of the lower class persuades them that the cards are stacked against them, or reinforces their sense of worthlessness.

In effect, Puerto Ricans in Chicago have been given humiliation, insult, and embarrassment as a daily diet, and without regard to individual merit. They've become convinced that most whites never see them as individuals. The Puerto Rican has become noticed, of course—for in rejecting him/her, white society must thereby notice him/her. But the Puerto Rican, too often, is noticed only to be rejected. This sense of rejection by American society, a sense which dominates the underclass Puerto Rican's life, suggests that there is no use in trying.

A few more statements challenging the "failure" of Puerto Ricans to form viable organizations and structures are in order. First, it is very likely that such assessments are based on comparisons with inflated assumptions of the participatory behavior patterns of Americans as a whole. That is, in spite of Tocqueville's observations, Americans do not actively participate in voluntary political associations.

Second, the criticism that Puerto Ricans are incapable of forming viable political organizations is ill-founded. Puerto Rican organizations have been multi-functional in nature: not strictly political, not strictly economic, not strictly social, they have responded to all kinds of problems, perhaps to the extent of deflating at times their effectiveness in any single area. Normally the response of such organizations has been the "crisis issue" approach, which means that at a single point in time the organizations have been involved with a single issue which has reached crisis proportions. Thus, Puerto Rican ethnic organizations have not restricted their activities strictly to political affairs, but have ventured into matters of economics, civil rights, and so on.

The point to keep in mind when discussing the pattern of social participation and behavior among Puerto Ricans is that, in the case of organization building, for example, these structures have been established to contribute to the "natural" drives toward ethnicity by reemphasizing ethnic core values (history, traditions, culture) through symbolism (Puertoricanism). This has been done by encouraging mutual assistance through concerted community action, by generating forums and communication for discussion of group problems, by articulating group goals, and by generating resources and laying the groundwork for strategies of action. While not all Puerto Rican community organizations have been involved in all of these pursuits and activities, their involvement in one or more has contributed toward group goals.

It should be emphasized that the perspective from which the role of Puerto Rican organizations is viewed here is a practical and realistic one. The significance of organizations can be seen by analyzing its parallel (i.e., organization and/or the lack of it). Viewed in this light, any level of community organization is politically significant, since it will contribute to ethnic group cohesiveness.

Third, and most importantly, it should be understood that much of what is mistaken for apathy is simply a system of self-defense inherited by a people with a long history of being kicked around. It is not apathy, it is self-protection. Liebow, in his study of black street corner men, comes to a somewhat similar conclusion in suggesting that there may not be a lower-class culture. "Lower-class people of color act the way they do not because of historical or cultural imperatives. Instead the way of life of these men may be simply a reaction to the facts of their position and isolation in American society" (1967:208). How could one expect economically and educationally poor Puerto Ricans in the United States to behave in an achievement-oriented fashion after coming from such a tradition of exploitation? — after being forced immediately upon arrival into enduring the crippling handicaps of prejudice and discrimination imposed upon them by white America?

I will show that in contrast to the criticism which views Puerto Ricans in a passive light, Puerto Rican migrants and their children were very active in the life of their community. Indeed, Puerto Ricans in Chicago have labored with great effort and energy to establish an institutional life of their own in the face of impossible odds.

THE PUERTO RICAN FAMILY AND FRIENDSHIP NETWORK

As in other immigrant settlements, Puerto Rican communities in Chicago comprised a group life which revolved around family members and fellow ethnics who spoke the same language and shared the same culture. This form of family ties and group solidarity was shaped by two major forces. First, the Puerto Rican family structure was given form by the norms and ideals of the Island's traditional culture. Second, societal conditions, such as residential concentration and lack of external support systems, played a significant role in molding the family patterns and friendship networks. In the traditional Puerto Rican family unit, with its strong emphasis on familism, ties beyond the nuclear family were strong and extensive, and reciprocal rights and duties were connected with all relatives including grandparents, aunts, uncles, and cousins. A unique feature of this kinship network was the inclusion of non-blood relatives such as *compadres* (co-parents or godparents) who took on the rights and obligations more characteristic of relatives than friends and were referred to and regarded as kinsmen. *Hijos de crianza* (children of upbringing) were also part of the Puerto Rican family network. In short, the Puerto Rican family encompasses not only those related by blood and marriage, but also persons tied to it through custom.

The range of family ties expressed among new arrivals to Chicago is not surprising in view of the important function played by the family unit in the Puerto Rican society. The Puerto Rican family provided members with emotional security and a sense of belonging. In a real sense, one's personal identity was derived from his/her family, and family membership was essential in terms of defining one's place and identity in society. Fitzpatrick's (1971:79) description of the Puerto Rican family gives weight to this point: "The world to a Latin consists of a pattern of intimate personal relationships, and the basic relationships are those of his family. His confidence, his sense of security and identity are perceived in his relationship to others who are his family."

The cultural traditions of *el campesino* and *jibaro* (peasants) of Puerto Rico retained their vitality in Chicago's Puerto Rican barrios primarily through family and friendship interaction and communication. This intense feeling of group solidarity, based primarily on the family and fellow ethnics, caused the Puerto Rican to cling to neighborliness very consciously and tenaciously. One study respondent described this lively social life as it could be observed on a warm summer evening in one of the Puerto Rican barrios of the city. "The family groups and neighborly visits on the front doorsteps all along the streets occupied by Puerto Ricans were always lively.

People were always talking about the Island and certainly about the new society. It would be late at night and the men would be engaged in domino games or just *charlando* (playing around)."

Suttles (1968) provides a similar account in his description of a Puerto Rican neighborhood in the Near West Side. Although his over- all account of Puerto Rican life in Chicago seems contradictory — suggesting in sharp contrast to the findings of most studies on Puerto Ricans in the United States, including this one, that Puerto Ricans are progressively losing the cultural content of their ethnic tradi- tion, Suttles still says of the Puerto Rican social life (1968:1480):

> In all, there are thirty-four business places on the street. All but two of them are attuned to Puerto Rican trade. Most of these have their "hangers-on," women or men on the inside, young boys or girls at the doorway. A combined record shop and cleaners has a loud speaker that plays their popular music. In the summertime the men gather in front of this establish- ment, set up a table, and play cards. Nearby, tambourine and guitar music sometimes drifts out of a storefront church.

A reporter for one of Chicago's leading newspapers provides a corresponding account of Puerto Rican family life in this metropolis. When describing one particular Puerto Rican family, the reporter wrote: "Most of the Medinas' social life centers around the family — more than 100 relatives in Chicago — and Puerto Rican friends. . . . It is nothing for 15 or 20 relatives to drop-in on one evening, to visit on the front porch or climb the additional flight to the Medinas' apartment. Occasionally the girls bring friends home from school . . . but usually they are Puerto Rican friends *(Chicago Tribune,* 1961).

In addition to providing Puerto Ricans with a lively social life, the family and friendship network constituted the cohesive force essential for the formation and maintenance of the migrant ethnic community. This network not only cemented ties to other families, it also served as an intermediary to build ties between the newcomer and the larger American society. When Puerto Ricans arrived in Chicago, they understood little about the English language or the wider American society. They lacked contacts with potential Amer- ican employers and knew little concerning American labor prac- tices. They had migrated to Chicago without the leadership of a professional class which could be directly connected to society's major institutions and structures. The church and clergy leadership, which had played such a significant function for other Catholic immigrant groups such as the Irish (Biddle, 1976), Polish (Lopata, 1976), and Italians (Femminella and Quadagno, 1976), for instance, were not transplanted to the new society by this Spanish-speaking population. Nor was the labor boss which had existed among Italians, Greeks, Austrians, Turks, Poles, Bulgarians, and others a part of the Puerto Rican migration experience. The Puerto Rican family and ethnic network compensated for these handicaps and became the method by which Puerto Ricans began to overcome their strangeness in this midwestern city.

The importance of the Puerto Rican family and friendship network to the newcomers is clearly reflected in the comments of one of my study's respondents: "Puerto Ricans could not have migrated here with ease unless there were friends or relatives waiting for them. The *jibaros* would take care of each other even if they didn't have a job for a year." How significantly far-reaching this system was for the migrants is also clearly shown in the accounts of two respondents concerning their quest in finding a job and an apartment, respectively:

> I had a cousin who came to live in Chicago around 1948. He wrote me several times asking me to come to Chicago where there was plenty of work. I decided to try it out. I arrived on Tuesday, November 9, 1951 and by Thursday of the same week I was already working. My cousin took me to where he worked, and helped me to fill out the application. He spoke to his boss, I was hired two days later. I've been working at the same place now for 32 years.

> I was one of the Pioneros [pioneers]. I came to live in Chicago when there were just a handful of us. In fact, I came here not knowing anyone. I was very fortunate that at the airport, while waiting for my luggage, I met another young Puerto Rican. We talked for some time. I told him that I did not have relatives in Chicago and I needed a place to live. He told me not to worry because he would help me find an apartment. He brought me to Milwaukee Avenue where I found a room in the same building where he lived.

Thomas Hall, a correspondent for the *Chicago Tribune*, provides an analogous account of the Puerto Rican family unit in Chicago. Recognizing the many problems and challenges facing a predominantly rural population encountering an urban area for the first time, the reporter suggests that Puerto Ricans learn to cope with their way of life by relying on the family:

> When a member of the family arrives every one of his kinfolk, blood or marriage, must be there to meet him. He must be taken in hand, housed where there is no room, and fed where there is nothing to eat. Finding work for the newcomer is a family project. Buying winter clothing (something unknown in tropical Puerto Rico) is another. If the family's resources are inadequate, the neighborhood lends its aid. The grocer, the bartender, and the beauty parlor operator relay bits of information on apartments and jobs openings. (*Chicago Tribune* 1968)

The strength of the family network can be further inferred from the characteristics of the Puerto Rican migrants: Puerto Rican emigration to Chicago was seldom comprised of whole families. The settlement of Puerto Ricans in this urban setting, as well as in other cities, was initially organized by single individuals—single and married young men mainly from the *campos* (rural areas) of the Island who poured into America's cities looking for work. Those who were married would make the journey alone, and after a few years, would send for their wife and children. Even a decade after the arrival of the first large group of Puerto Rican newcomers to Chicago, the 1960 Census showed an imbalance in the ratio of single male and female Puerto Ricans living in Chicago. Out of a total of 4,958 single persons, 14 years old and over, listed by the Census as city residents, 3,228 (65 percent) were male.[6]

The individual pattern of the Puerto Rican migration reveals something of its nature and motivation. Men were more likely to emigrate because of long-standing patriarchal traditions in the Puerto Rican society; it was virtually unthinkable to permit a single woman to travel abroad. In fact, within the Puerto Rican family, the father or male figure was dominant. He made the decisions and was responsible for making a living—a feat that involved skills of wit as well as hard labor to protect the family from the threat of desperate poverty. The sex-role definitions of traditional Puerto Rico rejected the idea of women leaving home and community social control for educational or work experience, even at the cost of the economic contribution they could make to the family. By accepting the responsibility for the economic welfare of the members of the family, the father was expected to make the journey to work regardless of its location. Because the economic conditions in Puerto Rico were so deplorable, married and single men were forced to travel throughout the Island and even across the Atlantic to the United States in search of work.

Individual migration represented a leading strategy for reducing expenses while establishing a financial base in the new society. The purchase of food and winter clothing, for instance, since limited to one person, was considerably lower relative to the expenses accrued by an entire family unit. Another example of the benefits of individual male migration can be found in the acquisition of rental units. In some cases, men would rent single apartments and rooms, paying very little weekly or monthly. Some men were taken in as boarders by friends, others came to live with relatives, while many others shared the same apartment. These and other similar advantages appeared to have encouraged and fostered a process of individual migration among Puerto Rican men.

This practice of migrating as individuals rather than as entire family units serves as further evidence of the significant role played by the ideology of return in the lives of the migrants. Men emigrated alone in order to return to the Island in the shortest time possible. "Why bring the entire family if we are going back to Puerto Rico in the not too distant future?" was the common view of the Puerto Rican migrant. As long as Puerto Ricans perceived emigration as temporary relocation, individual migration represented the best and surest way to accumulate the necessary capital which would enable a fast return home.

Another characteristic of Puerto Rican emigrants was their age range. The 1960 Census data indicates very clearly that most of the men who emigrated to the mainland were young. The Census shows that 22 percent of the men were between the ages of 18–24 years and 35 percent were in age range of 25–34 years. Over 23 percent of the women were in the first age range; another 31 percent in the second.

As with the case of the sex of the emigrants it is not difficult to understand why those who chose to emigrate tended to be young. American employers preferred young men and women who could work long hours in jobs in the declining blue-collar sector of the economy. In addition, the age of the emigrants might have been partially influenced by the Puerto Rican goverment's migration policies, which may have encouraged the younger surplus labor to try their luck in the mainland. It is not difficult to see that the more adventuresome younger men would be attracted to oversea emigration.

FIRST BARRIOS

As noted above, Puerto Ricans began migrating to Chicago in significant numbers during the 1950s and 1960s. According to the 1960 Census, there were 32,371 Puerto Ricans living in the city. Ten years later, this number more than doubled to a total of 78,963 residents. Several reports dealing with the wider Spanish-speaking population in Chicago have disputed the official count of these groups on the basis of undercounting practices by the Census Bureau. Two observers suggested the following figures for 1970 after examining the official enumeration for Spanish-speaking residents for that year:

> Beginning with the official 1970 Census figures of 247,857 and 324,215 [Spanish-speaking] for the city and the metropolitan area . . . respectively, if we assume that the under-counted population was about twice that of the Blacks but, conservatively, lower than some national surveys, and use a figure of 16%, the corrected number are 287,514 for the city and 376,089 for the Metropolitan area. (Walton and Salces, 1977:4)

In any event, it is safe to say that the Puerto Rican population increase between 1950 and 1970 was, indeed, substantial. During this twenty-year period, several sizable Puerto Rican barrios, usually of a few square blocks each, sprang up in various parts of the city. Beginning with the initial group of Puerto Rican migrants in the 1940s, Puerto Rican newcomers usually settled in or near the center of the city (Padilla, 1947). In a series of articles for the *Chicago Sun-Times*, Watson and Wheeler indicate that there were several major initial communities of Puerto Rican settlement in this area during the 1950s: Lakeview, Near North Side, Lincoln Park, and Uptown (Sept. 12-20, 1971). The two writers also add that another group of newcomers settled in the Woodlawn community in the city's Southside.

Data obtained from the Office of the Commonwealth of Puerto Rico in Chicago, a community social service agency established by the government of Puerto Rico in this and other American cities to assist the newcomers adjust to their new environment, provides further definition of the largest areas of settlement in the city during the 1950s. I collected the addresses of people who visited this agency for job placement and other services for a period of five years, 1955–1960, and clustered then according to community areas. The data yielded the following information: Uptown 6; Lakeview 36; Lincoln Park 54; Near North Side 170; and Woodlawn 37. Map 1 shows the geographic location of the leading communities of Puerto Rican settlement in Chicago during the 1950s.

The 1960 Census also shows the concentration of a fairly high number of Puerto Ricans residing in other communities in the city. In Logan Square, the number of Puerto Rican residents totaled 561; in West Garfield Park the number reached 993; 3,676 lived in East Garfield Park; and another 7,162 comprised part of the Near West Side community. The geographical distribution of these additional ethnic enclaves are shown in Map 2.

In addition to the fact that housing discrimination limited Puerto Ricans to certain areas of Chicago, their concentration in these communities is also an indication of the proximity of these areas to the workplace. Puerto Rican newcomers attempted to make the journey to work as short as possible. The accounts of several of my study's respondents serve as evidence of this pattern of residential concentration. One respondent, who shared an apartment with several friends in a large building on LaSalle Street in the Near North Side community, provides an insightful account of the relationship between place of residence and work.

> For a period of more than five years, I worked as a dishwasher at several hotels downtown. At first I lived near Adams and Ashland and rode the bus to work. This got a little expensive

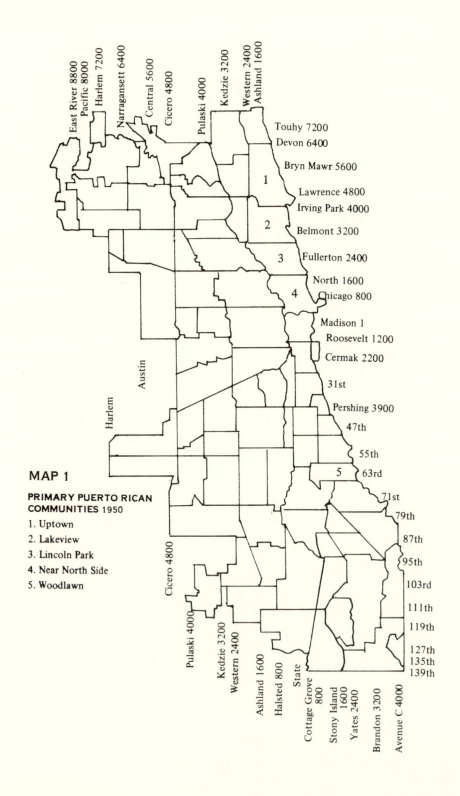

East River 8800
Pacific 8000
Harlem 7200
Narragansett 6400
Central 5600
Cicero 4800
Pulaski 4000
Kedzie 3200
Western 2400
Ashland 1600

Touhy 7200
Devon 6400
Bryn Mawr 5600
Lawrence 4800
Irving Park 4000
Belmont 3200
Fullerton 2400
North 1600
Chicago 800
Madison 1
Roosevelt 1200
Cermak 2200
31st
Pershing 3900
47th
55th
63rd
71st
79th
87th
95th
103rd
111th
119th
127th
135th
139th

1
2
3
4
5

Austin
Harlem

MAP 1

**PRIMARY PUERTO RICAN
COMMUNITIES** 1950

1. Uptown
2. Lakeview
3. Lincoln Park
4. Near North Side
5. Woodlawn

Cicero 4800
Pulaski 4000
Kedzie 3200
Western 2400
Ashland 1600
Halsted 800
State
Cottage Grove 800
Stony Island 1600
Yates 2400
Brandon 3200
Avenue C 4000

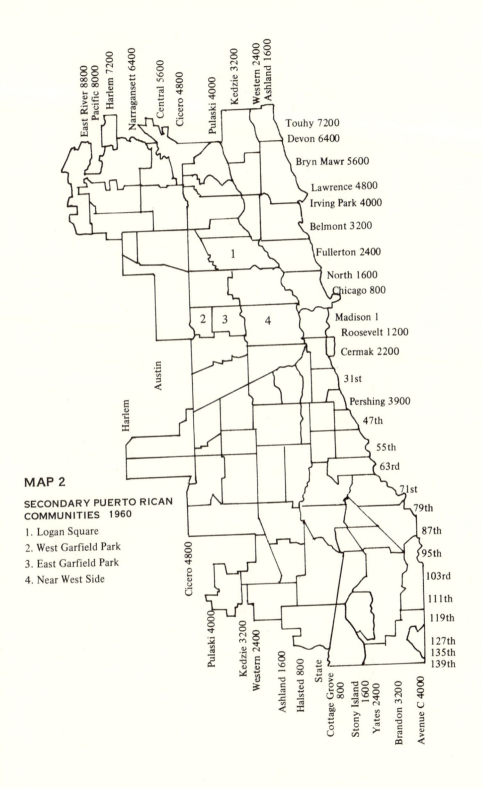

East River 8800
Pacific 8000
Harlem 7200
Narragansett 6400
Central 5600
Cicero 4800
Pulaski 4000
Kedzie 3200
Western 2400
Ashland 1600

Touhy 7200
Devon 6400
Bryn Mawr 5600
Lawrence 4800
Irving Park 4000
Belmont 3200
Fullerton 2400
North 1600
Chicago 800
Madison 1
Roosevelt 1200
Cermak 2200
31st
Pershing 3900
47th
55th
63rd
71st
79th
87th
95th
103rd
111th
119th
127th
135th
139th

1

2 3 4

Austin

Harlem

Cicero 4800

Pulaski 4000
Kedzie 3200
Western 2400
Ashland 1600
Halsted 800
State
Cottage Grove 800
Stony Island 1600
Yates 2400
Brandon 3200
Avenue C 4000

MAP 2

**SECONDARY PUERTO RICAN
COMMUNITIES 1960**

1. Logan Square
2. West Garfield Park
3. East Garfield Park
4. Near West Side

after a while, and since I could live near these hotels, walk to work, and save me that amount of money, I took an apartment with a couple of friends who were looking for the same kind of arrangements. In those days, we made little money, so we tried to save as much as possible.

Another respondent, who came to live in Chicago in 1948, provides a similar version. He lived in several places that were all near his place of employment but recalled best living in Woodlawn where he could walk to work most of the time:

> I was one of the few Puerto Ricans that got a job in the steel mills. Many of us came to Chicago with intentions of working in the mills but most of us never got past the front door of the personnel office. At that time most of the minority people hired were Mexicans and a few Blacks. But I was one of those lucky ones. I lived about ten blocks from the mills. In those days I could walk that distance and much more. I moved to this *barrio* because it was close to my job. In fact, I did not even know that other Puerto Ricans lived there.

The patterns of Puerto Rican urban settlement do not appear to have been substantially different from the patterns of settlement of early European immigrants. Ward (1971:105) notes, for instance, that from the mid-nineteenth century to World War I, "the central concentration of urban employment . . . strongly influenced the location and characteristics of the residential areas of new immigrants, most of whom sought low cost housing close to their place of employment." Thus, early Puerto Rican newcomers to Chicago concentrated, in part, near the center of the city in correspondence to the distribution of available employment opportunities and low cost housing.

In all areas of settlement, Puerto Ricans lived interspersed among whites and in some cases among blacks; there were few all-Puerto Rican communities. For example the 1960 Census shows that there was a total of 581 Puerto Ricans and 122,595 whites living in Uptown; 1,191 and 115,018 in Lakeview; 2,699 and 50,569 in Near North Side; and 2,181 and 84,604 in Lincoln Park. However, in the majority of the cases Puerto Ricans lived in segregated ethnic enclaves within these communities. In their analysis of trends in racial and ethnic segregation in Chicago, Taeuber and

Taeuber (1964) found that the index of segregation for Puerto Ricans in the 1960s was 66, second only to black's 82. Thus, the fact that Puerto Ricans might have shared certain communities in the city with other groups does not mean that they lived in integrated communities.

THE DIVISION STREET AREA

Beginning in 1960 a pattern of mobility and ethnic concentration began to operate among Puerto Ricans in Chicago. A movement towards the near northwest side of the city emerged which left some of the original barrios, particularly those of the west and south sides, with a very small, almost unnoticeable number of Puerto Rican residents. Using data from the 1960 and 1970 Census, Chicago's Department of Human Resources' report on "Chicago's Spanish-speaking Population" provides estimates of the population changes that occurred in these communities (1973). In terms of actual numbers, according to the report, the greatest loss occurred in the Near West Side. A total of 9,104 Puerto Ricans moved from this area between 1960 and 1970. And in terms of percentages, the Garfield Park communities experienced the largest drop of Puerto Rican residents. Out of 5,722 Puerto Ricans listed in the report as residing in East Garfield Park in 1960 only 284 were counted ten years later. This represents a loss of 95 percent of the Puerto Rican residents. In West Garfield Park, where the Puerto Rican population had equaled 2,620 in 1960, the loss of 2,449 residents during the ensuing ten year period represents a drop of 93.5 percent of the Puerto Rican residents from that community.

A similar decline occurred in Woodlawn. Only 191 Puerto Ricans were counted as residing in that community in 1970, a decrease of 91.7 percent or a reduction of 2,120 Puerto Ricans from the previous decade. In the Near North Side area the loss was relatively modest. Out of 3,433 residents counted in 1960, 1,452 were still living in the community ten years later. This equals a decline of 57.7 percent of the Puerto Rican population in this particular area.

There are several reasons for the movement of the Puerto Rican population from the west and south sides of the city to the north side. As for the Near West and Near North sides, the shift in population was influenced by contrasting conditions. In the Near West Side, the problem of gang warfare and delinquency served as the leading reason. There were four major ethnic groupings living in this community during the 1950s and early 1960s. Italians were the most numerous and hegemonic group, giving the area the reputation of being an "Italian neighborhood." Mexicans and blacks represented the next two largest groups, while Puerto Ricans comprised the smallest population in the Near West Side. Friction between the various groups was constant. According to Suttles, who studied this community during the mid-1960s, "for a long time the area [had] received special attention because of its delinquency rate and reputation as a problem area within the city" (1968:18). Suttles estimated the existence of 32 "street corner groups" in this area, making the Near West Side one of the target areas of the "Chicago Youth Development Project." This program brought in street workers and community organizers with the aim of reducing delinquency. It was primarily this concern for the youth which led many Puerto Rican families to move to other parts of the city in search of what they perceived as less hostile environments. Parents were simply afraid for their children.

The situation was different in the Near North Side, an area referred to by Zorbaugh (1929) as *The Gold Coast and the Slum*. This area had been the home of Chicago's wealthiest families as well as the city's largest slum district around the turn of the century. Puerto Ricans, like other groups before them, were attracted to the Near North Side by its cheap hotels and rooming houses on State, Clark, Wells, LaSalle, and other steets along the Chicago River. During the 1950s the penetration of business and industry was changing the Near North Side; it became one of the leading sites in the city for urban renewal renovation (Berry, et al., 1976). Thus, with the clearance of land for urban renewal and accompanying leaps in the real estate prices, Puerto Ricans were forced to relocate to other parts of the city.

In the case of the East and West Garfield Parks and Wood-lawn, the departure of Puerto Rican families is attributed to a set of interrelated circumstances. With the relocation of manufacturing and industrial employment to suburban areas during the 1950s and 1960s, there was a rapid decline of whites, accompanied by the expansion of the black community into these areas. The Woodlawn and the West and East Garfield Parks communities became a natural focus of black settlement in Chicago due to the dire housing needs of the black community and the general real estate policy of racial control. On all indices used to measure community instability (physical deterioration, high unemployment, deficiencies in community services, and the like), Woodlawn ranked among the most disadvantaged of the city's seventy-six community areas by 1960 (Kitagawa and Taeuber, 1963). Table 8 illustrates how the arrival and expansion of the black population in East and West Garfield Parks and Woodlawn paralleled the decline of whites between 1940 and 1960.

By the time of the arrival of Puerto Ricans in Woodlawn and East and West Garfield Parks, blacks were beginning to achieve ascendancy over these communities.

Insofar as the Woodlawn community was finally incorporated into the "Black Southside Belt" and East and West Garfield Parks into the "West Side," the streets, businesses, schools, and recreational facilities were all marked off as the exclusive domain of blacks. In fact, through The Woodlawn Organization (TWO) and the West Side Organization (WSO), blacks began to give deeper meaning and precision to their interests in these communities as well as in the wider context of the city. At the same time Puerto Ricans were becoming equally convinced that blacks would never voluntarily yield any of the benefits or resources vested in the west and south sides. The small number of Puerto Rican residents in these areas seem to have given up any further thought of remaining there. Puerto Ricans became even more convinced that they were expendable.

TABLE 8

Population Shift in the West and South Sides, 1940–1960

COMMUNITY	RACE	1940	1950	1960
Woodlawn	Black	12,107	31,329	72,397
	White	59,438	48,368	8,450
West Garfield Park	Black	24	23	7,204
	White	48,392	48,328	38,151
East Garfield Park	Black	2,990	11,695	41,097
	White	62,704	58,144	25,409

Source: Kitagawa and Taeuber (1963).

There is little doubt that one other major reason for the shift of population among Puerto Ricans is directly related to racial problems or social misunderstandings with blacks. Puerto Ricans felt that blacks were especially apprehensive of their presence in these areas and often attributed their conflicts with blacks to cultural differences. In general, Puerto Ricans felt that they were being regarded with suspicion, if not as enemies. This kept members of the two groups from joining forces and commiserating with one another over a common dilemma.

In more specific terms, the movement of Puerto Ricans from East/West Garfield Parks and Woodlawn was directly related to conflicts between Puerto Ricans and blacks, which in turn, can be attributed, in part, to different cultural practices. The most obvious restriction on communication and interaction between these two ethnic groups was their difference of language. For the most part, Spanish was the working language for the everyday life of Puerto Ricans. Some of my study's respondents make the claim that most of the time blacks found the behavior of this Spanish-speaking group incomprehensible, thus providing little ground for peaceful exchanges. As one respondent stated when discussing Puerto Rican–black relations in East Garfield Park: "Blacks could never understand why we were so interested in things that were happening in Puerto Rico or why we spoke Spanish all the time. They assumed that we did not have an interest in any community activity or learning their language. The problem was that our community concerns included certain things that our families, relatives, and friends were going through at that time in the Island."

Puerto Ricans in West and East Garfield Parks, many of whom had lived among whites in these areas before the massive arrival of blacks there and had experienced a tremendous amount of racial discrimination and prejudice, came to realize that their way of life was not accepted by either white or black Americans. They found themselves between both groups, being subjected to the ugly pressures of race prejudice on both sides. Distrust and misconception of Puerto Ricans who refused to choose the "white" or "black" way of life were quite pervasive.

Clara Rodriguez (1980:27) makes a similar observation regarding the experience of Puerto Ricans in New York:

The early-migrating Puerto Ricans entered a biracial society that strictly associated white with positive and black with negative. The migrating Puerto Rican saw that this association permeated every aspect of American life. . . . The result of this situation was that the migrant Puerto Rican held on to his cultural identity very strongly and rejected racial identification on American terms. This prompted a bitter reaction from the black community capsuled in the words, "Trouble is they (Puerto Ricans) won't call themselves colored and we won't call them white." For the migrant Puerto Rican this racial identification, and all it implied, was not only foreign to his cultural and perceptual frame of reference, it was also damning.

The American racial scheme expected Puerto Ricans to define themselves as whites or blacks, the standardized categories for color in the United States, with no allowance for the Puerto Rican's mixed heritage of Indian, Spanish, and African. In effect, identification as white or black would serve as the locus of orientation to concepts of self and others, to values, and life styles. For Puerto Ricans, these identifications created a great deal of confusion and ambivalence as they began to take on the malignancies of American society. This is not to suggest that Puerto Ricans were or are free of racial prejudice or had not experienced racial discrimination before leaving the Island. I agree with Samuel Betances (1971:6) when he writes: "The migrant Puerto Ricans . . . have brought with them certain experiences and outlooks on the issues of race and color. . . . The first generation grew up in an island which historically has experienced 'whiteness' as a positive value and 'blackness' as a negative one. . . . While blackness may not be as negative as in America, it is still negative enough to be a source of embarrassment in many instances of Puerto Rican life." Despite the practice of racism in Puerto Rico, often referred to as "mild discrimination," Puerto Rican migrants were totally unprepared to deal with the racial relations operative in America upon their arrival. And, the effect of American racism was and continues to be quite devastating.

The overwhelming majority of Puerto Ricans responded to conditions in West and East Garfield Parks by moving to another area in the city where a small number of migrants had begun to settle. They hoped to establish their own "little Puerto Rico" in Chicago.

They began to follow a northern path which united many of them in what became the city's first large Puerto Rican ethnic enclave.

One thing that is certain about the movement of Puerto Ricans in Chicago during the 1960s is that it bears little resemblence with the contention found in the "Chicago School" or human-ecology conception of ethnic residential segregation as an aspect of status differences among groups which would disappear with social mobility. Park (1967:60) propounded this position forcefully when he noted that "changes of economic and social status . . . tend to be registered in changes of location." Burgess (1923) and Cressey (1938) also argued that newcomers in each immigrant wave shifted from central-city areas toward peripheral residential communities at the same time that they moved upward economically and socially. While some economically and socially mobile Puerto Ricans may have moved to more fashionable and desirable residential areas, the majority of them, however, were driven to one clearly delineated area of settlement in the city. The largest Puerto Rican ethnic enclave, located in the near northwest side of the city, was formed as a result of this population shift.

Westtown/Humboldt Park are the official names for the two adjacent communities that house this Puerto Rican barrio. This name is almost artificial since it is seldomly used by the local residents. Instead, the popular name used for the area is "Division Street." The name includes an adjoining residential area and a commercial strip as well as the street proper. Map 3 shows the location of the Division Street Area within the wider metropolis. (A smaller, but similar offshoot in the Lakeview area also had begun to house another large number of Puerto Ricans.)

The development of present day Division Street started in 1837 when the eastern portion of the Westtown Community Area was included within the first city limits of the city of Chicago. Several old Indian trails which ran through the near northwest side later became important thoroughfares—Grand, Ogden, Milwaukee, and Elston Avenues. In 1848, Chicago's first railroad, the Galena and Chicago Union, followed the southern boundaries of Westtown along Kinzie Street. In the following years the community grew slowly, mainly near the railroads and also close to the factories that were being built along the river and along Milwaukee Avenue. Completion of the Logan Square and Humboldt Park branches of the

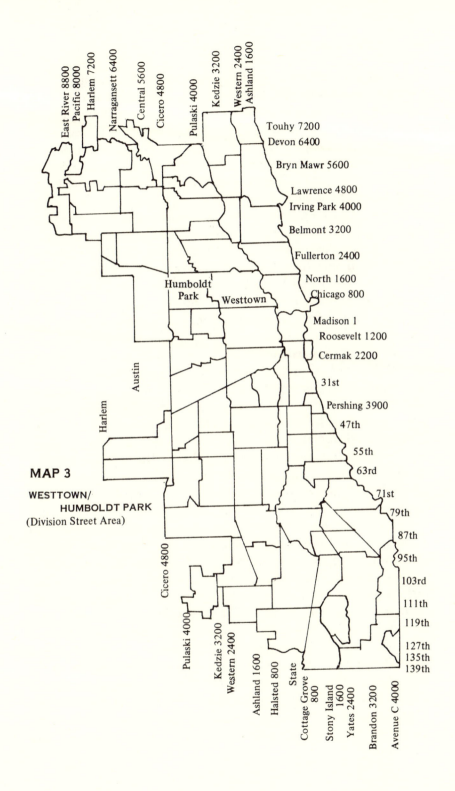

East River 8800
Pacific 8000
Harlem 7200
Narragansett 6400
Central 5600
Cicero 4800
Pulaski 4000
Kedzie 3200
Western 2400
Ashland 1600

Touhy 7200
Devon 6400
Bryn Mawr 5600
Lawrence 4800
Irving Park 4000
Belmont 3200
Fullerton 2400
North 1600
Chicago 800
Madison 1
Roosevelt 1200
Cermak 2200
31st
Pershing 3900
47th
55th
63rd
71st
79th
87th
95th
103rd
111th
119th
127th
135th
139th

Humboldt
Park
Westtown

Austin

Harlem

MAP 3

WESTTOWN/
HUMBOLDT PARK
(Division Street Area)

Cicero 4800
Pulaski 4000
Kedzie 3200
Western 2400
Ashland 1600
Halsted 800
State
Cottage Grove 800
Stony Island 1600
Yates 2400
Brandon 3200
Avenue C 4000

elevated lines in 1895, as well as the extension and installation of streetcar lines during the 1890s and early 1900s, brought the community more adequate rapid transit facilities and contributed to the development of Westtown. The community achieved residential maturity in the early 1900s, and according to the 1940 Census, 58 percent of the dwelling units were in residential structures built before 1900. As of 1960, only one percent of the housing units was in structures built since 1940.

For a very long time the Westtown community had been an important area of residence for foreign-born persons and natives of foreign or mixed parentage—particularly Polish. The Polish concentration in Westtown declined significantly over the years. In 1930, persons of Polish stock comprised 49 percent of the total population of the community. In 1960, persons of Polish background continued to be the dominant ethnic group followed by Russians, Italians, and Germans.

For Puerto Ricans, the Division Street Area served as the leading area of first settlement throughout the 1960s and for another large number of newcomers during the 1970s. During the former decade, for example, near one-fourth (7,948) of the city's Puerto Rican population already lived in Westtown. In the latter period, on the other hand, this number increased to 42 percent of the city's Puerto Rican population: a total of 33,166 Puerto Ricans were counted by the Census of that year as residing in this community.

Initially, the Division Street Area was comprised of a few sections of the Westtown/Humboldt Park community. Twenty-one (58 percent) of the thirty-six Census tracts in the community had a Puerto Rican population which represented less than 6 percent of the total population in each tract. Ten tracts (27 percent) had a Puerto Rican population between 6.0 and 12.9 percent of their total populations. Of all the Census tracts, numbers 298 and 299, located in the northeast side of Westtown, housed the largest concentration of Puerto Rican residents in the community in 1960: a combined total of 1,093 residents. This particular area stretched from Division Street on the south to North Avenue on the north, and from Leavitt Street on the east to Western Avenue on the west. Another sizeable concentration of Puerto Ricans (664 residents) was found living near the center of the community in Census tract 309. On the southeast corner of the community, Census tracts 317 and

318z combined to house another 613 Puerto Rican residents. Several smaller contingents were located in other parts of the Westtown area. Map 4 illustrates the location of the several Puerto Rican enclaves in the community in 1960.

As a whole, the various Puerto Rican barrios scattered throughout the city were neighborhood centers of activity of comparable size and make-up; Division Street, however, overshadowed all others. Division Street represented the typical Puerto Rican "*colonía*" so well described by Hernández-Álvarez (1968). The *colonía* was the familiar base where the migrant's native language was spoken, his customs and traditions were practiced and, thus, allowed to remain intact. In short, the *colonía* provided a milieu for Puerto Ricans in which they could imbue their lives with meaning. It was here that the Puerto Rican migrant shopped *en la tienda* or *bodega* (the ethnic grocery store), purchasing those very essential consumer goods. Puerto Rican restaurants, barber shops, and taverns were also very important commercial enterprises as well as serving the function of social institutions. Not only the first forms of entrepreneurship among the early settlers, the ethnic stores, restaurants, barbershops, and the like nurtured close interactions among Puerto Rican newcomers, and reproduced older forms of community and familial organization. In short, the physical structure of the community fostered the reconstruction of ethnic ties.

It was also on Division Street that *La Prensa*, a Spanish newspaper published in New York and distributed in Chicago and which preceded the publication of the local migrant press, could be purchased. *El Teatro San Juan* (The San Juan Theatre), the city's first Puerto Rican theatre, was located on Division Street. The famous Division Street Y.M.C.A. was located near the eastern-most boundary of the community on Division Street. Weightlifters like Sergio Oliva (Mr. Universe) and, of course, lesser known individuals from the neighborhood often "pumped iron" at the Division Street "Y." Since 1966 the Puerto Rican Parade has been filing along Division Street after completing its magnificent display of Puerto Rican traditions in downtown Chicago. Here was the site of the "Division Street Riots" of 1966, the first Puerto Rican civil disturbance in the city.

In recent years, new developments have maintained Division Street's reputation as *the* Puerto Rican community in the city of Chicago. A new and very modern high school was built on the cor-

MAP 4
PUERTO RICAN SECTORS ON DIVISION STREET

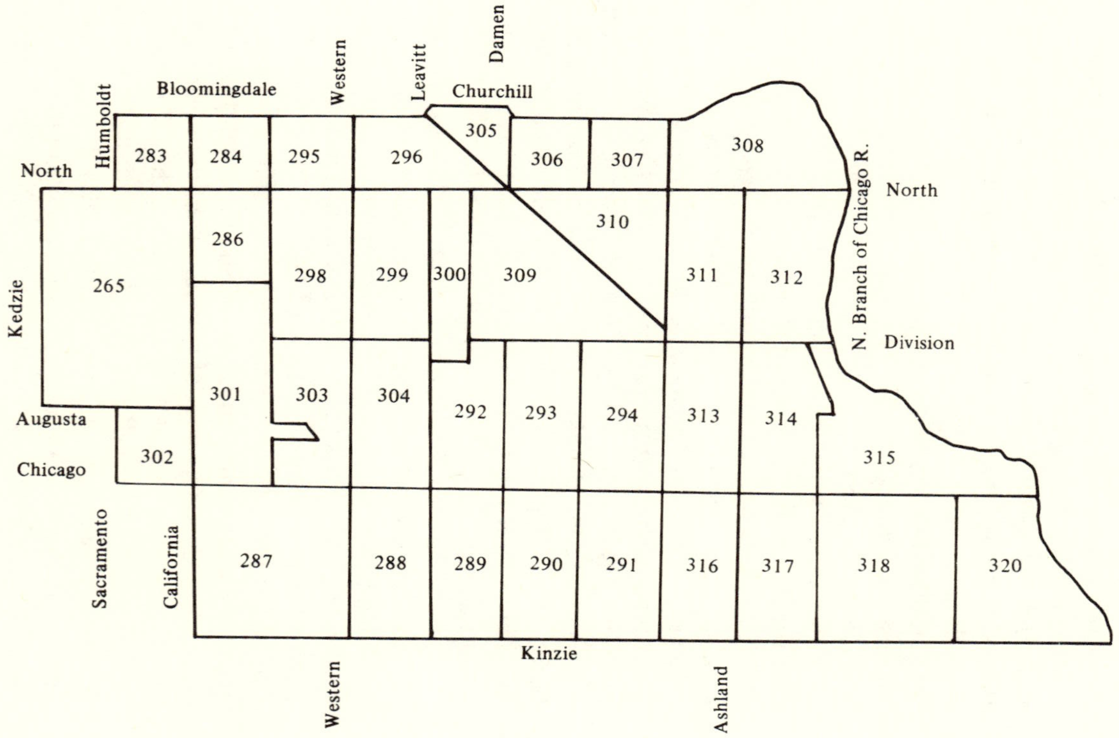

North

N. Branch of Chicago R.

Division

315

320

318

Ashland

317

316

308

312

314

311

313

307

310

294

291

Kinzie

306

293

290

Churchill

Damen

305

309

292

289

Leavitt

296

300

Western

299

304

288

Western

295

298

303

Bloomingdale

284

286

301

287

Humboldt

283

302

California

North

265

Sacramento

Kedzie

Augusta

Chicago

ner of Division Street and Western Avenue by the Board of Education in the mid 1970s. The school, named Roberto Clemente after the hall-of-fame Puerto Rican baseball player, is eight stories tall and takes up one square mile in actual space. Across the street from Roberto Clemente High is the Park District's new and modern recreational facilities, staffed primarily by Puerto Ricans. Part of these facilities includes the high school's own baseball field which has been the "home park" of the city champions for several years—the large majority of players on these teams have always been Puerto Ricans. José de Diego Academy, the city's first bilingual education academy, faces the baseball field directly north. As a whole, the surrounding city tends to authenticate their claim by referring to these structures and the area in general as a Pueto Rican community and by holding Puerto Ricans responsible for whatever happens with them.

Although Puerto Ricans know that residential segregation in the Division Street Area has had implications of inequality and inferiority (that it implies subordination), and that the metropolitan press has always pictured Division Street as an impoverished Puerto Rican slum, a bizarre world of gang wars, of radical plots, and of murder, Puerto Ricans have adjusted and learned to pride themselves on their community. Division Street is el barrio and this has come to mean not only an "area of minimum choice" but also a focus for strong positive feelings and sentiments. This emotional appreciation is nowhere better revealed and illuminated than in the poetic words of a second-generation Puerto Rican who later went on to become one of the most respected leaders in the Puerto Rican community:

> summer's here, shining, burning
> the litter on division steet through which I walk,
> and illuminating the dirty tenement buildings
> adding a new light to my 'barrio's' drabness
>
> but nevertheless, the less, the less,
> they laugh, they sing, they dance;
> and toil, and work and try to exist
> in the excrement of their poverty
> (Carmelo Rodriguez, 1973:13).

Elizabeth Colon, a second-generation Puerto Rican poet writing in the early 1980s, also reflects this sentiment of love and hope for

el barrio. In her poem, "Predators Dash," written with a "dose" of
the "Spanglish" idiom which is quite common among Puerto Ricans
born and/or raised in American cities, she presents a vivid picture
of two very different sides of Puerto Rican life in Division Street
(1983:10–11).

I walk, same path
A daily ruteen
Looking up in the sky whaching the birds sing
I become
So mermerized
Morning melodies
Stray cats soom by
Preying on rats
All big and fat
I've seen the flash
Of nightmare blast
The street is an alley
There is no back
Garbage can blues
But, I become so
Mermerized
Dream the street of steel and concrete
Pavement smooth and so complete
Dogs are released never being fed
As they take to their night post
The predators dash
Cats are the prey
Bodys are buried
After A Team tear just the legs
Yes, it sounds so gross
But you should see
In the morning
When the children are going to school
These same dogs
Trot by their side
Wouldn't hurt a fly
With a predators dash still in their eyes
Yah, I walk this path
Garbage can blues

But
I have dreams
My mind creates for me
Sensations
My feet become peddles
And race through the screen
Right out of the blues
Graffiti imprints
Are loud and clear
If one wishes to hear
Wishes:
When you wish upon a star
Never wonder
Who you are
Like
A diamond in the sky
You were born to rise and shine
And your dreams are not too
Far

The importance of "localism" in the Division Street Area can hardly be emphasized enough. The sense of a local spatial identity includes both local social relationships and local places. It is this sense of localism as a basic feature of working-class life and the functional significance of local spatial identity which have been stressed by a number of studies of the working class (Young and Wilmott, 1975; Mogey, 1957; and Gans, 1963), and are documented by many aspects of this study's data. In this respect, it may be safe to suggest that there existed a strong association between positive feelings about the Division Street Area and the extensive social relationships or positive feelings about other people in the neighborhood.

The Division Street Area eventually came to be seen as a cultural and symbolic manifestation of an evolving collective identity. Marc Fried is correct in saying that extensive contact with area people, use of local resources, friendship and a sense of neighborhood, long residence, and good housing are important determinants of residential satisfaction and a collective life (1973:85). This same point is made by Drake and Cayton (1962, vol.1) in their classic study of black community life in Chicago. The two authors note that black inhabitants of the ghetto did not view their institutional life as inferior to other distinctive local life-styles; indeed, "they expressed considerable pride in it, viewing it as evidence that they, as well as whites, can create a collective life. . . . They do not ordinarily experience their social separateness as oppressive or undesirable. Black metropolis is the world of their relatives and friends" (1962 vol.1:122).

In this way, the people of the Division Street Area also have a sense of community or peoplehood—most Puerto Ricans refer to their neighbors of common cultural heritage as *mi gente* (my people). They possess what some sociologists call "consciousness-of-kind." Again, they are largely shaped by the community surrounding and supporting them and the families in which they grow up. In essence, the Puerto Rican community can be best described, in Alba's terms "as a collection of primary networks in which individuals are linked through the relationship of kinship or friendship or by virtue of being neighbors. The networks of this description are abstractions of the quotidian interactions between people, as represented, for example, by the social event of a visit" (1976:1033). This community is both open to the great impersonal process of institutional form and growth that amalgamates in American society and yet closed enough to make its residents vividly aware of the cultures and attitudes of a given place, time, class, and locality.

It's important to add another salient point to this discussion. The creation and persistence of the Puerto Rican community are not simply random outcomes of three decades of Puerto Rican migration nor have resulted from natural increases. The crowding together in el barrio has not only been caused by the desire of Puerto Rican community residents to share common cultural and linguistic traditions, it reflects as well a systematic pattern of discrimination imposed by the dominant white society. Puerto Ricans are indeed loosely bound together by a common heritage; they are tightly bound together by a common set of grievances. The increasing concentration and persistence of Puerto Ricans in the Division Street barrio environment is no accident. It is the result of both racial discrimination and ethnic solidarity. In this regard, the Division Street Area is structurally equivalent to the Puerto Rican nation. The situation in the Division Street Area as well as that in Puerto Rico were characterized by asymmetrical exploitation—the raison d'etre of a colonial relationship. A great complex of laws in Puerto Rico and institutional racism in Chicago facilitated the exploitation of Puerto Ricans in both societies, keeping them politically, socially, and economically inferior and dependent.

Another very important reason for viewing the Puerto Rican barrio from a positive stance, or at least with a minimum of middle-class bias, is that there is a great deal of social integration within the Puerto Rican community, even if we do not see very much social integration between the Puerto Rican and white communities. It appears that the well-articulated position of Puerto Rican-white social polarization is yet another reason the present-day social scientist continues to place this strongly felt pathology stereotype upon the Puerto Rican community. Such a predilection emerges from the position in the field of race and ethnic relations which places social integration in a nearly synonymous position with racial integration, the bringing of Puerto Ricans into positions of equal status with whites in society. This is not the sense in which I will use the term in this analysis. I would prefer that social integration be used as an important term descriptive of the idea of community; it stands for the internal stability of a given community of people, not necessarily the stability of relationships of that community with other communities. In other words, whatever the personal and social costs of living in el barrio, as opposed, let's say, to living in a suburb, can it be said of the residents of the Puerto Rican community that they are living in a place which does not reject them or alienate them from one another, which accepts their style of social interaction?

The traditional categories employed for an understanding of the ethnic neighborhood are clearly too narrow in the case of the Puerto Rican community in Chicago. The Division Street Area was not just a "staging ground" or "decompression chamber" for the processing of immigrants into the larger society (Fried, 1973; Fitzpatrick, 1966), nor did it become "disorganized" as a result of contact with American culture (Park, 1967; Guest, 1977; Feagin, 1974). These perspectives, which quite obviously have an assimilationist bias and implicitly regard the ethnic neighborhood as an artifact of the immigrant experience, cannot account for the persistence of the Puerto Rican community in Chicago.

The Division Street Area has persisted well beyond the period of initial settlement, absorbing social and cultural changes in the process. The interests and needs of first- and second-generation Puerto Ricans have been met by a variety of institutions and organizations developed in the community. The present period suggests that the neighborhood-based Puerto Rican community is a historically specific form of urban ethnic community. The reasons are broadly related to the solidarity among Puerto Ricans of all ages. And the major reason for this togetherness rests on the salience of Puerto Rican ethnicity in the city of Chicago.

Mayor Daley greets Puerto Rican girls during the celebration of La
Fiesta de San Juan. (photo courtesy of Gabino Moyet)

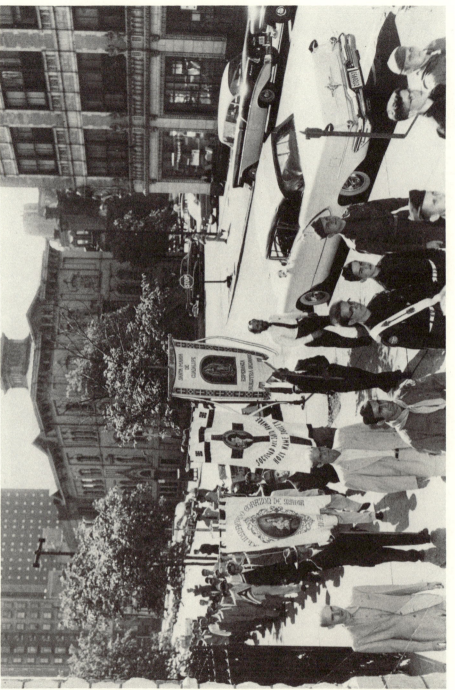

Early Puerto Rican Day Parade celebrated along 63rd Street (photo courtesy of Gabino Moyet)

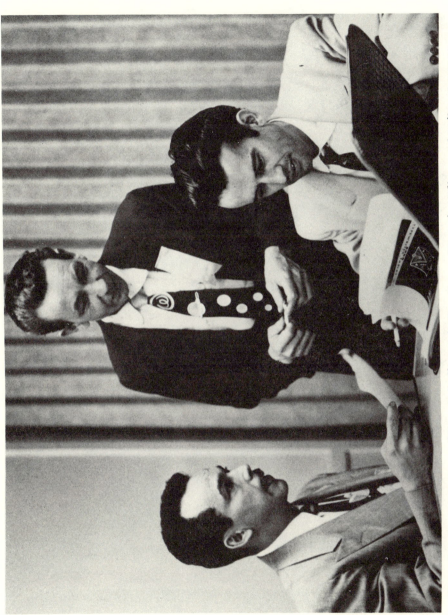

Three leading members of Los Caballeros de San Juan: Nazario, Elias, and Vélez, 1955 (photo courtesy of Gabino Moyet)

A city-wide meeting of Los Caballeros de San Juan, 1958 (photo courtesy of Gabino Moyet)

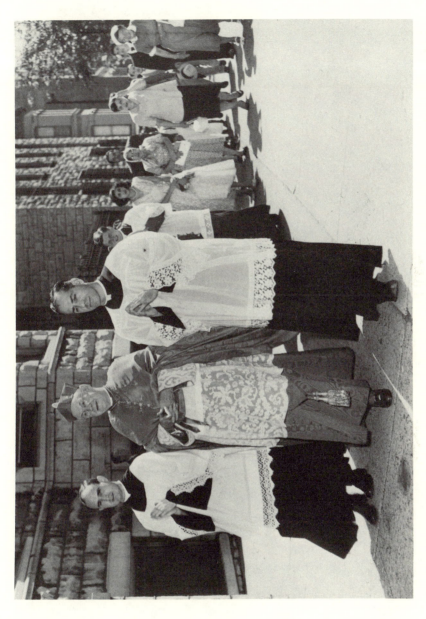

Cardinal Samuel Stritch and members of Los Caballeros de San Juan in a religious procession, 1957 (photo courtesy of Gabino Moyet)

A meeting of the Federation of Puerto Rican Organizations, 1958 (photo courtesy of Gabino Moyet)

A Puerto Rican baseball team, 1958 (photo courtesy of Gabino Moyet)

A float in the Puerto Rican Day Parade, 1973 (photo courtesy of Torres de Jesús)

Salsa singer Willie Colón approaching stage at Puerto Rican Day Celebration, 1984 (photo courtesy of Miguel Arroyo)

The crowd at Humboldt Park, Puerto Rican Day Parade, 1984 (photo courtesy of Miguel Arroyo)

3

Organizational Response to
Ethnic Oppression

Like many European immigrants before them, Puerto Ricans came to Chicago and other American cities from different regions, villages, and towns of their homeland. Unlike these earlier groups, however, most Puerto Rican newcomers to the United States already shared a consciousness-of-kind as Puerto Ricans before their arrival. Their initial contact with various forces of American colonialism in the Island had made many Puerto Ricans keenly aware of their economic marginality and supposed racial inferiority long before mass emigration to the mainland. Of course, this underclass or inferior minority status was greatly reinforced by several major structural factors and conditions on the mainland. In response, Puerto Ricans converted this stigmatized classification into a positive sense of Puerto Rican ethnic-conscious identity and behavior—*el Puertorriqueñismo*. These various sources of conflict will be discussed and analyzed after examining some of the characteristics of the city of Chicago, with emphasis on the patterns of industrial and technological change and urban development which preceded and at times paralleled the arrival of Puerto Ricans.

CHICAGO'S SOCIAL AND ECONOMIC CONDITIONS

By the time Puerto Ricans came to live in Chicago, this midwest metropolis had already astounded the world with its economic and population growth. The city's population surpassed the three million

99

mark by 1930, overtaking older and established cities like Philadelphia, Pittsburgh, and Boston. This growth in population secured
for Chicago the distinction of "second city" and gave rise to a friendly
rivalry with New York, "the Great Metropolis." Immigration from
different parts of the European continent contributed significantly.
"By 1890, 77.9 percent of [the city's] population was foreign born
or of foreign parentage. The Germans, Irish, and Scandinavians
were . . . the largest ethnic groups in the city, but after 1890, increasing numbers of Poles, Lithuanians, Czechs, Italians, and Eastern European Jews entered the city" (Spear, 1967:4).

Between the years 1850 and 1870, this midwest metropolis
along with New York, Boston, Philadelphia, Pittsburgh, St. Louis,
and Cleveland became America's "central cities" — older urban areas
whose economies were based on factory production. During this
period of industrial accumulation, American capitalists "turned more
and more toward making profits through industrial production
itself — through the direct manufacture of commodities that they ex-
changed on the market" (Gordon, 1978:37). That is to say, the process of capital accumulation began to unfold in a spatially structured factory environment. In the words of Mumford (1961:458),
"The factory became the nucleus of the new urban organism. Every
other detail of life was subordinate to it. Even the utilities, such
as the water supply, and the minimum of governmental offices
that were necessary to a town's existence often, if they had not been
built by an earlier generation, entered belatedly: an afterthought."
Viewed somewhat differently, Ashton (1978:65) adds, "historical
experience had taught capitalists that the factory was the most profitable, if not the most efficient and humane, method of organizing
production."

The central city became provisionally the particular geographical form and spatial pattern of relationships taken by the process
of capital accumulation. As Chicago, New York, and the others
became the central locus for factory manufacturing (industrial accumulation) in the United States, this mode of production was centralized near downtown areas, near to vital coal and iron resources
and to good intra-regional transportation and commercial linkages
established in previous decades (Hill, 1976). In addition, the centralization of factory production was usually a prerequisite for attracting a large factory labor force. Since most workers either walked

or utilized mass transit to get to their jobs, factories that did not locate in central cities were not within commuting reach of their potential labor force. Ashton (1978:66) provides the following explanation for the subsequent urban centralization of the working class:

> The rapid and continued growth of factories and industry swelled the urban population and further crowded the slums. Thousands of people left the countryside and streamed into the cities. Doubtless some were attracted by the excitement of city life or the promise of better wages. But many had no choice. Expanding urban land use pushed farmers off the land. And the uneven development characteristic of the capitalist market process resulted in the destruction of many small regional centers of trade and finance. Rural entrepreneurs as well as farmers increasingly became part of the urban proletariat.

The drive for capital accumulation and the need to expand the basis for profit led to the emergence of "monopoly capitalism." Under monopoly capitalism, businesses grew and consolidated into global enterprises. Their organizational and spatial structures and relations for production, distribution, and management shaped a hierarchical network of local, regional, national, and international urban centers. In other words, the hallmark of monopoly capitalism was the concentration of capital in fewer and larger business enterprises which could exercise considerable control over access to inputs, including raw materials and financing, and over markets and prices.

As monopoly corporations emerged on a base of large-scale production, a dual labor market segmented into primary and secondary sectors became the order of the day.[1] During the early years of the factory system the labor force had progressively taken on a homogenous character; craft jobs were compressed into semiskilled operative work and almost all factory workers were subjected to the same discipline of factory control. In turn, the unceasing homogenization of the labor process was generating the tensions manifest in the great labor movements of the early twentieth century. Mass labor revolts and strikes were rapidly becoming part of the urban life of American workers. To meet this threat employers actively and consciously fostered labor market segmentation in order to "divide and conquer" the labor force. Capitalists attempted to construct an urban environment which would allow for efficient production and distribution of goods and services, profitable investments, and continuous reproduction of a divided but reliable work force. In the view of Mollenkopf (1981:324): "As antagonism between capital and labor mounted, capital responded with generous applications of factory power in its many forms: wage cuts, unemployment, Pinkertons, labor-saving technology, and an increasingly finely-graded division of labor." Or as postulated by economists Reich, Gordon, and Edwards (1977:110):

> The central thrust of the new strategies was to break down the increasingly unified workers interests that grew out of the proletarianization of work and the concentration of workers in urban areas. As exhibited in several aspects of these large firms' operations, this effort aimed to divide the labor force into various segments so that the actual experiences of workers were different and the basis of their common opposition to capitalists undermined.

Along with segmentation in the industrial structure, there developed a corresponding dualism on racial lines. During this period of economic expansion, certain jobs became "race-typed," segregated by prejudice and by labor market institutions.[2] This racial segmentation forced the large majority of black workers migrating to the north into certain industries and into particular firms within those industries. While arguing that a racially segmented labor market in a city like Chicago is an important factor in understanding how racial differences have been systematically maintained, Baron and Hymer (1977:190) maintain:

> The racial divisions in the Chicago labor market are visible in many dimensions, by occupation, by geographic area, by firms, and by departments within firms. . . . Some firms have absolute racial barriers in hiring, with blacks being completely excluded. Within all industries and even in government employment there is unmistakable evidence of occupational ceilings for blacks. Within single establishments that hire both whites and nonwhites, black workers are usually placed in particular job classifications and production units. A good rule of thumb

is that the lower the pay or the more disagreeable and dirty the job, the greater the chance of finding a high proportion of blacks.

The arrangement of a racially divided labor market forced the overwhelming majority of black workers to offer their labor services at a reduced rate. From this point of view, as suggested by Michael Reich (1977:184), racism principally takes the form of wage discrimination rather than employment discrimination: racism enables capitalists to employ black workers at a lower wage rate. In a similar way, Baron (1975:52) maintains that racial discrimination enables monopoly corporations to decrease the cost of the business cycle by using black workers as a reserve army. When the economy contracts, capitalists can more easily lay off excess workers since a racist society is more willing to accept higher unemployment if the unemployed are disproportionately black. Also when the economy expands, there is a ready labor supply that can be hired at the existing wage rate. Baron (1975:53) concludes that the higher costs of a privileged white labor force are more than compensated for by the presence of a reserve army of workers.

As the period of monopoly capitalism progressed, employers also turned to a relatively new means of division, the use of "educational credentials." For the first time, educational credentials were used to regularize skill requirements for jobs. Employers played an active role in molding educational institutions to serve these channeling functions. Bowles (1973) indicates that new educational requirements helped maintain artificial distinctions between factory workers and those in routinized office jobs and helped generate some strong divisions within the office between semiskilled white-collar workers and their more highly skilled office mates. In general, the educational prerequisites increasingly served to screen out poorly educated and trained workers from certain blue-collar jobs, and of course, from white-collar occupations.

In spite of these developments, the industrial expansion of urban America during the late nineteenth and early twentieth centuries still required an abundant supply of the cheap and unskilled labor that European newcomers came to represent. In Chicago, for instance, the burgeoning steel mills, freight warehouses, meat packing, mail-order establishments, retail stores, construction work, and literally thousands of other tasks provided blue-collar unskilled and semi-skilled employment for hundreds of thousands of European immigrants and their children. In the words of historian Humbert S. Nelli (1970:9): "Whatever their place of origin, European immigrants and native Americans as well poured into the lake metropolis [Chicago], lured by economic opportunities." Regardless of the various attempts made by employers to prevent the urban labor force from advancing their interests from a collective working-class perspective, the growth of the industrial economic order in various cities provided the American labor force, particularly European newcomers, with a relative degree of economic security, a ray of hope not for themselves but possibly for their children. Hence, the plenitude of stable unskilled employment furnished the "tool" necessary for entry into higher levels of the economic order of the American society.

In contrast, by the time of the mass migration from the Island in the late 1940s and early 1950s, all these tendencies together had created such tightly fixed arrangements that Puerto Rican workers' point of entry into the labor market was destined to be at the bottom of the occupational hierarchy of the secondary labor sector. Not only were these jobs low-paying, involving dirty and unsafe work, but they were of short duration and had little advancement potential. Just as important, during the period of mass migration from Puerto Rico, the traditional blue-collar unskilled and semi-skilled jobs were in steady decline as major economic activities in America's central cities.

During the post–World War II "modern era," nation-wide socioeconomic changes and technological developments were influencing investment in manufacturing and industrial production in other, more profitable locations. Among these new sites were suburban areas outside of older cities, the Sun Belt of the American South, and the greener pastures of Europe and the Third World, including Puerto Rico. Although these changes began to unfold during the 1920s, they were slowed down by the Depression and World War II. It was after the war that they came into their own. William Wilson notes several national trends responsible for intensifying this migration of capital and the subsequent alteration of the economic structures of older American cities during this period (1980:9):

Following World War II, fundamental technological and economic changes facilitated the increasing decentralization of American businesses. Improvements in transportation and communication have made the use of open and relatively inexpensive tracts of land outside central cities more feasible not only for manufacturing, wholesaling, and retailing but also for residential development. The traditional central-city multistory factories have been rendered obsolete with the introduction and diffusion of single-level assembly line modes of production. Concurrent with the growing cost and limited availability of land, tax rates rose, traffic congestion increased, and vandalism and other crimes that multiplied the operating costs of city industries mounted; many firms, previously restricted to the central-city locations near ports, freight terminals, and passenger facilities, began to rely more heavily on truck transportation and to locate in outlying sites near interchanges, the expanding metropolitan expressway system, and new housing construction. Moreover, the use of the automobile has freed firms from the necessity of location near mass transportation facilities in order to attract a labor force.

Chicago's social and economic portrait after World War II, indeed, fits Wilson's characterization of American cities. Several reports by Chicago's Department of Development and Planning concisely describe several of the major trends taking place in the city. For example, "The Mid-Chicago Economic Development Study" (City of Chicago, 1966: vol.1:48) notes:

> Differential population and economic growth between America's various regions is an integral characteristic of the marketing component of our economy. Between 1920 and 1950, the Far West and Southwest were the two most rapidly urbanizing regions in the nation. The food processing industry, which is market-oriented began to move westward during the period. At the same time technological changes made small-plant operations more economical than large-plant operations. By 1954, Los Angeles County, California, had more meat packing plants than Cook County, Illinois, although those in Cook County were generally much larger. The westward movement of the

meat packing industry, halted in Chicago for more than fifty years by railroad transportation marketing, took the form of decentralization after 1919 and especially after World War II.

Mollenkopf, a sociologist of post–World War II urban development, adds several other factors responsible for the relocation of manufacturing production outside of central cities during this time. He suggests that suburban factory movement was often undertaken because business executives believed that they would have fewer labor problems and greater social control over production outside the cities (1978:120–22). Also, after World War II, business leaders and policy makers feared a return to Depression conditions, and suburban development was used as a way of stimulating demand, production, and investment to create economic growth (1978:130–31). Mollenkopf (1976:117) adds another cause of industrial relocation: dissatisfaction with the growing financial costs of dealing with city machine politicians prompted businessmen to move from the city and support reform government.

At the bottom of the decentralization of industry was growth — a general strategy for accumulating capital. Obviously, the decentralization of industry, on the other hand, led to the loss of hundreds of thousands of jobs from these major cities. In Chicago, the inner city felt the tight pinch of declining industrial employment opportunities. DeVise (1980:63–4), for example, shows that during the 1960–1970 decade (the period of greatest population growth and expansion among Puerto Ricans in Chicago)," [the city] lost 211,000 jobs, a 13 percent decline, and the suburbs gained half a million jobs, a 71 percent jump. . . . The 1960 ghetto lost 26 percent of its local jobs, while the 1970 ghetto extension dropped 22 percent of its jobs. At the other end of town, the white outer zone lost but 2 percent of its jobs."

The problems created by the relocation of industries outside of midwestern and northeastern cities and the disproportionate loss of jobs was also compounded by the lack of industrial growth and/or expansion in these metropolitan centers. The Mayor's Committee's study "Mid-Chicago Economic Development Study" addressed two major problems related to this issue. First, it revealed the existence in the city of large numbers of technologically obsolete and/or deteriorating buildings, and second, it admitted that in many areas of Chicago there was inadequate land for expansion or new development of industry. These older industrial districts were characterized as an "unattractive environment" surrounded by areas of very high unemployment particularly among non-whites (City of Chicago, 1966). A different report, the Comprehensive Plan, published a year later by the Department of Development and Planning, noted that the retail sector of the city's economy was also generally weakened through all areas of the city. According to this particular report, the city of Chicago sat in the center of an economic region that was growing very slowly (City of Chicago, 1967:61–2).

With the decentralization of industry, America's oldest cities experienced a new stage of growth: a shift from a base in goods-producing manufacturing to industries such as transportation, government, public utilities, trade, finance, and services. Variously termed the "service industry," "advanced monopoly capitalism," "post-industrial society," or "the corporate city," this economic order is characterized by a transition from the factory to the office building as the basic unit of social organization and capital accumulation. Mollenkopf (1976:118) defines this transformation as a "shift in private sector activities from production to administration (research, education, finance, information manipulations, entertainment, etc.).

After World War II, older U.S. cities were in a fiscal crisis caused by declining industrial employment, increasing suburbanization, and migration to the cities by impoverished surplus labor. In response to this crisis and in defense of threatened central city land values and investments, "pro-growth coalitions" of downtown businessmen, "progressive" mayors, planners, newspaper editors, construction unions, real estate interests, and others were assembled. With business and corporate initiative, political leadership by new pro-growth mayors, and increased local and Federal funding, this coalition launched a series of highway and urban renewal projects designed to modernize downtown areas and make the city economy grow and prosper. In short, post–World War II economic growth required a reshaping of the metropolitan area and the bold and powerful were able to reorganize their environments along more profitable and useful lines.[3]

By the late 1950s, city planners in Chicago had already concluded that the city's economy was to be transformed into one which emphasized specialized methods of production, distribution, and marketing (City of Chicago, 1958). A joint report by the business community of the city and Richard J. Daley, the newly elected Mayor, showed that since manufacturing would continue to gravitate to outlying, previously vacant land in suburbs and other areas, Chicago's economic future rested on a predominant service industry base. Particular emphasis was made toward buttressing the strengths of the Central Business District (CBD) or Loop; that is, the CBD was expected to be the growth sector of Chicago's economy. All means of access to the CBD were to be improved and the city was to do everything possible to encourage further office space construction to maintain and accentuate Chicago's position as a regional financial and administrative headquarters. An article in *Commerce* magazine indicates that between 1950 and 1962 over ten million square feet of office space was added to Chicago's Central Business District, making the total around thirty-eight million square feet in 1965. The report also shows that between 1965 and 1977 another thirty-two million square feet of office space was built, increasing the total to near eighty million square feet in 1977 (1978:24).

Berry and his colleagues (1976:71) make the following observation regarding the decision to convert the downtown area of Chicago into the headquarters for the city's new economic activity:

> It was the declining fortunes of the Loop and particularly of the State Street shopping core during the 1950's that sparked a series of actions by the downtown business community that, with the active support and participation of the city government, helped realize the growth potentials afforded by the growth of the service industries and the continuing concentration of headquarters and administrative functions in the downtown areas of America's cities.

Chicago, as well as others of America's major and older cities, began to experience a shift in population after World War II: the flight of white middle-class families to the suburbs and the massive arrival of blacks, Spanish-speaking, and other poor populations. Fusfeld and Bates (1984:93) point out that "intrametropolitan migration has been highly selective. It has disproportionately been young, employed, and white populations of central cities that have resettled in suburban peripheries, leaving the old, unemployed, and black inhabitants behind." City planners in these cities viewed this change as a problem that could only compound the other problems of industrial relocation and economic obsolescence already faced by these urban centers.

The way that the city of Chicago dealt with this problem is found in yet another report by the Department of Development and Planning. The department's "Comprehensive Plan" addresses the problem of population shift in the city by focusing completely on retaining a higher percentage of middle-class families (City of Chicago 1964). It was clear to the planners that Chicago could not remain economically, and for that matter socially, viable if it became overwhelmingly populated by the black, Spanish-speaking, and unemployed poor. The planners argued that Chicago would not be able to rejuvenate its economy without a strong and stable white middle class which, after all, represented the major part of the work force that was to be employed in the growth sectors of Chicago's new economic activities. On this basis, most of the policies designed to improve the social and economic conditions of the city benefitted significantly and disproportionally the white middle-class populations of the city. The residential areas of the city were to be improved for all income groups, but particular concern was given to middle-income residential areas. City services were to be improved, and particularly schools. Construction of single family dwellings was to be encouraged and middle-income housing was to be stressed in all further urban renewal sites. It is significant that the plan identified the obsolete railyards adjacent to the Loop as the location to encourage residential development—and this meant essentially middle-income housing (City of Chicago, 1964:17, 31; and 1967:24).

The strength of this emphasis on serving the needs of the middle class is shown by contrasting what the Comprehensive Plan proposed to do for the "disadvantaged." Noting that such persons were concentrated in the same areas of the city, the plan proposed a coordinated and unified set of social services, as well as the physical improvement of these areas, to break the "cycle of poverty." What was emphasized was job training, public housing, and community improvement (City of Chicago 1966:12). It is important to note that job training has never been characterized by great success, and community improvement has always been quite innocuous. It is also the case that in cities like Chicago, as suggested by Berry, et al.

(1976:55, 62), minorities tend to be served last and with the poorest quality of city services.

The relocation of U.S. manufacturing economic activities and the subsequent development of service economies with an emphasis on the proliferation of white-collar and professional jobs presented structural barriers for Puerto Ricans and other urban poor populations in their quest to secure permanent employment and participate more equitably in the institutional life of the larger American society. The cycle of prosperity enjoyed by white-collar professionals as a result of post–World War II economic growth widened the disparity between urban poor populations and the white middle class in America's largest cities. This point is strongly emphasized by James Pitts in his discussion of the effects of industrial expansion on the emergence and growth of "race consciousness" among blacks in the United States:

> From the 1940s onward major American cities were restructuring themselves into a new matrix of inequality. Dimensions of urban development that had been emerging since the earliest decades of the twentieth century were now further congealed by the unequal distribution of benefits from postwar economic growth. This continued expansion of the national economy shows up, in part, as growth in job opportunities and wages for a middle class, but also as contraction of opportunities for economic advancement and political leverage for many at the bottom of society. (1982:162)

THE PUERTO RICAN WORKING CLASS

Racial discrimination, the movement of jobs to locations outside Chicago, and rigid educational requirements kept the Puerto Rican labor force out of the primary labor market and fixed into occupational classifications in the declining and stagnant sectors of the economy where many still remain today. Anthropologist Elena Padilla's (1947) study of the first large group of Puerto Rican migrants to Chicago in the late 1940s provides substantial evidence of this by showing that many of the newcomers were employed in the restaurant business as busboys, sweepers, kitchen help, waiters and the like.[4] During this and subsequent decades the large majority of Puerto Rican workers were employed in the business sector as messengers and delivery men or in stock rooms and packaging areas of many stores. Yet another large number found jobs in the janitorial labor force of the city. According to the 1960 U.S. Census Report on the "Social and Economic Data for Persons of Puerto Rican Birth and Parentage," the majority were employed in three leading categories — "operatives & kindred" (45.7 percent), "laborers" (13.7 percent), and "service workers" (11.7 percent). Less than 10 percent of the entire work force was located in the categories of skilled or above (9.8 percent). Table 9 shows the overall concentration of Puerto Rican workers in the labor force of the city of Chicago during this period.

The non-Spanish-speaking occupational structure highlights the disparity which began to emerge between Puerto Ricans and other groups in Illinois' largest metropolis during the 1950s. In comparison to the Puerto Rican working class, the 1960 Census indicates that white semiskilled workers found in operatives and kindred occupations constituted only 20 percent of the work force. Conversely, 31 percent of the white work force was located in the technical oc-

TABLE 9

Puerto Rican Occupational Profile — 1960

Occupation	Percent
Professional, technical & kindred workers	1.6
Farmers and farm managers	0.0
Managers, officials & proprietors	1.2
Clerical & kindred workers	5.2
Sales workers	1.8
Craftsmen, foremen & kindred workers	9.0
Operatives & kindred workers	45.7
Private household workers	0.0
Service workers except private household	11.7
Farm laborers & foremen	0.5
Laborers except farm and mine	13.7
Not reporting	9.0

Source: *U.S. Census*, Economic Characteristics of Persons of Puerto Rican Birth and Parentage, by Age, for Selected Standard Metropolitan Statistical Areas, Chicago, Il.: 1960, Table 13, p. 100.

cupational categories (see Table 10). Even the occupational break-down for blacks, considered at that time relatively new to the city, illustrates the low status attained by the Puerto Rican working pop-ulations (see Table 11). Black workers were more evenly distributed in the intermediate and lower job categories than were Puerto Ricans. Their percentage as operatives (26.4 percent) and skilled craftsmen and foremen (10 percent) far exceeded the Puerto Rican in both categories. Thus, when compared to the non-Spanish-speaking pop-ulations of Chicago, Puerto Ricans came to occupy and continue to hold the lowest economic-occupational levels in the city.

The Puerto Rican family's response to their dire economic cir-cumstances during the 1950s and 1960s altered traditional patterns of employment and familial work responsibilities. The most dramatic change in the family occupational structure was the entrance of Puerto Rican women as co-principal contributors to the family's survival. The changing patterns of the urban labor market made it difficult for Puerto Rican male workers to become reliable or ade-quate bread winners. No longer able to subsist solely on the income of the husband, the Puerto Rican woman was forced to enter the unskilled labor market of the metropolis. Virginia Sánchez-Korrol's

TABLE 10

White Working-class Occupational Profile—1960

Occupation	Percent
Professional, technical & kindred workers	11.2
Farmers and farm managers	0.4
Managers, officials & proprietors	10.5
Clerical & kindred workers	9.3
Sales workers	7.4
Craftsmen, foremen & kindred workers	20.7
Operatives & kindred workers	20.0
Private household workers	0.1
Service workers except private household	7.0
Farm laborers & foremen	0.2
Laborers except farm and mine	5.8
Not reporting	7.2

Source: *U.S. Census*, Occupation of the Experienced Civilian Labor Force by Color, of the Employed by Race and Class of Worker, Chicago, Il.: 1960, Table 122, p. 960.

observations regarding the role played by Puerto Rican women in New York's Spanish-speaking *barrios* during the 1920s and 1930s is also applicable here: "Puerto Rican females in New York emerged not as stereotypical Latins relegated to second-class, bound by children, church and home, but as active, vibrant women determined to keep family life intact while shouldering their share of financial burdens" (1980:48). In addition to the many tasks carried out in the roles of housewife, wife, and mother, as well as in voluntary community activities, the Puerto Rican woman joined the "paid labor force" of American society.

The large majority of Puerto Rican women in Chicago found employment primarily as operatives and kindred workers (see Table 12). This involved performing tasks such as assemblers, laundry and dry cleaning operatives, packers and wrappers, spinners and weavers, and the like. It is also quite probable that like Puerto Rican females in New York City, Puerto Rican women in Chicago became involved in income-producing jobs in their homes. Childcare, taking in lodgers, and piecework are examples of occupations which would have allowed women to secure supplementary income for their families.

TABLE 11

Black Working-class Occupational Profile — 1960

Occupation	Percent
Professional, technical & kindred workers	2.8
Farmers and farm managers	0.2
Managers, officials & proprietors	1.8
Clerical & kindred workers	9.6
Sales workers	1.7
Craftsmen, foremen & kindred workers	10.0
Operatives & kindred workers	26.4
Private household workers	0.4
Service workers except private household	14.6
Farm laborers & foremen	0.7
Laborers except farm and mine	14.3
Not reporting	18.1

Source: *U.S. Census*, Occupation of the Experienced Civilian Labor Force by Color, of the Employed by Race and Class of Worker, Chicago, Il.: 1960, Table 122, p. 960.

Overall, Puerto Rican male and female workers increasingly filled certain labor positions in the declining sector of the urban economy. Firms which continued their operations in the city were dependent upon a pool of cheap labor which the Puerto Rican community furnished. Puerto Rican workers did not experience any special employment barriers in the menial jobs of the low-wage sector. In fact, employers were extremely pleased to have and keep this stable work force. A letter sent to the head of a barrio organization by the owner of a dry cleaning store in late 1957 reveals how important the availability of Puerto Rican labor was to this firm:

> Last April through your office we employed Tomas Delgado, a Puerto Rican. We have subsequently employed nine more or so, we now have a total of ten Puerto Ricans working for us.
>
> Frankly, they have 'saved our life' because they have offered us a source of miscellaneous labor which we never had before.
>
> Our experience with these people has been very good. We have found them to be honest, industrious, very clean and very co-operative. They are not only good employees, but we are also very fond of them, largely I think because of their

TABLE 12

Occupational Profile of Puerto Rican Female Workers — 1960

Occupation	Percent
Professional, technical & kindred workers	2.5
Farmers and farm managers	0.0
Managers, officials & proprietors	0.4
Clerical & kindred workers	8.0
Sales workers	1.9
Craftsmen, foremen & kindred workers	2.5
Operatives & kindred workers	63.0
Private household workers	1.6
Service workers except private household	6.8
Farm laborers & foremen	0.0
Laborers except farm and mine	2.4
Not reporting	11.5

Source: *U.S. Census*, Economic Characteristics of Persons of Puerto Rican Birth and Parentage, for Selected Standard Metropolitan Statistical Areas, Chicago, Il.: 1960, p. 95.

willingness to do whatever is asked of them in their courteous manner.[5]

In a story for a *Chicago Daily News'* series on Latin-American residents of the city, reporter Larry Green noted that some Chicago area companies recruited Puerto Rican men to work in factories, housed them in unheated railroad boxcars or barracks and shacks, then laid them off before other workers when business slowed. In one typical case, according to the reporter, Puerto Ricans were brought to work in an Illinois munitions plant that the owners knew would be shut down since the Korean War had just ended (*Chicago Daily News*, 1970:4). "In the strong trade unions like plumbing, electrical work, carpentry and bricklaying," Thomas Pietrantonio, a Puerto Rican editor of the *National Labor Journal*, told a *Chicago Sun-Times* reporter, "the Puerto Rican doesn't stand a chance. They won't let him in. But he's welcome in the machine shops where there is a lot of risk. Take a look sometime when you're down on Division St., and if you don't see a couple of guys within an hour's time with a finger or two missing, I'd be surprised" (May 16, 1969:22).

The economic contributions made by the Puerto Rican working class to the declining, blue-collar American urban economy were recognized in New York in the early 1950s. Peter Kihss, a correspondent for the *New York Times*, made the point that "Puerto Ricans are filling tens of thousands of jobs opened up by residents who have moved up in the economic scale or even departed to the suburbs. Puerto Ricans have enabled many of the city's businesses and industries—hotels and restaurants, garment trades, department stores, machine operations, maintenance—to carry on" (1953:2). In a similar way, some New York city officials stressed the importance of cheap labor from Puerto Rico to the city's economy. In the words of Emmanuel Celler, a Democratic Representative from New York: "We should not discourage them (Puerto Ricans) from coming. We need them for the hard chores and rough work. If they don't come, most of our hotels, restaurants, and laundries will close" (*U.S. News and World Report*, 1959:12).

A distinctive aspect of the jobs available to the Puerto Rican working class was that both white and black Americans tended to reject them in favor of more desirable employment. By 1950 most white Americans were fully integrated in the institutional life of the city while blacks were beginning to improve their economic status in trades and municipal employment, leaving little incentive for either to remain in industries that were stagnant. In a more general way, Castell (1975:54) notes that it is often argued that immigrant and migrant workers are necessary because the local population is unwilling to do certain kinds of work. He adds:

> In fact this is only a half-truth. While it is certain that immigrants do carry out the most arduous, the worst-paid and the least-skilled jobs, it does not follow from this that these jobs though necessary, have been given up by other workers. Such jobs are not given up because they are 'dirty' and 'soul-destroying' (since the jobs taken can hardly be said to be 'fulfilling') but because they are less well-paid.

In the same light, in his discussion of the view held by both black and white labor toward the low-wage sector, Wilson (1980: 165) stresses: "Many of these jobs go unfilled as fewer black and white workers are willing to accept an economic arrangement that consigns them to work that is not only dead-end and menial but does not provide a decent wage." Thus, the concentration of Puerto Ricans in low-paying, undesirable jobs led to little occupational contact with other ethnic working-class populations. Since Puerto Ricans in Chicago were not perceived as a major economic threat by white or black workers, and since they constituted a rather small proportion of the city population, they tended to be relatively invisible to the larger society.

This period of fluid racial/ethnic relations between Puerto Ricans and other groups in Chicago proved to be short-lived. As the physical Puerto Rican barrio expanded and the population increased rapidly during the late 1950s and early 1960s, Puerto Ricans became ever more conspicuous. The indifference with which they had been regarded in the early years changed to hostility. Ethnic tensions, police brutality, and the rise of a racist doctrine began to determine the status of the city's Puerto Rican population. Since the employment of Puerto Ricans in non-competitive economic sectors caused very little friction with other groups, racial/ethnic antagonisms between Puerto Ricans and whites, in particular, became related to social, political, and community-related concerns.

RACIAL FRICTION FLAREUPS

Housing Discrimination

From the outset, housing discrimination and police injustice were the leading forces responsible for fostering an antagonistic group relationship between Puerto Ricans and whites. Puerto Ricans were trapped in the most run-down residential sections in their communities not only because of poverty but also because of a stringent pattern of housing discrimination. The unwillingness of whites to tolerate Puerto Ricans as neighbors had far-reaching results. Since Puerto Ricans were so limited in their choice of housing, they were forced to pay higher rents in those buildings that were open to them. Some landlords began to divide up large buildings into smaller "kitchenette units"—usually two or three rooms each—and increase their income substantially by renting to ten or twelve families rather than to five or six. Suttles' (1968:148–49) discussion of a Puerto Rican neighborhood in the Near West Side is one example of the housing conditions experienced by many Puerto Ricans in Chicago:

> It is fairly easy to see why the Puerto Ricans . . . were able to first establish themselves on Harrison and Ashland. Along Harrison the buildings are probably the most deteriorated of any in the area and have long been blighted by the area's heaviest concentration of industry. The east side of Ashland is flanked by a line of old mansions that are inappropriate to the income level of local people. These mansions have been divided and subdivided into numerous flats. At the same time, both the mansions on Ashland and the apartment houses on Harrison are so huge that they are outside the range of local ownership. Thus, a lack of local ownership and a scarcity of other renters opened them to the Puerto Ricans.

A former resident of the Puerto Rican community of Woodlawn offers a similar account:

> I came to Chicago in 1952 and lived in *la barriada* 63 [the neighborhood on sixty-third street]. Initially, I lived with my brother-in-law. However, when I began to search for an apartment later on to bring my wife and children to live with me,

I was unable to find a large or roomy place. In those days, it was difficult for Puerto Ricans to find decent size apartments. You would find that the rental ads in the newspapers would indicate "for whites only," or "Puerto Ricans are not allowed" (no se admiten Puertorriqueños). Eventually, I ended up renting a kitchenette apartment, a three-room apartment which was originally six-rooms but it had been divided for Puerto Rican families. When my family arrived from Puerto Rico, I rented another kitchenette in the same building because I could not find an apartment anywhere else. We lived like this for quite some time. In fact, I found a larger apartment much later because the owner of this particular building confused me for Greek or Italian.

But it was the rapid increase of Puerto Rican population during the 1960s and the subsequent spill-over of el barrio into the adjacent areas of the near north and northwest communities of Westtown/Humboldt Park, Lakeview, and Lincoln Park which produced the major racial flareups between Puerto Ricans and whites. The housing situation in el barrio had deteriorated so rapidly over the years that on July 26, 1967, Mr. Juan Díaz, Director of the Spanish Action Committee of Chicago (SACC), went before the Housing and Urban Affairs Subcommittee of the Senate Banking and Currency Committee in Washington, D.C. to present a statement regarding this state of affairs. Speaking in support of the proposed Home Ownership Bill, which promised to allow the participation of the poor in the renewal and redevelopment of their community, Mr. Díaz said:

> The housing problem is very bad psychologically for Puerto Ricans who are struggling to adjust to American society. It is bad when a man who is working hard to make ends meet and is spending $125 a month on housing must come home from work to an apartment that is overcrowded, with rats and cockroaches, with water running down the walls and with poor ventilation. . . . For the past five years, various community organizations in our neighborhood, including SACC, have been trying to solve our housing problem, and the result has been only frustration among our people. We have found that when tenants have tried to get their buildings rehabilitated, their

landlords have taken action by offering them favors or harassing them into moving.

Perhaps the most serious case, and the one which provides the most insight into the nature of the housing situation faced by Puerto Ricans, occurred in the Lincoln Park community in the late 1960s. Puerto Ricans were no strangers to the community; for many years a small number of Puerto Rican families had established an ethnic enclave on the western section of the community along Armitage Avenue. From the beginning, the reaction of white residents in Lincoln Park to the Puerto Rican presence was basically straightforward: "Ship them back to Puerto Rico." The remarks of a white resident of Lincoln Park, printed in one of the city's major newspapers, is to the point: "If they [Puerto Ricans] really want to stay, why don't they get a job and save their money to buy a house like the rest of us had to?" (*Chicago Today*, 1969).

As the Lincoln Park community emerged as Chicago's hottest real estate market outside of lake front or downtown property during the 1960s, all of its neighborhoods and residents were directly affected. Investors and speculators as well as individual middle-class families were attracted to Lincoln Park by its proximity to the Loop and lake front (Lincoln Park is located three miles north of the Central Business District). Its picturesque nineteenth-century architecture, the burgeoning development of the nearby old town entertainment and shopping district, and the presence of DePaul University, McCormick Theological Seminary, and a number of large hospitals were further attractions.

Large amounts of urban renewal funds earmarked for the redevelopment of the Lincoln Park community also contributed in attracting people to this area of the city. One city newspaper reported that on June 9, 1965, the Federal Housing and Home Finance Agency (HHFA) approved a capital grant of $10,200,000 for the initial phase of an urban renewal project in this area of the city (*Chicago Sun-Times*, June 23, 1969:28). The formal beginning of the renewal of Lincoln Park took place in 1956, when the Lincoln Park Conservation Association (LPCA)—an organization of community residents designed to work for the improvement and conservation of that area—requested the Chicago Community Conservation Board to designate the community as an urban renewal area. The request was approved in July of the same year, and plans for a General Neighborhood Renewal Plan (GNRP) for the Lincoln Park community were initiated. The GNRP was to be implemented through several relatively small projects which were to be carried out over a fifteen year period. The projects were clustered into two major, but separate, projects simply called Projects One and Two. Project One was started during the summer of 1965 with the southeastern end of Lincoln Park as its target site. Project Two of the Lincoln Park GNRP included a substantial portion of the area remaining after the completion of phase one. The area in the western boundaries of the community designated for Project Two was approximately in the heart of the Puerto Rican ethnic enclave.

Out of the 6,729 residential structures in the GNRP area, 1,765 (26 percent) were slated for clearance, with 621 of these (9 percent of all structures in the community) located in the Project One area. While Puerto Ricans represented the second largest ethnic/racial group in Lincoln Park in 1961 with 1,898 or 7 percent of the households (the white population was numerically dominant with 22,991 or 88 percent of occupants of housing units), 34 percent of all Puerto Rican households were involved in clearance operations in the area (*Chicago Tribune*, 1969). Thus, for Puerto Ricans, redevelopment of the Lincoln Park community seemed like a repeat of the Near North Side's Carl Sandburg Village urban renewal project just south of Lincoln Park. As noted in the preceding chapter, Puerto Ricans had been forced to move from the Near North Side by the federal bulldozer in the late 1950s. The situation of Puerto Ricans in Lincoln Park was different; this time they refused to go. The comments of a young Puerto Rican best explains the shift in behavior among Puerto Rican residents of this neighborhood: "Where would we go if we have to leave, and why should we have to keep moving while other people stay?" (*Chicago Today*, 1969).

Attempts to displace Puerto Ricans were met and denounced by the Young Lords, a former street gang which became a community organization in 1967. Comprised primarily of second-generation Puerto Rican youth, the organization was aided by the support of Bruce Johnson, minister of the Armitage Avenue Methodist Church. A young man himself (30 years old), Bruce Johnson was one of the leading forces of encouragement for the Young Lords as he strongly urged its members to resist the pressure of redevelopment in their neighborhood.

The leading activities undertaken by the Young Lords were meant to oppose the forces that sought to push them out of Lincoln Park. The organization used physical force, vandalism, protest, and similar actions to scare off those who opposed the presence of Puerto Ricans. The Young Lords' approach was based on the premise that the only significant resource Puerto Ricans possessed was the capacity to make trouble—to disrupt institutions of the established system and produce sufficient political reverberations to force the authorities to respond.

The first of the organization's disruptive actions occurred May 16, 1969 when the Young Lords and two other community groups took over the administration and classroom buildings of the McCormick Theological Seminary at Halsted and Belden Streets. Classes at the 250-student seminary, operated by the United Presbyterian Church, were suspended for four days as the Young Lords' occupation of the campus lasted almost a week. During the occupation of the McCormick Seminary the Young Lords publicized the attempts to displace Puerto Ricans from the Lincoln Park community, charging that the seminary was a prime force in this displacement. The Young Lords demanded the seminary "to provide funds for low-income housing in the community, a children's center, a cultural center for Latin Americans and legal assistance" (*Chicago Sun-Times*, May 16, 1969:46). This action was taken primarily to dramatize the plight of the poor in the neighborhood and to demand that McCormick Seminary and other institutions become involved.

A month later, the Young Lords became involved in efforts to establish a day-care center in the basement of the Armitage Avenue Methodist Church. The organization asked church officials for permission to run the day-care center, and although Bruce Johnson was receptive to the idea, the small congregation of whites and Cubans said no. As a result, the Young Lords acted on their own and occupied the church. The take-over had been preceded by a sit-in which began June 11, 1969 and ended four days later with the occupation of the church. White residents of Lincoln Park opposed the opening of the day-care center and requested city inspectors to conduct an investigation of the site to determine if it was in compliance with state regulations. City inspectors found eleven violations, including one which required raising the basement floor three feet. Although the total cost for correcting the various violations was estimated at $10,000, the day-care center opened in August, 1969. The overall program included, among other services, a breakfast program—the first of its kind in the community.

The organization's most notable activity, however, revolved around a plan to establish a "poor people's" housing project on an urban renewal site on the westside of Lincoln Park near Larrabe and Eugene Streets. Knowing that the Department of Urban Renewal had approved the construction of a housing plan on this site, the Young Lords proposed that 40 percent of the housing units be set aside for poor families. Further, the organization demanded the rents be subsidized by the U.S. Department of Housing and Urban Development under Section 8.

The Lincoln Park Conservation Community Council (LPCCC), a group of community residents named by Mayor Daley to oversee and approve government urban renewal in the community, opposed the poor people's housing project with a plan of their own. The LPCCC's plan, primarily aimed at middle-income families, called for setting aside only the Federal Housing Authority minimum of 15 percent low-income family units. After the announcement of the LPCCC's plan, the Young Lords agreed to disrupt any open meeting held by this group of community residents to seek support for its plan. In July, several meetings were disrupted by violence when members of the Young Lords stormed the stage of meeting halls and refused to allow the agenda items to be discussed (*Chicago Tribune*, December 14, 1969).

The poor people's plan was turned down by the Department of Urban Renewal (DUR) on February 11, 1970. In an open meeting in the council chambers in city hall, the board rejected the bid to build a housing project for low- and moderate-income families. The Department of Urban Renewal voted to award construction of a 70-unit project which provided 15 percent of the housing for poor people.

A riot almost broke out in the council chambers following the DUR's decision. The *Chicago Tribune* reported that one person was subdued by five policemen after he leaped over a spectator's barricade and jumped from one row of empty aldermanic desks to another in an apparent attempt to reach the area where the board members were sitting. It was also reported that policemen moved in to hold back a dozen members of the Young Lords who also jumped from the spectators' area in an attempt to reach the arrested man (February 12, 1970).

Although the Young Lords lost this battle, their confrontation with the Lincoln Park Conservation Community Council and their involvement in other related activities pointed to the new response among Puerto Ricans to their housing situation. Puerto Ricans were forced to protect their "turf," or face displacement. This particular case suggests not only the way of life experienced by some Puerto Ricans but the circumstances which awaited the growing number of Puerto Rican newcomers and their children during the ensuing decades. Similar instances of housing discrimination and inequality were experienced in Lakeview, Logan Square, and other northside communities during the 1970s and 1980s. This pattern of housing discrimination has been an ongoing part of the urban life of Puerto Ricans in this midwest metropolis.

Police Injustice

The nature of group relations between Puerto Ricans and whites in Chicago was also heavily influenced by the actions of the police toward barrio residents. From the start, policemen treated Puerto Ricans in Chicago with a great deal of resentment and enmity. During the period of adjustment to the new society, many of the newcomers were arrested under any suspicious circumstances, and were more likely to be accorded discourteous or brutal treatment at the hands of the police. For example, there were instances when policemen arrested some of the migrants because, when stopped and questioned about their names and citizenship status, they would use two last names when identifying themselves, i.e., *Mi nombre es Luis Rodríguez Martínez* (My name is Luis Rodríguez Martínez). The policeman would assume that this was a ploy on the part of the Puerto Rican to prevent "American authorities" from finding out who he was. According to many of my respondents, these incidents were quite common in el barrio and led to many unnecessary arrests and embarrassing moments for the Puerto Rican newcomer.

One of the earliest and most revealing incidents of police brutality occurred in the summer of 1965 and involved the beating of two Puerto Rican men, Celestino A. González, 25 years old, and

Silvano Burgos, three years older, both of 2847 W. Division Street. An article in the *Chicago Daily News*, "Cops Brutal In Arrest: Latin Group," (August 2, 1965) reported that the two men were standing on the corner of Mozart and Division about 11:15 P.M. on July 23, 1965 when the police came to chase children away from an open fire hydrant. The pair informed the newspaper that they went into their home as they saw the police drive up and were pursued by the officers, who broke down the door to enter the house. González and Burgos were both arrested and charged with aggravated battery, resisting arrest, reckless conduct, and disorderly conduct. While in custody, the two men were brutally beaten by the police. González's account of the incident, printed in one local community newspaper, describes the treatment he received from the policemen:

> They handcuffed me in my room and took me to their car by pushing me and threatening my life. They took me to a hospital on Leavitt near Division where the policeman who broke the glass of my door was going to be treated. They pulled us out of the car and took us to a washroom in the hospital. There we were beaten savagely. The next stop was a park near the hospital where I was, once again, beaten up. Finally, I was taken to a police district where several policemen hit me like crazy; I fell to the floor and everyone that passed by hit me. I was bleeding terribly and I lost my consciousness, when I woke up, I was in Cook County Hospital with my hands and feet tied to a bed. (*El Puertorriqueño*, August 11, 1965:3)

The González and Burgos' case created a flurry of community responses. One organization, which assisted the newcomers in dealing with the challenges of a new urban setting, complained to Mayor Richard Daley about this and other incidents of police brutality and injustice. In a letter to the Mayor, the organization urged an investigation of this particular case and also stressed:

> We by no means intend to give the impression that this is an isolated case. The complaints of Spanish-speaking residents within this area revolve around not only the several accusations of irresponsible beatings, but also a complete lack of concern on the part of the police in the protection of Latin-American residents. We would not mention this if cases could not be documented through witnesses from both the commu-

nity and various commissions responsible ultimately to you and to the city. (reprinted in *El Puertorriqueño*, August 11, 1965:11)

Such cases set the stage for police-Puerto Rican relations in Chicago as the lines of cleavage were already being sharply drawn. On the one side, a generalized belief in police brutality and discriminatory law enforcement was widespread and gaining strength within the Puerto Rican community. On the other side there was a denial of these charges by the police and elected officials. In concrete terms, a belief on the part of a Puerto Rican about to be arrested that the arrest would involve the use of force had the consequence of an attempt to avoid or resist arrest, thus increasing the probability that force would in fact have to be used. A belief on the part of the police that resistance could be expected also produced a behavior in which force would in fact be used.

The whole matter of police-Puerto Rican relations in Chicago is a complicated one. Police brutality came to mean more than the excessive use of physical force during an arrest, the manhandling of suspects in the police station and in jail, and the other physical acts usually associated with the term brutality. It also referred to arrests, questionings, and searches of Puerto Ricans by police without apparent provocation, the use of abusive and derogatory language in addressing Puerto Ricans, such as the word "spik," and a general attitude toward this Spanish-speaking group which was an affront to its sense of dignity.

ORGANIZATIONAL RESPONSE AMONG PUERTO RICANS, 1950–1965

Puerto Rican contact with the white society during the 1950s and early years of the 1960s accelerated the growth of Puerto Rican consciousness. The Puerto Rican ethnic identity converted whatever residual regional/town differences that may have existed among the new arrivals into a sense of peoplehood. Manifestations of Puerto Rican peoplehood and/or ethnicity were operative in a variety of ethnic-conscious attitudes and organizations. Puerto Ricans were forced to develop and staff a parallel set of personal and social services, neighborhood businesses, and communication networks to meet the tastes and needs of a growing Puerto Rican population.

The most significant response among Puerto Ricans during this period was their development of community organizations. Several community organizations developed which sought to provide guidance and leadership for neighborhood residents. Members of each organization believed their contributions to be the most significant and vital to the whole ethnic group. The community organization became basic to the success of the Puerto Rican community in Chicago by providing identification, political styles, and core values, contributing to group cohesion by enhancing the ethnic group member's subjective identification with the group.[6] For instance, the Office of the Commonwealth of Puerto Rico was established in Chicago in 1948 by the government of Puerto Rico to provide employment services and orientations to the Puerto Rican newcomer to Chicago. Another early organization was the Puerto Rican Congress, which was established in 1951 basically as a cultural and social organization. A large number of "town clubs," such as El Club Vegabajeno, El Club de Lares, El Club de Manati, and others, also represent some of the structures established by Puerto Rican residents during the 1950s. The overall function of the town clubs, like that of the earlier social agencies, was primarily social and cultural.

Los Caballeros de San Juan

The chief expression of social organization among Puerto Ricans in the 1950s and early 1960s was found, however, in one particular community organization, Los Caballeros de San Juan (The Knights of St. John). The significance of Los Caballeros among Puerto Ricans was first of all institutional, and only secondarily a matter of cultural transmission and/or perpetuation as in the anthropological sense. Los Caballeros presented the primary means by which Puerto Ricans began to structure a self-conscious community for ethnic advancement and betterment. The church service became a symbolic rite of affirmation of one's ethnic association and a vehicle for preserving the ethnic language and cultural traditions. The embryo of what was to later become a diverse Puerto Rican community had its inception in the growth of Los Caballeros.

In general, Los Caballeros had strong religious connections and its programs and activities were linked directly with the parish church, church membership being a prerequisite to organization membership.[7] The organization, founded by the Catholic Church and Puerto Rican lay persons, was chartered in 1954 in the State of Illinois as a fraternal and civic entity for Spanish-speaking men. It was always dependent on voluntary support and its structure, leadership, and liturgy were shaped to meet pressing human needs. Members of Los Caballeros found meanings for personal and communal life in the cultural symbols and the religious ideas that their leaders believed were marks of a shared inheritance and, hence, of a common peoplehood.

Los Caballeros provided an extensive personalizing of religious faith—not to be confused with making faith private or individualistic. While the experience of uprooting and resettlement was a remarkably solitary one, and the traumatic aspect of it affected each person individually, the thrust of the organization was not to make individual experience the measure of faith but to enlarge the sense of personal involvement in one's religious community and its systems of belief and prescriptions for behavior. Group consciousness and activity flowed from the church, which did not exist primarily to spread Christianity to the world, but rather, to cultivate the ethnic solidarity of the group. Crucial to cultivating this solidarity was the collective conversion of Puerto Ricans, binding the group into a self-sustaining "convenantal" community. Puerto Ricans were not practicing a transcendent faith calling for the brotherhood of all saints; they were practicing a culture of faith oriented around nurturing an ethnic community of feeling and aspiration, which looked inward toward preserving the integrity of the group.

As different parishes began to serve diverse family, group, and individual interests they came to represent for the migrants communities of commitment and, therefore, arenas of social change. The religion pursued by Los Caballeros, in other words, was, above all, an instrument of self-expression for the Puerto Rican community. It was in essence more social than religious. For the organization, Christianity was accompanied by a symbolism of Puerto Rican ethnicity or nationality. This symbolism was formed and cultivated by a sensitivity to ethnicity or nationality that extended to people who were often detached from religion. It created a "backwash" of fixed impressions and attitudes, which were for quite some time difficult to efface.

The establishment of Los Caballeros cannot be equated with

the creation of the "national parish" by German, Italian, Polish, and other Catholic immigrants. Unable to participate on an equal footing in the existing English-language parishes and other religious structures of American society, European Catholic immigrants rallied around their common identity, saints, and priests to protect their self-respect and their piety. The "national parish" represented the establishment of a major institution on the part of these immigrants to preserve the religious life of the old country. Los Caballeros, on the other hand, was just simply a community organization with a religious tone—a voluntary association sponsored by the Catholic Church in Chicago. Puerto Ricans in Chicago were served by priests who had worked almost exclusively with English-speaking congregations.

The initial location of Los Caballeros was in the Woodlawn area. The organization was headed by Leo T. Mahon, an Irish Catholic priest who had been assigned to Woodlawn to work there with the expanding black population of the community. However, when several Puerto Rican residents of Woodlawn visited Father Mahon and requested that he help them organize a program and some activities to improve their conditions in this community, he sought and was granted permission to work with this group of newly arrived migrants. According to Father Mahon, they decided to form an organization that would do for Puerto Ricans what other social agencies and religious organizations had done for European immigrants—to help with work and wages, health and housing, the difficulties of adjustment of an essentially rural population to the conditions of a city environment and to modern life. The Father also stressed that since racial prejudice made the Puerto Rican situation distinct from the experience of European immigrants, the organization set out to engender in Puerto Ricans a counter feeling by directing the energies aroused by racial antagonism into constructive channels.

The organization advocated a policy of ethnic expediency and conciliation; it tried to make the most out of the conditions of racial discrimination and appealed to the conscience and goodwill of the white community, especially the employing class. Los Caballeros attempted to advance a doctrine of solidarity or cooperation between the white and Puerto Rican populations. Just as important, it attempted to bring the Puerto Rican migrants into the mainstream of the city's life while at the same time respecting and encouraging their cultural tradition.

This particular strategy combined some of the basic tenets of the assimilation and cultural pluralism theories often used by sociologists to discuss group adaptation and relations in American society. In terms of assimilation, Los Caballeros' program called for a direct attempt to become involved in the larger American society by adopting, to whatever extent possible, the customs, attitudes, and language of white America. Reflected in the Church's statements was a deeply rooted conviction that Puerto Ricans had to become Americans as soon as possible by adopting a Catholicism like that of the Irish and other European immigrants. This approach presupposed that between the migrants and the larger American society there was some incompatibility in role expectations and in role demands. If the ultimate success of Americanization, from the Church's point of view, was the attainment of a new, stable status-image—the acquisition of new skills, performance of new roles, and the reformation of self-image—then clearly it entailed full acceptance and participation in the "absorbing society." Puerto Ricans were expected to accept and perform the universal roles of the American society. In other words, the Catholic Church was perceived as being capable of helping Puerto Ricans "cleanse" themselves of their assigned underclass identity or inferior minority status. It was anticipated that the traditional assimilationist program of the Catholic Church, which in large measure was responsible for the Americanization of European immigrants, could indeed perform the same function for Puerto Ricans.

The Catholic Church's assimilationist response to Puerto Rican newcomers was not surprising since this institution historically has been perceived as the essential vehicle for the Americanization of "foreigners." The process of Americanization embodied in the religious work of the Catholic Church did not involve the beliefs and rituals associated with the traditional church, but instead, had come to mean

> the American Way of Life that supplies American society with an "overarching sense of unity" amid conflict. It is the American Way of Life about which Americans are admittedly and unashamedly "intolerant." It is the American Way of Life that provides the framework in terms of which crucial values of

American existence are couched. By every realistic criterion the American Way of Life is the operative faith of the American people. (Herberg, 1955:88)

Simultaneously, the organization gave voice to an ideology of ethnic solidarity and self-help which urged Puerto Ricans to develop skills and organize their own economic and civic institutions. Long before other community organizations began to deeply affect Puerto Rican ethnic consciousness, Los Caballeros had fashioned an organization to sustain the cultural traditions of the newcomers. It supported the efforts of priests and lay leaders to help the members of local congregations find in their faith the moral resources to improve their situation in the new society. Thus, Puerto Rican ethnic consciousness fortified by religious faith took hold of the imagination of many new arrivals, and affected most precisely that group which comprised the majority of early emigrants to Chicago.

To achieve this dual role of "Americanization" and "cultural pluralism," Father Mahon outlined a concrete program of coordination, investigation, education, religious service, and labor relations. Primarily, the initial efforts of the organization were directed at organizing the different Puerto Rican barrios in the city. The task of "community organizing" was assumed by *jibaros* (peasants), who a few years earlier had toiled the soil of the mountains of the Island. In background, the majority of these men were self-made people with no more than rudimentary formal education. Lester Hunt and Nicholas Von Hoffman, two Saul Alinsky-trained organizers hired by Los Caballeros to work and teach Puerto Ricans certain specific skills in community organizing, describe the educational background of Puerto Ricans in their concise essay on "democracy" and the newcomers' interpretation of the concept:

> Coming as they have from the farm and hills of backwood Puerto Rico, the newly arrived have found Chicago a strange and frightening place. They have not been fortunate enough to come with the education or knowledge that could help them out of their dilemma of being country folks in the big city. Almost none of them speaks English well, many can hardly be thought of as speaking it at all, nor do they have the advantage of being well educated in their own mother tongue. Their Spanish vocabulary is small, writing in it comes hard.

Their general education is about on the same level, fourth or fifth grade, we estimate. (1957:182)

The 1960 Census also provides insight into the educational attainment levels of Puerto Rican newcomers to Chicago. Of 11,204 enrolled males, only 9 percent had completed four years of high school, as had 7.3 percent of 9,173 women. For male emigrants, the median of school years completed was 7.9, for women the number was slightly lower, 7.2 (see Table 13).

The participation of these politically ambitious newcomers in Los Caballeros provided them with the opportunity to develop leadership skills and a group following. In fact, this "elite," the founders and leaders of the organization, went on to dominate Puerto Rican life well into the 1960s; they ran the social affairs, organized the civic ventures, and acted as spokesmen for Chicago's Puerto Ricans in matters of group concern.

After receiving a few weeks of training in community organizing by the two hired consultants, the community workers would walk around an area populated by Puerto Ricans, observing things and asking people they met to come to the office of Los Caballeros for a visit and to bring a friend. The community workers used these early contacts to get the feel, as well as the acceptance, of the residents of the neighborhood. They tried to learn what their neighbors

TABLE 13

Number of School Years Completed, 1960, 14 Years Old and Over

		MALE		FEMALE	
		NUMBER	PERCENT	NUMBER	PERCENT
Elementary:	1 to 4 years	2,012	18	1,834	20
	5 and 6 years	2,087	19	1,834	20
	7 years	1,201	11	937	10
	8 years	1,974	18	1,333	15
High School:	1 to 3 years	2,109	19	1,562	17
	4 years	1,004	9	668	7
College:	1 to 3 years	315	3	204	2
	4 years or more	120	1	92	1
Median School Years Completed		7.9		7.2	

Source: *U.S. Bureau of the Census*, Social Characteristics of Persons of Puerto Rican Birth and Parentage for Selected Metropolitan Statistical Areas, 1960.

were up against, and they looked for ways to help out. As indicated earlier, the organizing tactics included maintaining the ethnic personality type by organizing the group around religious and cultural symbols and the newcomers' experience or situation in American society.

The geographic dispersion of the Puerto Rican communities during the 1950s made the community workers realize that in order to be more effective, the organization needed to expand into these different areas of the city. As a result, it was decided to augment the initial organization with *concilios* (councils or branches of the umbrella organization). By 1960 there were 12 concilios servicing Puerto Ricans throughout the city of Chicago. There were times when one particular barrio was the site of two concilios as was the case in the Near West Side and Lincoln Park. Each concilio represented an ecological unit, a community of families and an organized church membership.

Los Caballeros and its concilios provided a wide range of services and assistance to Puerto Ricans. They directed needy cases to city's social welfare agencies, supplied legal advice and employment, and provided for newcomers at their arrival in Chicago. Its most frequent and visible function was the provision of social-recreational activities such as picnics, dances, baseball leagues, and the like. The leading social-recreational activity of the entire organization was the celebration of El Día de San Juan (St. John's Day). Beginning in 1956 and lasting until 1966, when the event was changed to include the participation of newly formed organizations and institutions not connected to Los Caballeros and subsequently renamed La Parada Puertorriqueña (the Puerto Rican Parade), El Día de San Juan represented the major social activity and celebration for the Puerto Rican community. (The same applies for present-day Puerto Rican Parade.) These events were meant to be and continue to represent one of the leading political activities among the city's Puerto Rican residents—a show of unity and power. Professor Rosa Estades has referred to this event in the context of New York City as symbolic unity: "for most Puerto Ricans . . . the Desfile [the Parade] represents a powerful show of strength and solidarity that far outweighs its negative aspects. For them this is one day when pride in their own identity overrides all other emotions. The sufferings and conflicts are forgotten—members of all factions join on this day and with a smile on their faces they march up Fifth Avenue, proud to be Puerto Rican" (1980:82).

Although not as visible as its social-recreational activities, Los Caballeros accepted a struggle on the political front as the most promising means of attaining equality for Puerto Ricans. Through the use of the ballot and the courts strenuous efforts were exerted to gain social justice for the group. Full faith was placed in the ability of these instruments of democratic government to free this population from social proscription and civic inequality. Under this banner Los Caballeros fought for full equality for Puerto Ricans, involving the eradication of all the social, legal, and political disabilities which drew a line of distinction between Puerto Ricans and other groups.

Los Caballeros carried on its struggle valiantly. By becoming directly involved in several major issues, it contributed immensely toward the enhancement of Puerto Rican life in the city of Chicago. In 1960, Los Caballeros organized and rallied Puerto Rican voters in support of the "Viva Kennedy" Democratic campaign. It is claimed that the organization was able to register over 30,000 Puerto Ricans for these elections, a participation which enabled Democratic candidate John F. Kennedy to win the city of Chicago. In effect, Los Caballeros brought to light the significance of the Puerto Rican political power in this midwestern city. (The significance of the Puerto Rican vote was once again manifested in the early 1980s when most Puerto Ricans supported Harold Washington's mayoral candidacy, serving as, according to some commentators, the election's "swing vote.")

The other more notable involvement of Los Caballeros was with the issue of wage garnishment as it pertained to the Puerto Rican consumer. For some time Puerto Rican families had been victims of "easy credit plans" which resulted in the garnishment of their wages when payments on purchased merchandise were not made or were stopped. Los Caballeros became involved in efforts to protect Puerto Rican consumers from falling prey to these credit schemes.

Their lack of shopping sophistication and their vulnerability to easy credit allowed many Puerto Rican families to encounter serious difficulties as consumers. The institution of credit and the special forms it took during this time in low-income areas, like the Division Street Area, provided consumption opportunities for Puerto

Rican families. This group of "proletarian consumer" families limited their shopping to the immediate neighborhood; they were not particularly conscious of quality and they did not shop around before buying. It was not expected that any of the families would shop for durable goods in the downtown department stores and discount houses. They went instead to the local stores and to appliance chain stores that advertised easy credit plans.

Symbolic of their narrow shopping scope was yet another consumer practice frequently found among Puerto Ricans and members of other underclass groups—buying from door-to-door peddlers, the men with the traditional slogan of a "dollar down, a dollar a week." These peddlers served as purchasing agents for these families, getting them practically anything they needed. Unlike most of the local merchants and the more bureaucratic stores that offer credit, most of the peddlers did not use installment contracts. These men were not interested in building up a clientele. Once the contract was signed, this kind of salesman gave or mailed the customer a coupon book with instructions for making monthly payments, and then he would disappear.

Thus, it was not unusual to observe different salesmen coming to the home of a newcomer daily, to show him or his wife some merchandise and to offer to finance it if certain papers were signed. Other salesmen would stop potential customers at factory gates or push their goods at bus stops and trap Puerto Ricans into signing for the merchandise. In many cases Puerto Ricans agreed and signed the documents although the contracts were complicated and written in English. Auto dealers, for example, would sell Puerto Ricans used cars at double the price they were worth, quickly repossess the car when a payment was missed, and then resell it for the same price, while the Puerto Rican buyer was sued for the balance.

The victimization of Puerto Rican consumers by these various easy credit schemes is epitomized in the case of William Rodríguez in 1960. A *Sun-Times* report, "Debt trap: Some can't spring it," summarizes this particular case. After having his wages garnisheed three times before, a different creditor was threatening court action against Mr. Rodríguez. He also had several outstanding debts which he was unable to pay. "William Rodríguez," writes the *Sun-Times'* correspondent, "didn't know where to get help and, deep in despair, he went for a walk to think things through. He wandered through his neighborhood for several hours. Then he stopped at a drug-store, bought some rat poison and ate it as he walked home. When he got there, already in terrible pain, he told his wife he couldn't take any more hounding by creditors. Four hours later he was dead" (*Sun-Times*, Sept. 30, 1971).

William Rodríguez's suicide was followed by a great outcry for credit reform on the part of Los Caballeros, influencing the formation of a "Credit Squad" in 1960 by the Municipal Court. The aim of the Credit Squad was to crack down on credit law abuses. When complaints came in, plainclothes policemen assigned to this unit would check for violations of the retail credit laws. This reform was finally followed eleven years later by a law that sharply limited the amount of a worker's earnings that could be taken under garnishment or wage assignment.

As one examines the history of Puerto Ricans in Chicago it becomes evident that Los Caballeros emerged as a central and creative force in the life of the migrant community. Los Caballeros attempted to provide a common religious establishment where a group of people would learn to waive their individuality in favor of the common welfare—Puerto Ricans were urged to adopt a world view and attitude shaped by religion. It was assumed that since the large majority of Puerto Ricans were Catholics, Catholicism was a natural and largely unexamined preference. This view, however, overlooked the fact that for Puerto Ricans the Catholic Church in the Island was an institution far removed from their lives. Fitzpatrick (1971:116) indicates that the distant and alien nature of the church in Puerto Rico resulted in the Puerto Rican having an internalized sense of Catholic identity without formally attending Mass and receiving the sacraments. In more general terms, he notes that throughout all of Latin America, Catholicism means personal relationships with the saints and a community manifestation of faith, not the individual actions and commitments expected in the United States.

This is not to suggest that the Church did not play a vital role in the rites of passages, signified by baptism, marriage, and burial. But to those forms of religious observance which were highly prized by American Catholics—regular attendance at Mass, confession, and Holy Communion—Puerto Rican jíbaros were less attentive. While women frequented the church for Mass, men rarely attended except for social and cultural activities. Thus, for the large majority of Puerto Rican men Los Caballeros came to signify another social club. The magnet that pulled many to the activities of the various concilios was primarily "socials," i.e., participation in El Día de San Juan, baseball and domino leagues, and the like.

That Los Caballeros rendered valuable services for Puerto Rican newcomers can scarcely be disputed, nor, can the prominent role of the organization in developing or training many of the foremost leaders of the Puerto Rican community be denied. As one former leader of Los Caballeros remarked: "If there had been no religious organization, there would not be a Puerto Rican movement today." By facilitating ongoing contact among Puerto Ricans, the organization helped perpetuate or reproduce the Puerto Rican culture, language, and cohesiveness in an otherwise foreign society. For more than a decade, Los Caballeros was the lifeblood of the Puerto Rican community in the city of Chicago.

While the organization can be considered the first line of defense behind which Puerto Ricans could organize themselves and preserve their group identity, Los Caballeros participated in a movement which sought the elusive but ultimate goal of equality by means of accommodation. The leaders of the organization gave the appearance of accommodating or compromise leadership, holding their positions primarily because they were acceptable to the city's white power structure. They were also accepted by Puerto Ricans because accommodation was regarded as the most practical and effective mode of adjustment in the existing power situation. The price for the organization's assistance in the migrants' struggle to survive and prosper in urban America was conformity.

Beginning in mid-1960, Los Caballeros began to experience decline. Its ability to speak for the Puerto Rican community faded because its ideology and tactics were considered by community residents to be out of touch with the needs of the period. At a time of social upheaval and unrest in the Puerto Rican community Los Caballeros continued to advocate a non-violent or peaceful assimilationist approach. The organization was not organizing people, thus people began to turn away from membership rolls or participation.

In the final analysis, Puerto Ricans became just another "immigrant group" for the Catholic Church to accommodate, and this ambivalence disillusioned many Puerto Ricans. The church hierarchy saw the discrimination against Puerto Ricans, but it did not condemn it as part of American society. Instead, it sought to do charity by trying to alleviate suffering by serving as a buffer without attacking institutionalized racism. The Church could not, due to its own relationship with American society, help the Puerto Ricans resist the violation of their culture and personal identity.

The Migrant Press

Another major institution organized by the Puerto Rican newcomers during this period of adjustment was the "migrant press."[8] Several leading newspapers were started during the early 1960s which serviced the whole ethnic group. Chicago's first Puerto Rican newspaper, *El Centinela*, began in 1959 and lasted until 1960, at which time it was replaced by *Prensa Libre*, which lasted less than a year. *La Gaseta*, the next Puerto Rican newspaper to be published in Chicago, was founded in 1964. A year later its name was changed to *El Puertorriqueño*. The first three newspapers began and remained as monthly papers while *El Puertorriqueño* was published weekly. The language of the Puerto Rican press was Spanish, since one of its functions was to communicate with the newcomers who did not speak English.

All of these local papers functioned as guides, coordinators, and promoters of national cultural pride. They served as intermediaries between the emigrants and the institutions and inhabitants of the new society, a bridge between life in familiar Puerto Rican society and that in strange urban America. They intended to help newcomers interpret the issues and events of the day and to provide them with the information needed to operate in the new American society. In addition to the dual function of reporting news and stimulating ethnic consciousness and solidarity, this local migrant press provided identifiable leadership for Chicago's Puerto Rican neighborhoods and voiced demands and complaints of individuals and groups. The maximum impact and value of the Puerto Rican newspapers lay within their ability to satisfy a desperate need for reasonably accurate information about the old homeland and the new society.

El Centinela grew out of the common goals of the Catholic Church and was an outspoken organ of Los Caballeros. This newspaper, which was under editorship of Juan Sosa, one of the founders and first President of Los Caballeros, dealt primarily with problems of adaptation while serving community interests. Some of this religious journalism, like that of the other local papers, ventured into social problems and was perceived as an agent of community welfare and progress.

In *El Centinela*, Puerto Rican newcomers always found wise advice and moral and material assistance. This newspaper provided them with useful information on American customs, laws, and politics. A section of the paper called, *"El Padre Mahon Dice"* ("Father Mahon Says"), was always filled with a wide range of suggestions of this kind. In one particular column, Father Mahon used the hypothetical case of two recent arrivals from the Island, referred to simply as José and Juan, to better illustrate to the readers the "do's" and "don'ts" of assimilation. Juan was portrayed in the story as someone who, in the course of three months since arriving from the Island, had already adapted a street-like manner. José, on the other hand, typified a family-centered individual. While Juan would spend part of his salary in socials with friends or to buy himself a car, watch, television set, etc., José's lifestyle did not require these particular items. The latter was content with living in a small apartment, making sacrifices and saving his earnings to purchase a house "later on." When going to a party or to Sunday Mass, unlike Juan, José would always take his wife and children. "This is why," notes Father Mahon, "when a priest who knows José talks to another American about Puerto Ricans he would say: obviously Puerto Ricans are good people and good Catholics" (*El Centinela*, January 8, 1959:2).

In another column, Father Mahon called attention to the idea of the "fifth freedom." He suggested that advanced medicine, modern technology, equal educational opportunity, and a system of democracy, as they all existed in the United States in 1960, provided the four major freedoms otherwise not available to most of the world's population. In such society, however, slavery was still a salient feature as the act of "sin" always resulted in the enslavement of some members of that wider community, depriving them from enjoying the other four freedoms. The only way to free oneself from this enslavement, proclaimed the Father, is by adhering to the fifth freedom: "It doesn't matter the sin you've committed, you can still free yourself from it through confession and agreeing and complying with the small punishment imposed by the priest" (*El Centinela*, February 1, 1959:3).

Other articles in *El Centinela* aimed to educate readers on how to be wise consumers. Be a patient shopper, compare prices in different stores, save and use discount coupons as much as possible, were typical suggestions. In several other cases the newspaper instructed the newcomers to avoid buying merchandise on credit and not to sign blank documents for any items.

In addition, *El Centinela* would always feature some of the major social events sponsored by Los Caballeros. Dances and banquets were frequently brought to the attention of the readers. For instance, in the paper's very first edition in 1959, the organization's annual banquet for that year appeared in the lead front-page story. It was reported that the banquet was going to be celebrated at the Palmer House downtown and that Dr. Jaime Benitez, then president of the University of Puerto Rico at Rio Piedras, would be in attendance to receive an award as the "most distinguished Puerto Rican citizen of the year." Most of the article provided highlights of Dr. Benitez's major accomplishments.

El Centinela was used quite often as a recruiting arm for Los Caballeros. Editorials urging residents of the Puerto Rican community to join and participate in the activities of the organization were commonly featured, while others were critical of barrio residents refusing to become part of the rank and file of Los Caballeros — the city's most important and prestigious organization.

> One of the factors that hinders our ascending progress in this metropolis is the negative attitude of our people to participate in important and prestigious activities that are promulgated and supported by our organization. It is something to lament the antipathy that our people show toward these types of activities, which can be perceived through the scarce support or input they offer them (*El Centinela*, April, 1959:4).

As far as the publisher of *El Centinela* was concerned the obvious solution to the problems faced by the Puerto Rican migrants in urban America lay in adapting themselves to the American system. Thus, the newspaper tried to encourage the newcomers to adopt habits appropriate for adjusting to life in urban America, particularly in the years of the migration period.

EL PUERTORRIQUEÑO

A year after the defunct *Centinela* was replaced by *La Gaseta*, there emerged in the Puerto Rican community *El Puertorriqueño*. Appearing first in 1965, *El Puertorriqueño* lasted longer than any other Puerto Rican newspaper in the city of Chicago. It was terminated in the early 1980s when its publisher became ill.

Unlike Los Caballeros' newspaper, *El Puertorriqueño* emerged as an outspoken political paper. In the words of one of my study's repondents who was also a writer for the paper, "*El Puertorriqueño era un periódico sin pelos en la lengua*" (*El Puertorriqueño* was a newspaper which stopped at nothing). In an interview, Mr. Alfredo Torres de Jesús, one of the founders of *El Puertorriqueño* and the paper's first editor, specifically outlined the newspaper's goals. The paper promised to describe the life of Puerto Ricans who lived in Chicago in all of its manifestations: intellectual, artistic, commercial, and industrial:

> The paper was started because there was a need to communicate the "issues" to Puerto Ricans in Chicago and to establish a Puerto Rican presence in this city. There was one or maybe two Puerto Rican radio announcers but there was no Puerto Rican program in itself. We established a very positive atmosphere which, I believed, raised the political consciousness of our readers. We wanted to get them involved in the problems in the community, problems such as education, housing, police brutality. There was no one there educating *el pueblo* [the community].

Although the content of *El Puertorriqueño* varied by editorial inclination, it typically took strong stands on community issues affecting barrio residents. The paper would note the needs, the pains, and the aspirations of the Puerto Rican newcomer who, in

America, fought an arduous struggle for existence. The paper, in other words, promoted the "cause." It also provided explanations for the various problems operative in the Puerto Rican community. In one particular case, an editorial called attention to the effects of external forces on circumstances faced by barrio residents:

> It's necessary that Puerto Ricans learn to speak the English language, after all, it is a very effective medium for conversation, but it cannot resolve our problems. The grave housing problem, the problem of unemployment, the school problem, the problem of dignity and respect, and others don't have anything to do with the language that we speak or don't speak. Our problem is rooted much more profoundly: we are victims of a series of problems that have gone unresolved for many generations. We are heirs of these many problems (June 1, 1966:1).

El Puertorriqueño displayed a great deal of interest in the economic and social situation of Puerto Rican newcomers. It supported labor against capital, feeling that the latter abused the former. When hundreds of Puerto Rican workers were laid off by Zenith Radio Corporation in the winter of 1966, the paper called for an investigation by the City of Chicago's Commission of Human Relations of such unjust actions. The editor was not only critical of Zenith Radio Corp. for dismissing Puerto Rican workers but he also condemned the workers' union (Independent Radio Workers of America— IRWA) for not protecting the interests of Spanish-speaking labor. "The IRWA," the columnist reported, "is involved in a struggle with another rival union for control at this firm, in the meantime the interests of Puerto Rican workers have been set aside" (Dec. 1966:2).

El Puertorriqueño was closely linked to life in Puerto Rico. It not only reported news and events from the Island and their relationship to Puerto Rican residents in Chicago, but it also called for the establishment of structures and programs which would reflect the cultural and social way of life of native Puerto Rico. The establishment of an institute for Puerto Rican culture, suggestively called La Casa del El Puertorriqueño, was strongly recommended in one editorial. This idea was to be modeled after El Instituto de Cultura Puertorriqueño of Puerto Rico and was meant to bring pride and exposure to the Puerto Rican culture in the city:

How wonderful it would be to build something that would make our children feel proud and happy of their Puerto Rican culture; that they will be able to say this was built by my parents. This would represent a symbol of the various collective efforts among Puerto Ricans in this city. How wonderful it would be to have our own "house" where during sad moments we would contemplate a particular cultural aspect from our beautiful Island and allow others to admire our treasures (June 6, 1966:6).

El Puertorriqueño became an established institution in the Puerto Rican community, wielding enormous influence over the thinking of barrio residents. During the formative years, this weekly was by far the most important agency for forming and reflecting public opinion in the Division Street Area as it served, spoke, and fought for the Puerto Rican population of the city.

The Puerto Rican press in Chicago primarily served the need for unity and understanding among new arrivals who lacked command of the English language. This function is, of course, not new to the Puerto Rican press, the newspapers of European ethnic newcomers to America had more or less the same purpose if not the same content (see Janowitz, 1952). These ethnic newspapers differ from standard American journalism by reporting news not covered by other papers and by commenting on topics and in areas into which the established media did not venture. They interpret the news differently and from an uncommon standpoint. Perhaps more like the black press and that of other ethnic/racial minorities, the Puerto Rican press led the protest against injustices — it was a journalism almost totally committed to a cause.

These papers are an admirable social and financial achievement on the part of the "old migration" which originated from the peasant and working class of Puerto Rico. *El Puertorriqueño* was not only Chicago's first Puerto Rican weekly, it continued even when other local papers began to flourish in the late 1960s and the ensuing decade. *El Puertorriqueño* did not undergo any striking or abrupt changes in format or function; it maintained its usual vigor in the face of innovations such as Spanish radio and television stations and programs.

By the end of the 1950s, Puerto Rican families in Chicago had achieved an enduring cohesion of community in which social organizations and agencies and cultural traditions played the largest part. The emergence of Puerto Rican migrant communities was not a reconstitution of old models, but rather, an accommodation to the life of the city. In other words, since most Puerto Rican newcomers were drawn from hundreds of *campos* (rural areas) and villages of Puerto Rico, the urban communities were no mere transplants of the old society. Rather, Puerto Rican migrants to Chicago set about constructing a "tangible organizational reality" within which newcomers could identify themselves and declare their solidarity as a people.

It was in this accommodation that the migrants developed distinctive orientation toward the problems and prospects of the city. The family, the neighborhood, the community organization became the principal agencies of social control and reform from the outset of the migration period to the present. These characteristics, then, have defined the new society of Puerto Rican migrants and descendants and structured the course of their lives.

The small size of the various Puerto Rican ethnic enclaves during the 1950s and early years of the following decade contributed immensely in bonding Puerto Ricans together. The concentration of Puerto Ricans in small size barrios influenced and reinforced continuing individual and group interaction and relationship. Further, this concentric residential pattern permitted community organizing, the listing of support and subsequent mobilization of individuals for community affairs, to be carried out more easily. It was significantly less difficult to organize a population which was concentrated in several blocks of a neighborhood than one which was geographically dispersed. Several members of Los Caballeros gave accounts of how, while "making the rounds in the neighborhood," they would learn about new families from other residents. It was not surprising that most Puerto Ricans knew and interacted with their neighbors.

4

Evolution and Resolution of Conflict

RIOTS ON DIVISION STREET

Los Caballeros de San Juan and the local community press raised Puerto Ricans' awareness of their ethnic oppression, heightened their expectations, and increased their impatience with existing racial/ethnic arrangements in Chicago. The oppressive conditions during the 1950s and early 1960s created the need for more aggressive political ethnic-conscious action than what had been exhibited during the adjustment period, but only an urban riot emerged as the initial political activity of the period. The "Puerto Rican Riot of 1966," as this uprising was called, represents one of the loudest expressions of Puerto Rican ethnic-conscious behavior among barrio residents. It also constitutes one of the most massive and sustained expressions of Puerto Rican dissatisfaction with their internal colonial situation. The Division Street Riot was a clear signal that Puerto Rican people would no longer tolerate the conditions under which they were forced to live and proved to be the pivotal Puerto Rican response to American life in this midwest metropolis.

During the summer of 1966 the city of Chicago became the site of the first major urban Puerto Rican riot in the history of the United States. The outburst was one in a series of urban protest riots which raged in American society, primarily among blacks, from the end of World War II until the last years of the 1960s. Puerto Rican behavior in Chicago during the summer of 1966 mirrored the dilemma of exploited, non-white people in the United States: whether to withstand the rejection of the majority in the hope that ameliorative action would bring rewards within the system or to

144

lash out and destroy the "hated environment," thus abruptly focusing the attention of the majority and bringing release for oneself.

The Puerto Rican riot occurred almost at the same time that various national and local governmental agencies were taking precautionary measures to head off rioting in major American cities. The two preceding years had witnessed some of the largest and most intense black disturbances ever—Harlem, Watts, Detroit, Philadelphia, etc. In order to prevent future outbursts, the Justice Department instructed its Assistant United States Attorneys to report on conditions in a score of communities considered particularly "inflammable". The Vice President's Task Force on Youth Opportunity authorized its field representatives to investigate potential troublespots and offer short-term recommendations. These findings were to be made available to federal agencies involved in the black ghettoes. Government officials throughout the country devised emergency programs to employ and entertain black youths and otherwise keep them off the streets, while local and state police departments aided by the F.B.I. prepared coordinated riot-control plans. (These measures were not designed to alleviate conditions in the ghettos but merely to prevent their manifestation.) Hence, it was with mounting apprehension that local and federal officials awaited the summer.

They did not have to wait long. The Puerto Rican riot erupted in June, and was followed by disturbances among blacks in battered cities previously stricken and cities hitherto spared, Omaha, Dayton, San Francisco, and Atlanta. The summer of 1966 was the most violent yet.

The Puerto Rican riot began June 12, 1966 when a white policeman shot and wounded a young Puerto Rican man, Arcelis Cruz, twenty years old, near the intersection of Division Street and Damen Avenue in the Westtown community. After the shooting, the situation at the Division-Damen intersection intensified when the police brought dogs into the fray and a Puerto Rican was bitten. For three days and nights, a Puerto Rican crowd demonstrated against police brutality. And each time the police tried to disperse the crowd, it only succeeded in arousing them.

From June 12 to June 14, Puerto Ricans not only defied the police, but also looted and burned neighborhood businesses, particularly those identified as white-owned. The city's Puerto Rican leaders pleaded with the rioters to return to their homes, but to little avail. The *Chicago Sun-Times* (June 14, 1966:1) reports that at one rally, organized during the second day of the riot and held at the intersection of Division Street and California Avenue, community organization leaders and clergymen urged the crowd of 3,000 to halt the violence. Immediately after the rally, however, rocks and bricks were thrown at policemen. Meanwhile the police department ordered all available personnel into the Division Street area to quell the rioting, and on June 15, order was finally restored. By this time, it was officially acknowledged that 16 persons were injured, 49 were arrested, over 50 buildings were destroyed, and millions of dollars accrued in damages.

Smelser's (1962, chap. 8) analysis on the causes of collective behavior and the forms which it takes is helpful in this context of shared cleavages, grievances, and hostilities. Smelser's analytic framework emphasizes a number of determinants of social action which must all be present at the same time for a riot to occur. In addition to socioeconomic factors, such as high unemployment, low income, well defined racial cleavages, and inaccessible and unsympathetic authorities, this perspective emphasizes the importance of a generalized belief in the population as a necessary determinant of collective action. It refers to a state of mind, formed over a period of time, which provides a shared explanation for the undesirable state of affairs and pinpoints blame upon specific agents or groups who become the target of hostility. Given the requisite conditions, individuals whose basic desires are thwarted and who consequently experience a profound, chronic sense of dissatisfaction and anger are likely to react to their condition by directing aggressive behavior at what is perceived as responsible for thwarting those desires, or at a substitute.

For Puerto Ricans in the Division Street Area the police represented that "substitute." The state of police-Puerto Rican relations before the riot was a major source of Puerto Rican frustration and accounts for the presence of a generalized belief which, following Smelser's approach, became the necessary ingredient in producing this collective action. For many years Puerto Ricans attempted, without any success, to bring to light the ample evidence of discriminatory beatings and humiliations, as in the case of González-Burgos described in the preceding chapter. The numerous hostile and abrasive encounters between the police and barrio residents, particularly those incidents perceived by the Puerto Rican community as inflammatory and as acts of injustice or insults to the Puerto Rican community, were the triggering events of the 1966 riot.[1] As psychologist Leonard Berkowitz points out in his discussion of civil violence among blacks: "[The police] are the 'head thumpers', the all-too-often hostile enforcers of laws arbitrarily imposed upon [blacks] by an alien world" (1968:48).

The society's bases of legitimacy and authority had been attacked. Law and order had long been viewed by Puerto Ricans as the white man's law and order, but now this characteristic perspective of a colonized people was out in the open. Puerto Rican residents of the Division Street Area shared a pervasive belief that policemen were physically brutal, harsh, and discourteous to them because they were Puerto Ricans; that policemen did not respond to calls, enforce the law, or protect people who lived in this community because they were Puerto Ricans. Their grievances about police brutality and inadequacy of protection yielded the deep sense of hostility and resentment prevalent among other ethnic minority groups in urban America.

Accounts given by Puerto Ricans to correspondents from the larger metropolitan press demonstrate the widespread and volatile reservoir of antipathy felt toward the police during this period:

> "Because the [police] don't understand us. They treat us bad because we don't know English—we cannot speak to them" (*Chicago Daily News*, June 14, 1966:3).

> "This is usually a quiet neighborhood. We've never had anything happen like this before. We Puerto Ricans are easy to get along with, but we are hard to mess with" (*Chicago Sun-Times*, June 13, 1966:2).

> "[Tell the] police, we are not supposed to be beaten up like animals. Til you show us you are going to do something to stop this, this thing can't stop because we are human beings" (*New York Times*, June 14, 1966).

On June 13, 1966, Janet Nolan—then director of a research project sponsored by the University of Notre Dame which aimed to examine and reveal the "coping mechanisms" used by Puerto

Ricans from the Division Street Area in overcoming poverty—conducted a "polling of opinions" as well as interviews with local residents. The following are examples of the views of some Puerto Ricans as revealed by Mrs. Nolan's field notes:

> They do not treat us like human beings. The Americans, because they are white and speak English better, think they are superior to us. It was necessary to act even though I think that it may now be worse for us.

> The presence of the police makes the people furious. If the police had not come, nothing would have happened. We need a peaceful protest. But the police makes this impossible.

> I think that police officers are all more or less the same. They treat us Puerto Ricans as if we were dogs and cats—as if we were animals and not real people. The detectives are very bad too. They have some plain clothes detectives who come and spy on the teenagers and take them to jail when they get out of line, sometimes for no reason at all. I know because this happened to me about a year-and-a-half ago.

> I have one of the best points of view actually about the situation between the Puerto Ricans and the city police. My opinion is that actually this all started not just a few weeks ago, but rather a long time ago, years ago. Actually the Puerto Ricans have not been treated the way they ought to be treated because, for what reason . . . ? For the simple reason that when a policeman sees a group of three or four Puerto Ricans standing on a corner he gets down from his car, pushes them around, and tells them to get away from the corner and that he doesn't like them and all that.

The testimonies of fifty-four witnesses at a public hearing held a month following the Division Street riot (Friday and Saturday, July 15–16, 1966) provide further evidence of the negative appraisals of police behavior by barrio residents. According to the summary report of the hearings entitled "The Puerto Rican Residents of Chicago, a Report on an Open Hearing," of six major problem areas identified by the witnesses, relations between Puerto Rican residents and the police was the most pressing and in most need of corrective action. In fact, one witness expressed the point that since the state of Puerto Rican-police relations was so incredibly poor, "a comprehensive community action program against social injustice" needed to be established in the community.

Yet the police became a main focal point for attack not only because of their attitude and behavior toward Puerto Ricans, but because they symbolized the despised invisible white power structure. Of the institutional contacts with which barrio residents had intimate contact — schools, social welfare and employment agencies, medical facilities, and business owners — the police embodied the most crushing authority.[2] For many Puerto Ricans, the police had come to represent more than enforcement of law; they were viewed as members of an "occupying army" and as an oppressive force acting on behalf of those who ruled their environment. Police officers came to represent the key agents crucial in maintaining the colonized status of Puerto Ricans. They were primarily responsible for enforcing the culturally repressive aspects of the values of white America against the distinctive ethnic orientations of Puerto Ricans and other non-white ethnics. In the final analysis the police did the dirty work for the larger system. Conversely, this means that the police, as the daily visible representative of a white-dominated society, sustained the full brunt of the accumulated frustrations and hostility of el barrio. In retrospect, the Division Street Riot was not merely a reaction among Puerto Ricans to police behavior and attitudes, but also to their total situation in the wider American society.

The riot on the Division Street Area stunned and shocked human relations experts and police officials who had earmarked other areas of the city as possible trouble spots for the summer 1966. The superintendent of police at that time, Orlando W. Wilson, told newspaper correspondents that he had ordered a report on racial tensions of both the Puerto Rican and Mexican American communities on June 7 and the investigation showed no signs of unrest in either community (*Chicago Sun-Times*, June 14, 1966:4). Ed Brooks, Commissioner of the Chicago Commission on Human Relations, said, according to the *Chicago Daily News* (June 13, 1966:1) that "there [was] no indication that something of this type could happen there." He also added: "To say that we were surprised would be a big understatement." A veteran of forty-three years of settlement house work in this area of the city informed a correspondent from the same newspaper of similar perceptions: "I must admit I was surprised and shocked myself. With all my knowledge of the area, I had no idea there were that many people living there. And I would have said there was no danger of any riot" (*Chicago Daily News*, June 18, 1966:3).

Some city officials and other critics of the riots used what social scientists have called the "criminal riff-raff" theory of rioting in explaining the outburst (e.g., Fogelson and Hill, 1968). According to this view, every large urban ghetto contains a disproportionate number of criminals, delinquents, unemployed, school dropouts, and other social misfits who on the slightest pretext are ready to riot, loot, and exploit an explosive social situation for their private gain and for satisfying their aggressive anti-social instincts. After meeting in City Hall with residents from the Division Street Area, Mayor Daley made a statement to the press appealing especially to the neighborhood parents to keep their children off the streets. "Such action should be taken," stressed the Mayor, "in areas where unthinking and irresponsible individuals and gangs are seeking a climate of violence and uncertainty that threatens lives and property" (*Chicago Sun-Times*, June 15, 1966). In a similar way, the Executive Director of a local settlement house said of the riot: "It wasn't planned, it wasn't organized. It was spontaneous. Most of the rebels were young fathers, and there were many small clusters active. But they weren't even in contact with each other" (*Chicago Daily News*, June 18, 1966:3).

Thus, according to city officials and others, the basic source of the trouble was not to be found among long-standing and well-established residents of the Puerto Rican community, an otherwise tranquil and satisfied populace. Such a view contained important advantages for city officials who widely espoused it. This point is explicitly made by Feagin and Hahn (1973:9) in their discussion of the riff-raff explanation of rioting:

> Civic leaders argued that this troublesome faction of the populace was quite small and did not detract from the "exemplary race relations" and harmony of the general community. Thus civic authorities could easily dismiss the sentiments of these groups. Moreover, from this point of view, the outbreak of rioting did not necessitate a radical change in existing city leadership.

The official climate of opinion regarding the Division Street riot is far from an adequate explanation of the outburst. In contrast, the evidence indicates that the rioters did not form an amorphous mass of riff-raff: a collection of criminals acting out private or individual frustations and hostility. Rioting on Division Street was a group activity in the course of which strangers were bound together by common sentiments, activities, and goals, and supported each other in the manner typical of primary groups. Let us not romanticize the barrio violence. I don't claim that everyone involved and everything done had rational motives. However, when city officials, the metropolitan press, and others viewed the violence as an uprising of the criminal element against law and order, these individuals chose to block their sensitivity to the sociological meaning of the riot. They failed to look seriously at the human meaning of the turmoil or understand what messages may have been communicated by the rocks and gunfire. Thus, looting as well as other riot activities were essentially group activities during which participants and onlookers experienced a sense of solidarity, pride, and exhilaration. They were bound together by shared emotions, symbols, and experiences which Puerto Ricans inevitably acquire in white America and which makes them address one another as *"hermano"* (brother).[3] In other words, the Division Street Riot seems to have served the same psychic function for Puerto Ricans as violence did for the colonized of North Africa described by Fanon (1963) and Memmi (1967)—the assertion of dignity and peoplehood.

Viewed from a different point, the Division Street Riot was the action of a people, poor and dispossessed and crushed in large numbers in el barrio, who rose up in wrath against a society committed to democratic ideals. Their outburst was an expression of resentment against racial prejudice, anger at the unreachable affluence around them, and frustration at their sociopolitical powerlessness. Puerto Ricans had gradually developed an urban consciousness—a consciousness of an entrapped ethnic minority. The sense of entrapment stemmed from the inability of the Puerto Ricans to break out of the urban ghetto and become part of the burgeoning middle class. There were the conditions of deprivation in the Puerto Rican community that since the 1966 riot have come to be widely recognized as very real grievances. Frustration and alienation accentuated by feelings of relative deprivation must be regarded as psychological factors that create a readiness for individuals to give vent to what Smelser calls collective behavior.

It was during this time that some Puerto Ricans sensed the possibility of improvement; in fact, they had become quite dissatisfied with their situation and rebelled against it. And "with rebellion," as Albert Camus (1967:247) puts it, "awareness is born," and with awareness, an impatience "which can extend to everything that [people] had previously accepted, and which is almost always retroactive." Puerto Ricans began to realize, perhaps for the first time in their lives, that the signs advertising "American egalitarianism" did not include them. Puerto Ricans found themselves on the outside looking in. Since coming to Chicago they had remained on the metaphoric margin, apart from, not a part of, the important positions of America's institutional life—they represented a population whose participation in the political and economic systems occurred at the lowest reaches of these structures. Thus, a population of Spanish-speaking people that used to see the proverbial glass as half full now saw it as half empty.

What were the rioters protesting? In a word: everything. The world about them, which doomed them to defeat and humiliation, and the weakness in themselves, which accepts humiliation, and so makes defeat inevitable. Something happened to Puerto Ricans in the Division Street Area (or in Spanish Harlem in New York or their equivalents in a dozen cities)—something which stifled the ambition and killed the spirit, and suffused the whole personality with despair and emptiness. Like the immigrants of old, Puerto Rican newcomers came in search of a better life. But their aspirations were quickly trampled on.

Despair and apathy, of course, are basic ingredients of any under-class community, and a good many problems attributed to Puerto Ricans because of their race or ethnicity in fact are due to their class. But there is a special quality to the despair of Puerto Rican barrio residents that distinguishes it from many others. For the Puerto Rican youngster growing up in the Division Street Area, the gates of life clang shut at a terrifyingly early age. The children become aware almost from infancy of the opprobrium Americans attach to color or to language. They become aware of it as they begin to watch television, or go to the movies; beauty, success, and status all wear a white skin and speak perfect English. They learn to feel ashamed of their color and language.

Puerto Ricans began vowing to fight to change their conditions and their way to power. There was a difference in both the tone and the tempo of their protest: the tone was bitter and the tempo frenetic. There had been times when expressions of anger, hatred, and hostility had burst out in the Division Street Area in the form of small acts of aggression against representatives of the dominant group or against other minority group members. But it was the collective support given this expressed hostility, permitting the spread and intensification of it in reckless defiance of police power, that made the outburst an instance of collective behavior that was more than just another race riot.

There is considerable theoretical speculation about the psychological sources of aggression, some of which has been applied to acts of civil disobedience such as riots. Psychologist Leonard Berkowitz (1968) views civil disorder as a special case of the more general category of aggression. Hence he suggests that in trying to explain why individuals would engage in civil violence we should examine the degree to which individuals are thwarted or frustrated in their attempts to reach the social and economic goals which they desire. Along the same lines, Ted Gurr (1968:53) writes:

> Underlying this relative deprivation approach to civil strife is a frustration-aggression mechanism, apparently a fundamental part of our psychobiological makeup. When we feel thwarted in an attempt to get something we want, we are likely to get angry, and when we get angry the most satisfying inherent response is to strike out against the source of frustration. Relative deprivation is, in effect, a perception of thwarting circumstances.

From a sociological perspective, Robert Blauner (1966:9) describes this collective action as "the crystallization of community identity through a nationalistic outburst against the society felt as dominating and oppressive." In a similar way, sociologists Bowen and Masotti state: "It is not necessarily the perception of an unequal distribution of values that moves men to civil violence, but rather the perception that the inequality in question is also unjust"

(1968:22). This view is also shared by Robin Williams, another sociologist and long-time analyst of race and ethnic relations in the United States. Against the background of the black riots of 1964, he said:

> It is difficult to sustain the nonviolent character of nonviolent social movements intended to substantially change the existing subordination and segregation of a minority group, especially if the movement is successful in initial attacks on limited objectives, and then confronts hardening resistance to broader and more crucial aims. When objectives are limited, the tactics can be such as to clearly show a direct connection between means and ends, e.g., the sit-ins to desegregate lunch counters. Selective pressure on the sensitive "pocketbook nerve" of business enterprises by a highly selected and well-disciplined organization often has brought specific, restricted gains. But as hopes rise such gains may be seen as illusory by those who fail to benefit and whose problems of employment and status worsen rather than lessen. Cynical alienation gains increased frustration. Hostility is more freely expressed, and the likelihood grows of expressive aggression. Actual outbreaks assume a run-away character and release a great variety of hostile and opportunistically predatory forces. (1965:23–24)

In the Puerto Rican community a sense of betrayal of expectations brought about a focus on the grievances of the past and present. The visibility of an affluent, comfortable, middle-class life made possible by a powerful mass communications system was in itself enough to induce dual feelings of resentment and emulation. The failure of society to effectively raise the status of those trapped in el barrio contributed to the smoldering resentments. The urge to retaliate, to return the hurts and the injustices, played an integral part of the Division Street Riot. In short, the 1966 riot erupted as a new generation of Puerto Ricans sensed that persuasion was not going to bring an end to subordination and oppression. They saw that the Puerto Rican community was far more powerless than the earlier successes of Los Caballeros might suggest. The Puerto Rican community took to the streets in defiance of both the obdurate white community and the older Puerto Rican leadership who had tried to win the battle for equality without bloodshed. Tired of promises of things to come, bitterly frustrated by ghetto-living, and seething with a hatred born of denial, they sought action.

RISE OF A POLITICIZED ETHNIC CONSCIOUSNESS

The 1966 riot represents a major watershed in the history of Puerto Ricans in Chicago. For one thing, it demonstrated the depth of Puerto Rican discontent, the extent of Puerto Rican anger and hate, and the ease with which Puerto Rican anger and hate could flare into violence. More important, the riot raised the anger to a new pitch. When the police dogs were unleashed on the corner of Damen and Division Street, every Puerto Rican in the city felt their teeth in the marrow of his or her bones. The explosion of anger and hatred that resulted for a moment, at least, broke through the traditionally alleged apathy of the poor and created an almost universal desire to act. The Puerto Rican poor were able to overcome the shame bred by a society which blamed them for their plight; they were able to break the bonds of conformity enforced by their jobs and by every strand of institutional life; they were able to overcome the fears induced by the city's police force.

Of course not all Puerto Ricans took up the banner of militancy. Indeed, many, perhaps even the majority, were frightened at the turn of events. Yet there is little doubt that sympathy for the sentiment underlying the "new militancy" touched all Puerto Ricans in the city. One of the more valuable group assets to emerge from the 1966 riot was an "awakening" among the masses of the Puerto Rican poor. This awakening led to an increased ethnic consciousness among Puerto Ricans: the partisan behavior and sense of group obligation that more and more Puerto Ricans began to exhibit in trying to overcome their conditions. Advocacy for Puerto Rican ethnic consciousness began to show up in various forms.

In addition to several peace rallies held at Humbolt Park, community leaders organized several major meetings during and after the riot to inform and interpret issues with residents of the community. The Latin American Boys Club, located on 1218 N. Washtenaw Street in the heart of the Division Street Area, became the leading site for these gatherings. At times, Puerto Rican leaders met there with police officials and human relations staff workers to devise ways to prevent future disturbances (*Chicago Daily News*, June 13, 1966). Several marches and demonstrations were also organized. On June 28, over 200 Puerto Rican residents of the Division Street Area marched five miles to City Hall to protest what they had come to interpret as police brutality and the failure of the city administration to recognize "Puerto Rican problems." The Puerto Rican community also rallied to show support for those arrested during the riot. The Coordinating Commission of Puerto Rican Affairs was formed to help bail out those who had been imprisoned. Hundreds of barrio residents jammed into the courtroom where Puerto Ricans arrested during the riot were being tried. A *Chicago Daily News'* story, "Judge's Warning: Respect the Police," indicated that, conversing in Spanish, the spectators provided constant moral encouragement to the defendants (June 13, 1966).

While the 1966 riot worked a readjustment of the social relations between the Puerto Rican community and the larger society, it dramatically affected the leadership, goals, and agenda of the post-riot Puerto Rican community. The Division Street Riot put the "old leadership," or "old guard"—members of Los Caballeros or of other community organizations of the 1950s and early 1960s—on notice that, while more Puerto Ricans might be inclining toward some form of assimilation, they were not in the least interested in idle dreams or obscure mysticism. If the old guard had nothing more substantial to offer, the people would devise ways and strategies to declare their hatred for the colonial situation imposed upon them. The Division Street Riot forced the old leadership to come to grips with the "real" problem or to write themselves off as irrelevant ethnic advocates. By their actions the "Puerto Rican rioters" were calling for a new leadership willing to confront head-on the problems arising from oppression and powerlessness, and who could speak to the needs of the Puerto Rican masses.

The post-riot period did witness a steady decline in the relative social status of some of the earlier Puerto Rican elite. Social standing and the legitimacy to speak on issues pertaining to the Puerto Rican community began to shift to a leadership not directly connected to Los Caballeros or community organizations of the early adjustment period.

The old establishment was also challenged by the increasing effectiveness of an emerging leadership comprised of few members of the old guard who had broken ranks and a large number of young, articulate, and brash new leaders. The leadership of the Puerto Rican community, no longer in the exclusive hands of first-generation Puerto Ricans, began to question the traditional goals of the programs led by the old guard. After 1966 the new leadership of Puerto Ricans increasingly gave voice to an ideology that challenged the assimilationist perspective of Los Caballeros and other early organizations. Like the old guard's approach, the new leaders assumed that the growing white hostility could be dealt with if Puerto Ricans developed and organized their own economic and civic institutions. On the other hand, this philosophy also called for counterattack; the new leadership emphasized protest against injustices. It began to mount broad and all-embracing attacks upon the forces of oppression of the larger American society. The lines between the two ideological camps were not always clearly drawn. At times, the issues were spelled out; at other times, they were only implicit. But regardless of the many variations and complexities, Chicago's emerging Puerto Rican leaders were engaged in a new and different approach directly related to the course of Puerto Rican development in the city.

The Young Lords represent one of the various activist, direct action, organizational efforts among Puerto Ricans in Chicago from the mid-1960s onward. Despite the Young Lords' political activism and a general increase of civic activities among barrio residents, in the main, the people of the Division Street Area were not in a position to establish action-oriented community institutions and organizations that would adequately meet the needs of the growing Puerto Rican community. Most Puerto Rican businesses were undercapitalized and the existing cultural and social service organizations and agencies lacked the financial resources to develop satisfactory facilities and to hire adequate professional staffs to deal with the many problems operative in el barrio. It was the indirect result of the expansion into the Division Street Area of "Community Action Programs" (CAP), established throughout the country during the early 1960s as part of the federal government's War Against Poverty, which contributed to the development of some of these structures as well as toward the growth of a new leadership.

The outburst of racial violence on Division Street during the summer of 1966 produced a political response from city officials in the form of community action programs to address the complex social problems of el barrio. In turn, these programs were used to produce a politicized and activist agenda by some Puerto Ricans. Federally funded Community Action Programs, channeled through the city's political system, then, became the leading mechanism for the institutionalization of barrio-based politics or activist social action. Several of the Community Action Programs established in the Division Street Area during this period were transformed from community service agencies into local political structures; they were used to politicize inactive barrio residents, i.e., welfare mothers, gangs, unemployed, school dropouts, and the like.

While residents of poor neighborhoods had used Community Action Programs as political access points before, what made the political transformation of these programs less difficult to realize was that by the time federal funds were extended into the Division Street Area the leading controversy, which had prevented minority groups from really manipulating the programs to their fullest advantage, had almost ended. In 1964 and 1965, at the start of the anti-poverty programs, there was an overriding concern with how poor people were to be involved in the local authority structures being established as part of the Community Action Programs. In the words of Greenstone and Peterson (1973:xiv): "Insofar as community participation seemed likely to redistribute political resources from an economically dominant entrepreneurial class to economically subordinate workers, the former could be expected to oppose, the latter to support community participation." In general, the community action controversy focused on questions of political authority and citizen participation.

More specifically, Title II of the Economic Opportunity Act of 1964 provided for the establishment of local Community Action Programs intended to stimulate local communities throughout the nation to develop and administer small antipoverty programs of their own. The most significant feature of the act was what is popularly know as the "maximum feasible participation clause." The act defined a community action program as, among other things, one which is developed, coordinated, and administered with the maximum feasible participation of one-third residents of the areas and members of the groups served. The law also provided that the federal government would pay up to 90 percent of the operating costs of the community action programs. The maximum feasible participation clause gave promise that the federal government would fund new and more representative political organizations. The act increasingly insisted both that the representatives themselves be of low-income or minority-group status and that they be selected independently, i.e., by elections or through local community organizations. Overall, it was assumed that by granting the poor increased participation in the decisions of agencies that allocated goods and services in their community, their access to these services would be increased.

But to keep local government support, the Office of Economic Opportunity "made private arrangements with mayors of some fifteen cities to clear all CAP grants in their jurisdiction through city hall" (Levitan, 1969:66). Hence, mayors of these cities wanted to retain control over the direction and allocation of the community action funds coming into their area and to prevent them from being channeled to community groups and organizations which were unfriendly to the mayors.

After the passage of the Economic Opportunity Act, the mayors followed a number of strategies in the attempt to prevent the poor from having an influential voice over the administration of Community Action Programs. In Chicago, where city officials successfully insisted that they themselves appoint and thus obtain a controlling influence over poverty councils, Mayor Daley initially appointed "public officials who almost uniformly were dependent upon the Democratic organization, and business and community leaders bound to city administration by a complex web of formal and informal relationships" (Greenstone and Peterson, 1973:20). He also tried to limit the number of poor persons who would be given positions on the local umbrella agency responsible for the allocation of most community action funds. Another strategy employed by Mayor Daley was to use the Community Action Programs to increase his own influence in poor neighborhoods. For instance, in order to obtain employment in the neighborhood-based city service agencies, like urban progress centers, neighborhood representatives needed letters of recommendation from their precinct captain. In other words, these centers represented another link to Daley's democratic machine.

According to Mogulof (1969:229), "this conflict was to be partially resolved by the Quie Amendment, adopted in 1966, requiring at least one-third of a Community Action Agency's board to be representative of the poor." Although it is safe to suggest that the mere issuance of an administrative guide was no assurance that the policy would be adhered to, in the end, Chicago and other cities did make some concessions and the maximum feasible participation clause was implemented to a certain degree in these cities. Mann (1966:22) indicates that six representatives of the poor were named by Mayor Daley in 1966 to the city's committee on Urban Opportunity, where there was no representation in 1964 and 1965. Thus, by the time Community Action Programs were introduced in the Division Street Area, the bickering over the programs had almost ceased. This allowed Puerto Ricans to concentrate on developing the programs rather than fighting with the mayor over the participation issue.

The most important CAP established by the city public officials and used by some Puerto Ricans to politicize area residents was an urban progress center. The Division Street Urban Progress Center, put into place immediately following the riot on Division Street, represented the first program of this kind to service any of the city's Spanish-speaking populations. It began as an outpost of the Garfield Park Community Center, but shortly thereafter became a service agency of its own. The initial location, 2120 W. Division Street, was near the spot where the civil disturbances had occurred a month earlier. Like other urban progress centers in the city, the neighborhood center was a multi-service program established to coordinate the activities of governmental and, at times, private agencies servicing the Division Street Area. Further, a series of Title II Community Action Program agencies, as well as others funded outside this title, were housed in the Center.

Many other programs from the arsenal of weapons used in the poverty war were also established throughout the Division Street community and housed in the Center. To close the gap between barrio residents and the nonpoor, manpower training—both institutional and on-the-job—was required. Hence, the Job Corps, the Neighborhood Youth Corps (NYC), the Manpower Development and Training ACT (MDTA), JOBS, and Work Incentive Programs (WIN) were either established or scheduled for rapid expansion into this community during and after the summer of 1966. Head Start, Teacher Corps, and Title I of the Aid to Education Act were also launched to assist the children of that generation in preparing for school and in receiving better and more schooling. Further, a Neighborhood Health Center was set into place to subsidize the medical expenses of welfare recipients and the medically indigent.

In short, the Division Street Urban Progress Center was a catch-all for projects to aid the poor — practically any effort aimed at reducing poverty could be found as part of the structural arrangement of the Center. Given this range, it was clear that the Center was not a program, but a strategy for combating poverty. When one examines the literature on the War on Poverty, it becomes very obvious that one of the prime goals was to give the lower classes, and particularly the ethnic minorities, a middle-class mentality rather than middle-class resources. Daniel P. Moynihan makes it clear in his report, *The Negro Family: The Case for National Action* (1965), that, in his view, the deterioration of the black family is at the root of their problems. In the 1960s, thousands of pages were devoted to the "culture of poverty" and how to break the "cycle of poverty." The argument ran: people can make their way out of poverty through changes in attitude, motivation, and willingness to make sacrifices. The policy, aimed more at changing the attitudes of mind than at offering material help, was a psychological assault to give the poor the motivation to work their own way out of poverty. As Charles Valentine (1968) has so ably shown, this was only a subtle way of blaming poverty on the poor.

The approach followed by social service agencies and social workers concentrated far too much on symptoms rather than on causes — and on symptoms seen and treated individually rather than in connection with other symptoms. This concern with symptoms has been a reflection of the preoccupation of the social work profession with case work and the study and treatment of individual maladjustment. The goal of the Division Street Urban Progress Center was to teach "maladjusted individuals" how to adapt themselves to society as it was, rather than to change those aspects of society that made the individuals what they were. In some instances, the services offered at the Center would simply substitute a new set of symptoms for the old.

It's little wonder that a larger number of social scientists as well as local residents of poor communities throughout the country acquired a growing sense of disenchantment with the War on

Poverty programs. An abudance of evidence is found that speaks to the limited impact these programs had on poor people. After reviewing governmental actions in post-1967 in such important areas as poverty, education, and housing, an Urban America and Urban Coalition report entitled, "One Year Later," concluded that "most actions and programs to meet ghetto problems and grievances had been, depending on the area, too limited, underfunded, or nonexistent" (1969:114–118). The Division Street Urban Progress Center represents a sample case of a policy which offered individualistic solutions to members of this aggrieved Spanish-speaking population, as opposed to structural solutions. Although Community Action Programs in general reinforced the status quo by coopting people into pseudo-conflicts rather than engaging their members in effective struggles, it was primarily the establishment of the Division Street Urban Progress Center which provided the impetus for political activism among barrio residents. Two separate dimensions of the Center facilitated this: (1) the employment of community residents as part of its staff and (2) participation in its advisory council by local community residents. More specifically, several staff and advisory council members of the Division Street Urban Progress Center used their position and status to politicize community residents on behalf of their interests.

Staff Activism

The general conviction behind the establishment of the Division Street Urban Progress Center was that it would provide area residents with assistance in resolving individual problems or by referring them to other facilities. For example, Puerto Rican families were encouraged to apply for public assistance and health care, while many others were helped to find jobs. For this, the Center hired several community residents as social workers and community aides. Since the large majority of the newly hired community workers lacked formal training in this field, they were compelled to learn welfare regulations, the working of social institutions, and how to obtain benefits for their new clients while on the job.

Recognizing that the claims behind the Center were not implemented by practical designs to solve poverty, several of the Center's service personnel turned militant as a way to "turn things around" in el barrio. Some staff members were quickly disillusioned with the Center, concluding that its services were spread too thinly to have a discernible impact on poverty. They agreed that by responding to the needs and problems of barrio residents through an anti-poverty policy, city officials in fact were offering these residents an ameliorative and cooptive strategy. These workers decided to organize the poor to protest the policies and practices of local agencies; in many instances, they led them. They were determined not to negotiate with their counterparts in local agencies (the school system, the welfare department) — they demanded responses favorable to their clients. It was felt that to have done anything else would have been to make themselves irrelevant to those who were presumably their constituents. These staff members developed a political consciousness and a truly conflictual strategy which offered, they thought, a stronger possibility for meaningful social change.

The most notable case of militancy and activism among the Center's staff was that of Hector Franco. A second-generation Puerto Rican and resident of the Division Street Area, Hector became a staff member of the Center in 1968, and resigned his position two years later. In an interview, Hector talked about how he became part of this service organization:

> Immediately after the Division Street Riot I interviewed and was hired for a job as community representative. I remember that I took a salary cut from my previous job to venture into something that I knew very little about. I did not know anything about community work; I did not know anything about social problems and what-have-you. They just needed Puerto Ricans to solve the problems of el barrio and that's how I got hired.

It wasn't long before Hector began to recognize the tragic circumstances of residents of el barrio. Working with cases pertaining to families receiving public aid, he discovered how some of the families he visited were often capriciously denied access to benefits, failed to receive their welfare checks, received less than they were entitled to, were arbitrarily terminated, or were abused and demeaned by other welfare workers. He also learned very quickly that the promise that such problems or grievances could be solved through the Center was false. Hector concluded that these grievances could only be solved through organizing, and the grievances could be used as the basis from which to organize these various families. In responding to the question, What was your job all about at the Center?, Hector provided insight into how he transformed his position at the Center into that of an organizer:

> At that time we were talking about the complex problems of the poor — their welfare rights, their right to a job, their right to public assistance if they could not work, their right to health services. We would go into the community and talk about all of these things to the people. However, it was just a matter of weeks after being out in the field that I came to the conclusion that the Center was not capable of correcting any of these problems; that the Center was established to quiet down the noise that we were making that summer. So we began to organize the people. Since the Center would not do what was needed, I and a friend took the initiative.
>
> We got together and organized a group of Puerto Rican and black families from Bell Street. We called the group Allies for a Better Community (A.B.C.), emphasizing the two allies and the need to preserve that area for the two groups. We were still working for the city at this time, however, we went ahead and began to fight St. Mary's [a hospital located in the Division Street Area near Bell Street]. St. Mary's wanted to move people out of the community to build a new building and a huge parking lot. When we learned of the hospital's plans, we sought help from two white community organizations — the Wicker Park Council and the Northwest Community Organization (N.C.O.). Each organization refused to attend to our cause because we were not a club. So we decided that instead of forming a club to join these racist people, we might as well establish our own organization

It was also during the time that he was employed by the Center that Hector learned formal community organizing. He enrolled and studied in the Saul Alinsky's Urban Institute for Community Organization. This experience, according to Hector, was the turning point in his career as a community worker. The skills and techniques learned during this two-year period provided Hector with the groundwork for a career in community work which still continues today. His organization Allies for a Better Community (A.B.C.) has been at the forefront of some of the leading events in the Puerto Rican community. A.B.C. was one of the few organizations to keep direct action as part of the social agenda of the Puerto Rican community.

Advisory Council Activism

One of the major organizations to emerge on the crest of the Puerto Rican riot of 1966 was the Spanish Action Committee of Chicago (SACC). Several Puerto Rican leaders tried to seize the opportunity presented by the rise of unrest in the Division Street Area to build a "formal organization" in the sure conviction that this was the order of the day. The disruptive protests which had characterized the Puerto Rican struggle during the summer of 1966 were quickly superseded by an emphasis on the need for "community organization," and SACC was one expression of that change. Its leaders and organizers, while animated by the spirit of protest, were nevertheless more deeply committed to the goal of building a mass-based permanent organization among barrio residents. Several similar efforts were followed in the 1970s but none gained the city-wide scope of SACC.

The Spanish Action Committee of Chicago was formed in June, 1966, "to enable local residents to identify in an organized manner the physical and social problems of the community, to interpret these needs to city agencies, and work toward implementing some community-based programs" (A Proposal to Develop an Urban Service Training Center, submitted by the Spanish Action Committee of Chicago, not dated). During its early period, only a cadre of volunteers constituted the membership of SACC. Mr. Juan Díaz, a former member of Los Caballeros, was its Executive Director, and there was a board of directors composed of local residents. But because of the temper of the times, this non-salaried hard core managed to bring out ever-increasing numbers of supporters for organizational activities. During this early stage, leaders of SACC concentrated on direct action, and the actions they led in the streets were generally more militant and disruptive than those of Los

Caballeros and of earlier groups. They seized upon every grievance as an opportunity for inciting mass actions, and channeled their energy into extensive pamphleteering and agitation, which helped bring community residents together and raise the pitch of anger to defiance. SACC organized boycotts, picket lines, and demonstrations to attack discrimination in access to a wide range of services. A summary report, prepared by SACC, indicates the more notable involvements of the organization during the period of 1967–1969:

1. *Relocation of Division Street Urban Progress Center to its present location from a store front.*

    SACC received complaints from local residents pertaining to the limitations and service problems of the then storefront Urban Progress Center unit. SACC took action by informing Dr. Dayton Brooks, Director of Chicago Committee on Urban Opportunities, that unless something was done about these problems, direct action would be taken on the part of the community. Dr. Brooks came and personally inspected the facilities and ordered that the present location, 1940 W. Division St., was more suitable for the Center.

2. *Creation of the Humboldt Park Recreation Committee.*

    In collaboration with more than twenty Puerto Rican community organizations and local residents, a series of meetings and pickets were organized against the Chicago Park District. Our demands called for the building of a large size swimming pool and improvement of Humboldt Park facilities and programs. Some improvements were made, however, the park district did not meet our demands of a new and large swimming pool.

3. *Removal of Policemen from 13th District.*

    SACC received various complaints about certain police officers who were using unlawful tactics and discriminatory actions against the Puerto Rican community. SACC's legal committee circulated a petition, gathering over 2,000 signatures. The petition was taken to the Internal Investigation Division of the Chicago Police Department, and after much examination several of these officers were removed from this district.

4. *Board of Education's Program is Defeated by Community Parents.*

After learning of a proposed boundary change and the potentially subsequent transfer of 300 students from Von Humboldt School, SACC arranged that the board's agency in charge of these changes meet with the Puerto Rican community. A public meeting was arranged and held at the school, the parents opposed all proposed changes. New boundaries for Von Humboldt School were never drawn.

SACC gained a wide and approving audience by articulating feelings which most Puerto Ricans shared but feared to voice in public. The success of SACC in mobilizing the barrio poor and receiving support from other emerging community groups and organizations resulted, principally, from its close affiliation with the Division Street Urban Progress Center—several members of SACC were also members of the Center's Advisory Council. This Council, comprised of members from local businesses and community service agencies, had a formal advisory role in program planning within the Division Street Area. From the beginning, members of SACC were represented in the Advisory Council's membership. There were times when one SACC representative was a member of the council; at other times, two SACC members served as part of the council's membership base.

Participation in the Center's Advisory Council provided these members with an excellent opportunity to learn a variety of political skills. They learned about the internal workings of this particular social service agency, the interrelationship between this agency and different levels of government, where to go to get things done, and the problems of funding and program support. Just as important, participation in the Center's Advisory Council kept members of SACC always informed of particular policies, programs, issues, and decisions concerning the Puerto Rican community. Members of SACC and other community representatives, serving on the Advisory Council, operated consistently as a voting block on contested issues and were able to win on key issues against the opposition of other board members. A coalition was also organized by SACC members to support common demands on internal issues within the

Center involving budget cut-backs, program choices, and personnel appointments.

When an issue of great significance to the Puerto Rican community could not be resolved or treated by the Advisory Council, the SACC members would turn to their own organization for a solution. The coalition established by the leaders of SACC and community representatives did become engaged directly in controversies involving other community service agencies.

The essence of the new militancy among Puerto Ricans was the basis for the formation of institutions and structures that could implement organized actions and concerted and coordinated programs to aid in the ascent up the ladder. Those who supported the new structures believed that the ethnicity that already existed among Puerto Ricans only needed to be strengthened to become a factor to be reckoned with.

THE REPRESSION OF PROTEST

While dramatizing both the complex problems confronting Puerto Rican residents of the city and the urgent need for solutions to the problems, the 1966 riot also marked the beginning of a new wave of Puerto Rican protest, one which is still underway today. The Division Street Riot put direct action on the agenda of social change in the Puerto Rican community. It made Puerto Ricans realize that protest could be used as an effective power tool, stretching its influence into the political process. However, as quickly as protest was introduced into the Puerto Rican agenda, city officials moved in to repress it.

The grudging support that had been forthcoming to the Puerto Rican community in the post-riot years in the form of Community Action Programs was now joined by an increasingly repressive local response to activism in the Division Street Area. The emergence of a militant leadership represented a direct threat to the established order, and therefore, had to be suppressed by any means the authorities thought necessary. There were countless instances of intimidation, harrassment, and surveillance directed at the Puerto Rican groups and individuals who were viewed as presenting a fundamental challenge to existing power relationships.

In the years which followed the riots of the mid-1960s law enforcement officials at all levels of government responded to what they perceived to be unacceptable political action. They initiated a stepped-up campaign of repression designed to diminish, in particular, the ongoing prospects for insurgency on the part of the black militants, the New Left, and other political activists. Writing in the early 1970s, Feagin and Hahn (1973:238) pointed out that "in the last decade a major local response to ghetto rioting, as well as to pressures generated by other types of collective violence, has been the law enforcement of repressive response." Professor Robert J. Goldstein notes (1978:429):

> During the 1965–75 period . . . the United States went through a period of political repression, which, at its greatest height in 1967–71, exceeded in intensity any other time in the twentieth century with the possible exceptions of the 1917–20 and 1947–54 periods. The social setting for this intense period of political repression was a background of political turbulence, dissent and violence unmatched in American history since the Civil War . . . Clearly the major catalyst for these developments was the American involvement in the Vietnam War, and the growing dissatisfaction with that involvement. However, the Vietnam War and the protests against it, alone, would probably not have led political authorities to institute political repression on the level that it reached had not the war been accompanied by other factors. Among the most important of these other factors were: the worst series of racial disorders in American history, accompanied by the increasing popularity of black militancy, symbolized by the "Black Power" movement, and the rise of the Black Panthers in the late 1960s; a startling rise in violent crime, which made "law and order" the favorite program of all three presidential candidates in the 1968 election; and the growth of a "counterculture" among American youth, who expressed their disdain for American society by adopting dress, hair, drug, sex and life "styles" that outraged older, conservative and more powerful Americans.

In Chicago political repression has been used extensively. Its official beginning started in May 1886 with the Haymarket bombing. Following this episode, the city's police department initiated a surveillance program in response to an anticipated fear of anarchist scare and radicalism — imaginary bombs, terrorist conspiracies, assassination, and bomb plots. Forty-four years later (in the summer of 1930), political repression in the city came to the attention of the populace as members of the unit moved to destroy individuals affiliated with organizations alleged to be influenced by communists, both nationally and locally. By way of illustration, Frank Donner (1982) details the treatment accorded the C.I.O. labor union by the city's surveillance unit when the former was believed to be infiltrated by Russia:

> During the thirties much of the energy and resources of Chicago's political police were concentrated on the labor movement and in particular the C.I.O. A labor detail with access to Chicago intelligence files played an important role in collaborating the employers in strike-breaking, not only by assaulting picketers and protecting scabs, but in supplying dossiers (usually for a fee) to the right-wing press (the Hearst *Chicago American* and the *Chicago Tribune*) discrediting striking unions and their leaders. Well into the strife-torn forties, the labor detail served as a defense corps for the A.F.L. unions embraced in "sweetheart" contracts with employers to repel C.I.O. organizing efforts as well as internal rank and file revolts against repressive A.F.L. union leadership. (pp. 5–6)

The emergence of Chicago as a center for organized crime following World War II coupled with the racial unrest of the early fifties led to the expansion and reorganization of Chicago's surveillance unit — eager veterans of the war and naval intelligence personnel contributed to this expansion and reorganization by joining the city's surveillance unit. During this period, a special unit was established to deal with organized crime, and a Human Relations and Security Unit was set up to gather information from newspapers, real estate brokers, and district commanders concerning the status of racial harmony and requirements for the prevention of vandalism. It also kept the department informed concerning the subversive and related activities of various groups, such as Communist, anti-Communist, Fascist, and anti-Fascist organizations.

But it was the social unrest of the 1960s which intensified political repression in Chicago. During this period the intelligence unit of the Chicago Police Department heightened its harrassment and intimidation of public demonstrations and protest activities and expanded its surveillance coverage of all shades of dissidents. The old Human Relations and Security Squad was absorbed into a newly formed Intelligence Division which in turn became part of the Bureau of Inspectional Services. The Subversive Section of the Intelligence Division was divided into "covert" and "overt" units and linked to a support section, "Files and Analysis." This section functioned through two teams, one assigned, among other duties, to subversive files and the other to analysis. In addition, the anti-radical intelligence operation was supplemented by a Special Equipment Unit devoted to communications as well as film processing. The routine overt practice was the physical monitoring of both indoor and outdoor meetings, identification of individuals through observation, taking down license plate numbers, tailing arriving and departing participants in meetings, rallies, or demonstrations, and, most important, tape recording and photography. With the increasing emergence of civic and neighborhood groups, the police surveillance network was extended to cover this new front. Referring to Chicago as "the surveillance capital of the United States," Frank Donner summarizes surveillance activities in the following way:

> Until its dissolution in September 1975 the political surveillance unit of the Chicago Police Department was the outstanding operation of its kind in the United States—whether measured in terms of size, number and range of targets or operational scope and diversity . . . The power of the unit and its freedom from accountability have been nourished by a super-patriotic "American" tradition, a socially conservative constituency rooted in compact ethnic neighborhoods, a repressive, boss-ridden political structure, a right-wing press, racism both within the police department and in the city as a whole and a corrupt police department. Beginning in the sixties, indiscriminate targeting and autonomy were further assured by the power needs of the Daley administration and its political machine which used the department's countersubversive resources as a weapon against critics. (1982:1)

It was in this atmosphere that the political repression of the Puerto Rican community in Chicago was initiated by local authorities. Typical of the wide ranging treatment accorded black and other activist groups in the late sixties and early seventies by the CIA, the FBI, the Defense Department, and local police departments throughout the country, the "policing of politics" expanded considerably into the Division Street Area following the aftermath of the 1966 riot as police intelligence units moved to gather information on activists and potential activists. Personal files were maintained on a large number of barrio residents. Equally revealing is the range of individuals who were surveilled either as primary targets or because of their alleged political activism. Any individual who attended a meeting in the community was listed as an activist or sympathizer. Even individuals who were considered only remotely subversive or whose personal and political activities were irrelevant to any legitimate governmental interests became targets of surveillance. A vivid illustration of the reasons for surveilling persons involved in community activities in the Puerto Rican barrio comes from the files of Obed Lopez. Although Obed Lopez is Mexican, he was initially classified as a Puerto Rican; and his personal life was the subject of a ten-day intensive surveillance by two intelligence agents. Their report for a sample day, records his going and comings, car and license number, when he parked his car and where, etc.:

> SUBJECT (Obed Lopez) drives a dark green Volkswagen, Il./Lic. # HK 5026 which he usually parks on the 1200–1300 blocks of California, the 2800 block of Division, or the 1200 block of Washtenaw while in the Division Street area.

> SUBJECT (Obed Lopez) is very difficult to keep under surveillance as he is very evasive. He will drive in circles, stop on occasion for periods ranging from 3–4 minutes, leave his auto and walk up a block on one side, and return on the other side to a point near his auto where he watches for anyone who might be following him, and just about any other tactic that might throw off a surveillance, moving or stationary. (Police Report, August 23, 1966)

The politics of Obed Lopez were analyzed by secret service agents in this way:

> Obed Lopez is presently heading up a Communist front organization known as the Latin American Defense Committee . . . (Police Report, September 19, 1966) SUBJECT (Latin

American Defense Organization), under the direction of Obed Lopez, is currently conducting a boycott of the National Food Stores at 2650 & 2311 W. Division Street, and has picketed both stores on three occasions in groups of three. The purpose of the boycott and picketing is to protest what they consider discriminatory hiring and personnel practices by the National TEA Co. in relation to people of Latin American extraction. In general, SUBJECT is using the National TEA Company as a scapegoat for a "Pilot Program" they believe will give them considerable influence in the community, especially among the small businessmen who they feel will support them as they are supposedly encouraging Latins to buy from Latin owned businessmen or businesses. (Police Report, September 28, 1966)

Subversive files were also maintained on Puerto Rican community organizations and groups composed of individuals exercising their rights of association and political protest. Groups like the Young Lords, Aspira, Inc. of Illinois, Organization for Latin Americans in Chicago, Latin American Defense Organization, Northwest Spanish Community Committee, Latin Boy's Club, and others were investigated. The files of the Organization for Latin Americans (OLA) are illustrative. The organization was involved in working with issues pertaining to housing, employment, and civil rights. Although its methods were entirely peaceful, it was accused in the intelligence reports of being communist and aiming to become the official voice of Spanish-speaking people in Chicago (Police Report, July 11, 1966).

Perhaps the most celebrated surveilled group was SACC.[4] SACC was subjected to a wide range of official control efforts by a unit of the Chicago Police Department's Intelligence Division also referred to as the Subversive Unit, the Security Section, or the Red Squad. The Subversive Unit used police officers as infiltrators to spy on the activities of SACC and at times to try to provoke organization members into foolish actions. There was an Intelligence Unit's police officer by the name of Thomas Braham who posed as a Spanish-speaking policeman; James Zorno was another surveillance agent who passed as a public relations person with expertise in the preparation of press releases. There were also four Spanish-speaking police officers: Victor Vega, Andrew Rodríguez, Alfredo Perales, and Edwin Olivieri. SACC was deemed worthy of infiltration primarily because, in the views of the Chicago Police Department's Intelligence Unit, its ranks were filled with communists and leftists. The role of the police agents was to encourage paranoia and internal dissension and to damage the public image of SACC.

The agents' entry into SACC was facilitated by the structure of the organization; it lacked resources and people willing to undertake the routine and time-consuming tasks required of activists. The agents brought badly needed skills and resources. It was assumed by SACC members that the agents' ties to institutions they claimed to represent would give the organization added strength of support. The entry of these informants into SACC was further facilitated by the fact that the organization was not comprised of a highly centralized, formally organized, tightly knit group of experienced activists, but was instead decentralized, with fluid task assignments and an emphasis on participation. Members were generally not carefully screened, and requirements for membership were minimal. This was all the more true in cases of social action—demonstrations, meetings, and marches—in which anyone could participate. The emergent non-institutionalized, social movement character of the struggle, as advanced by SACC, meant constantly changing plans, shifting alliances, and spontaneous actions. SACC's ideology stressed peaceful nonviolent means, reform, democracy, openness, an anti-bureaucratic orientation, optimistic faith in people, tolerance, community, and naiveté about government surveillance. SACC had nothing to hide; the group saw little reason to be suspicious.

Several "investigator's reports,' prepared for the Intelligence Division of the Chicago Police Department by undercover police officers and filed during the summer of 1966, reveal the direct and active part played by these officers in the ultimate dissolution of SACC. In one of the earliest reports the investigating officer indicates very explicitly that the objective of his undertaking "was to destroy the SUBJECT [Spanish Action Committee of Chicago], its leaders and community influence" (June, 1966). In another report dated August 19, 1966, the reporting officer noted: "I launched an all out anti-Ted Vélez, anti-Juan Díaz campaign amongst the original committee members of subject organization, with emphasis on the subversive intonations."

If the repressive actions directed at SACC were to be successful, the involvement of some of the organization's members were required in the plot. The undercover Red Squad officers used intimidation tactics to gain the support of a few organization members. The police officers convinced these members that the organization's involvement in communist-related activities would ultimately cause them a great deal of harm and pain. In particular, Ted and Myrta Ramírez were two SACC members identified by the infiltrators as prospective collaborators since, according to the police officers, both members were very dissatisfied with the way the organization was being run. One investigator's report, which details the content of a meeting between one police officer and Mr. and Mrs. Ramírez, demonstrates the scare of intimidating tactics used by the officers and, at the same time, the resistance expressed by these two SACC members to the idea of aiding the police with the expulsion from the organization of its alleged communists and leftists:

> [Police officer] then advised [Mrs. Ramírez] of the fact that communists are undisputed masters of deceit, and will seize on any popular or controversial issue for their own cause. [Mr. and Mrs. Ramírez] both seemed in agreement with this, but were slightly reluctant when the [police officer] said he would like their help in removing any communist influence from SACC. They feel that SACC has a lot of potential, and would never allow communists to take over, but would inform the [police officer] of the presence of any new or suspicious persons who might try to get into SACC. (August 19, 1966)

In an interview, Mr. Richard Gutman, the Attorney representing SACC, stated very clearly that those who defected from the organization were truly victims of the tactics used by Red Squad. He pointed out, for instance, that the undercover police officer who passed as a Spanish-speaking policeman convinced these members that SACC was a communist organization and that its leaders had been convicted of possession of narcotics. In the words of Mr. Gutman: "Ted and Myrta were victims too. They were used. The various police reports make it clear that Ted and Myrta did not necessarily want to quit SACC; this wasn't their idea. They were totally opposed to putting out the stuff about communism."

In any event, after several meetings, the police officers manipulated Mr. and Mrs. Ramírez into resigning from SACC and forming a competing organization. Shortly after the resignation of these persons, the American Spanish Speaking Peoples Association (ASSPA) was born. In another investigator's report, the role played by the surveillance officers in the formation of ASSPA is clearly stated:

> The SUBJECT was secretly organized by members of the Intelligence Division and composed of former members of the Spanish Action Committee of Chicago. Although the members know nothing of the part played by the Intelligence Division, they have been directed to a point where they will publicly denounce SACC and its leader, Juan Díaz and his followers and associates for acts not to the best interest of the Spanish-speaking community, and for the Communist influence they believe exists there. (August 31, 1966)

The undercover officers then proceeded, successfully, to convince members of the newly created organization to prepare a press release announcing the establishment of ASSPA. After examining the text of the original press release prepared by members of ASSPA, the police officer assigned to this investigation concluded that it was insufficient for the desired goals of the police department: "They did prepare a press release that said very little as to what their reasons were for resigning from SUBJECT organization, at which time I felt it necessary to ask for the assistance of a 'friend of the family' by the name of 'Dr. Baron,' an expert in the preparation of Press-releases, . . . [but] who is in actuality Officer James Zarnow" (Investigator's Report, August 19, 1966). The entire text of this release is printed below to provide insights into the course of direction former members of SACC were driven to follow:

> We, the members of ASSPA are for the most part, former members of the Spanish Action Committee of Chicago, who have arrived at the realization that SACC does not represent the Puerto Rican community or any of the Spanish Speaking as a whole. It has done nothing more than keep the Spanish community apart from the society it should be becoming a part of.
>
> SACC is being led by a man who is directed by individuals in New York who know nothing about Chicago, and only want to maintain discontent and anger among the Puerto Ricans who live in Chicago. It is influenced by some people who have Com-

munist philosophies and who have been before the hearings of the House Committee on Un-American Activities and Fair Play for Cuban Investigations. When organized, our group was dedicated to helping the Latin American peoples in Chicago; we were staff members, but every time we suggested methods to help make citizens of the people of our community, we found ourselves powerless. This was possible because the Director of SACC, Juan Díaz assumed dictatorial power over the organization. We have never been told where our financial aid came from; we were given no information regarding the amount of money the organization had; Díaz refused to keep records and made all decisions. To us, it appears that the only interests served by SACC were to the benefit of Juan Díaz and others who do not serve the interest of our country. We have since learned that this man Díaz is a convicted narcotic offender and of all things, he is presently the director of the Latin American Boys Club; and to our knowledge has no qualification as such director.

True, we are Puerto Ricans, Mexicans, Cubans and South Americans, but here, we are all Americans first. We should not be trying to set ourselves apart, but becoming part of the society we live in. Your descendants were strangers to the ways of their new land and many of them were not at first accepted, but they and their children eventually overcame this. They were assimilated into the society around them, as we and our children are and will be. SACC does not want this to happen; they want the Latin to feel apart, keep them angry, keep reminding that they are apart and make them believe they are not treated the same as other citizens. This is not true. Despite those people who preach hate, tell lies to incite us, we are progressing and are accepted more and more each day. We are learning these things and those of us who have learned are helping those who need help. We are not a minority group, we are a majority group, we are Americans.

The resignation of SACC members and the subsequent establishment of ASSPA was carefully and strategically staged by the undercover agents. The agents persuaded Bob Weidrich of the *Chicago Tribune* to use the press release and responses gathered from an interview with Mr. and Mrs. Ramírez "to expose SACC, Díaz and etc." (Investigator's Report, August 31, 1966). (It turned out that the undercover agents supplied the *Tribune* correspondent with the questions to ask during this interview. Also, one of the agents was present during the interview to provide the "correct answers" to the questions in cases when the two respondents' replies were not in line with the expected response.) In a two-part series, Weidrich reported almost exclusively on allegations regarding the involvement of communist individuals in SACC. He made the claim that "one reputed Communist" provided SACC with both financial and advisory support. This particular individual was said to have been a former "Fair Play for Cuba" committee official. Further, the reports charged that SACC was being taken over by outsiders: Puerto Ricans from New York who were also alleged as communist-affiliated and a Californian alleged to have been a "former head of the Young Communist League of California" (*Chicago Tribune*, September 3–4, 1966).

The police officers also arranged for Alfredo Torres de Jesús, a writer for *El Puertorriqueño,* to use the *Chicago Tribune* information for a local publication. A week later, *El Puertorriqueño*'s front-page, lead story was almost a complete translation of Weidrich's articles. However, Mr. Torres de Jesús sensationalized the story by calling it: "SACC ES NIDO DE COMUNISTAS" — SACC is a nest of Communists — (*El Puertorriqueño*, Week of September 9–15, 1966), contributing more severely to the damage and discredit of the organization.

The press played an indispensable role in the planned disruption of SACC. The combined articles attracted a great deal of attention. The publicized charges that SACC was communist-affiliated not only served to drive out some members (except for two, all other officers of the organization resigned their post), but also to scare off potential recruits and supporters. The charges made against SACC raised the cost and danger of being active in the organization, and supporters feared their careers would be ruined if they continued their affiliation. The testimonies of several of these supporters at a trial filed by SACC against the city of Chicago gives weight to this point:

> Those articles had a very great negative effect on SACC's reputation in the Puerto Rican community. Because of those articles, SACC gained a reputation for being controlled or in-

fluenced by communists. This reputation greatly decreased the Puerto Rican community's willingness to work with SACC. I quit SACC when I read in the newspaper that the organization was taken over by communists. . . .

There was a lot of conversation about [the newspaper] articles. People were very negative. They thought the information was real, and then nobody wanted to be associated with the Communist Party. I did not want to be associated with the organization, I stopped going to meetings. I did not want to be known as a communist.

There is little doubt that political repression, as manifested in surveillance and disruption activities, significantly disrupted and discredited SACC and thereby made the organization less attractive to members and sympathizers. A present-day member of SAAC informed me in an interview: "We were set back an entire generation. The Chicago Police Department hampered our growth. We had a very good reputation in the community before the smears in the *Tribune* and *El Puertorriqueño*." Similarly, Richard Gutman said: "The evidence clearly shows that SACC was the major group in the Puerto Rican community during the summer of 1966. But after the press publication, it never recovered its former position. It continued to function, it remained active, but it never regained its early form."

In addition, increased police repression significantly deterred some people from speaking out, demonstrating, or joining protest groups, and thereby weakened the capacity for political activism in the Division Street Area. Government and police officials demonstrated that open defiance by Puerto Ricans was extremely dangerous and often suicidal. Despite this, there is much evidence to suggest that political repression did not significantly deter protest activities in el barrio. Protests increased even as political repression increased, at least until 1975. Regardless of the various official repressive actions taken against members of barrio-based political activist organizations and groups, the organizer and mass-agitator types of leaders continued to represent a very important part of Chicago's Puerto Rican community.

5

Institutionalization of the Ethnic Minority Classification

The working class continued to represent the demographic and financial foundation of the Puerto Rican population in the 1970s. It also remained at the very bottom of the occupational ladder of the city's economy. During this time the Puerto Rican ethnic minority classification became institutionalized—it became a well-established and fundamental part of American society. It was also during this period that the Puerto Rican community witnessed the initial development of a distinctive class structure. The social and economic composition of barrio residents was becoming more diversified than it had been in the 1960s—a Puerto Rican middle class was beginning to take form. Leadership and ideological competition among those aspiring for ethnic primacy in el barrio had slowly but definitely taken shape. The rise of middle-class "intermediaries" resulted in their consolidation with the masses to overcome the pervasive inequalities of el barrio. Puerto Rican ethnic advocacy also showed up in a diversified manner as the new ethnic leadership began seeking different explanations and solutions to the urban situation. We will examine the reasons for the distributive change experienced by the Puerto Rican community in the 1970s, the ideological foundation of the emerging ethnic leaders, and the struggles involved in realizing some of these changes.

THE GROWTH OF AN EDUCATED ELITE

One of the leading reasons for the changes in the economic composition and leadership status among Puerto Ricans in the 1970s

180

was an increase in the attainment levels of education among barrio residents. More Puerto Ricans who were born or raised in Chicago went on to post–high school training, which identified them as members of the modern strata of white-collar workers and a professional leadership core. In the 1950s and 1960s few Puerto Ricans attended college — but then, few Puerto Ricans had access to higher education.

The increasing number of Puerto Rican students attending two- and four-year colleges and universities during the 1970s is revealed in the annual survey reports "On Campus Enrollment of Students by Race or National Origin in Illinois by Institution" compiled by the State of Illinois' Board of Education.[1] Although these official figures apply to all Spanish-surnamed students in the state, one can suspect that a large proportion of the students counted were Puerto Ricans. Further, while the proportions are very small relative to entire school populations, they are, nevertheless, substantial when compared to earlier periods (see Tables 14 and 15).

Of special interest here is the number of enrolled Spanish-speaking students in campuses located in the city of Chicago. One can assume that geographical proximity to home was one of the major reasons why the number of enrolled Spanish-speaking students was higher for local schools than for those campuses located outside the city. During the fall of 1973, the University of Illinois-Chicago Circle and Northeastern Illinois University were the four-year public institutions most attended by Spanish-surnamed students, with an enrollment of 725 and 345, respectively. The private universities with the largest number of enrolled Spanish-speaking students for that same year were Loyola and DePaul. Loyola reported 303 Spanish-surnamed students while DePaul reported another 221. (See Table 16 for the number of Spanish-speaking students enrolled in two-year colleges during this period.)

It would be incredibly naive to simply construe this increased enrollment as evidence of the egalitarian foundation of American society. On the contrary, the experiences of Puerto Rican college/ university students were filled with much friction. Puerto Rican youth who managed to "crack" through the university door learned very quickly that, like other major structures of the American society, the university needed to be challenged and forced to provide them with their desired wants and needs. Puerto Rican students believed

TABLE 14

Enrollment of Spanish-Surnamed Students in Illinois' Major Public Senior Universities

INSTITUTION	NO. SPANISH SURNAMES, ACADEMIC YEAR		
	1973	1975	1977
Chicago State Univ.	108 (1.8)*	145 (2.3)	140 (2.2)
Eastern Illinois Univ.	11 (.13)	28 (.31)	29 (.31)
Governors State Univ.	13 (.13)	29 (.63)	76 (2.1)
Illinois State Univ.	55 (.30)	56 (.29)	109 (.57)
Northeastern Il. Univ.	345 (4.59)	550 (5.9)	881 (9.1)
Northern Il. Univ.	164 (.82)	202 (.95)	203 (.95)
Sangamon State Univ.	8 (.28)	16 (.45)	7 (.21)
Southern Il. Univ.-Carbondale	36 (.18)	107 (.52)	82 (.38)
Southern Il. Univ.-Edwardsville	19 (.16)	33 (.27)	42 (.37)
University of Il.-Chicago Circle	725 (3.7)	1,116 (5.3)	1,402 (6.7)
University of Il. Medical Center	31 (.76)	43 (.95)	81 (1.7)
University of Il.-Urbana/Champaign	171 (.49)	248 (.70)	344 (1.01)
Western Il. Univ.	69 (.48)	87 (.61)	117 (.92)
TOTAL	1,755	2,660	3,513

Source: Illinois Board of Education, Data Book on Illinois Higher Education.

* =Percentage of Total School Enrollment.

TABLE 15

Enrollment of Spanish-Surnamed Students in Private Senior Universities

INSTITUTION	NO. SPANISH SURNAMES, ACADEMIC YEAR		
	1973	1975	1977
DePaul	221 (2.3)*	340 (3.1)	382 (3.4)
Illinois Inst. of Technology	NR	37 (.56)	101 (1.4)
Loyola	303 (2.2)	320 (2.4)	359 (3.1)
National Coll. of Ed.-Urbana	NR	129 (5.3)	72 (2.8)
Roosevelt	143 (2.1)	NR	193 (3.1)
TOTAL	667	826	1,107

Source: Illinois Board of Education, Data Book on Illinois Higher Education.

* =Percentage of Total School Enrollment.

the university represented that mechanism which would provide them with the particular skills needed to alter the historical pattern of oppression operative in el barrio. If the function of the university has always been to prepare all students for a more meaningful role in society at large, then Puerto Rican students insisted that it prepare them in a much more effective way for the kind of social transformation needed in the Spanish-speaking community. Universities and colleges were assigned the task of preserving the Puerto Rican perspective, while making a commitment to aid in the uplifting of barrio residents. It was imperative, the students concluded, that their university training be connected in some way with what was happening beyond the campus.

What Puerto Rican students understood far better than their parents is that the choice of a career involved more than a choice of how to earn a livelihood. They understood, viscerally if not intellectually, that the question, "What shall I do?" really meant "What shall I do with myself?," or rather, "What shall I make of myself?" And that also meant asking "Who am I? What do I want to be? What values do I want to serve? To whom, and to what, do I want to be responsible?" As Drucker (1969) rightly observes, "These are existential questions, for all that they are couched in secular form and appear as choices between a job in government, in business, or in college teaching." That the students' answers were not always

TABLE 16

Enrollment of Spanish-Surnamed Students in Two-Year Colleges

INSTITUTION	NO. SPANISH SURNAMES, ACADEMIC YEAR		
	1973	1975	1977
Central YMCA	165 (3.7)*	197 (4.9)	NR
Kennedy-King	37 (.44)	27 (.27)	41 (.36)
Loop	743 (6.3)	770 (4.8)	527 (6.4)
Malcolm X	73 (.44)	104 (2.6)	305 (4.6)
Mayfair	345 (8.8)	399 (5.9)	NR
Olive-Harvey	125 (2.4)	87 (1.5)	55 (.86)
Southwest	246 (4.9)	265 (3.2)	NR
Wright	438 (5.4)	430 (5.2)	464 (4.2)
TOTAL	2,172	2,279	1,392

Source: Illinois Board of Education, Data Book on Illinois Higher Education.

* = Percentage of Total School Enrollment.

relevant is less important than the fact that they were forcing society to confront the most fundamental questions of value and purpose. In the main, Puerto Rican students were making a direct connection between their demands for educational reform and the general demands of the Puerto Rican barrio for equality.

This was to come about as a result of the added emphasis given to the Puerto Rican ethnic presence on the campus. The realities of institutional ideology and life which the Puerto Rican students encountered upon entering the world of the university were inadequate to meet their felt needs. Puerto Rican students agreed about what was missing in the university experience and concluded that within the existing framework of the university they could not readily apply the tools of a scholastic discipline to the problems, the wisdom, or the experience of Puerto Rican people. Instead, the students believed that a "Puerto Rican curriculum" would give them the best opportunity to find the desired direction. The Puerto Rican curriculum was modeled after other ethnic studies programs of the period and called for the offering of instructional and service programs having to do with the history, the culture, the language, the art, and the psychological, social, and economic realities of this Spanish-speaking population.

As with other early instances of ethnic studies programs, the idea of a Puerto Rican curriculum was perceived by university administrators as a "radical, if not political, innovation" — hence their little regard for the students' proposal. As Puerto Rican university students began to reach a "critical mass," they rallied around their ethnicity and cultural tradition to form student organizations which would force the university to take cognizance of the fact that they "were there," and that they were there not to be lost in the predominant culture. All of the organized efforts were aimed at curriculum reform as well as establishing student admission and retention programs. Subsequently students insisted that members of their own ethnic group be hired to teach courses and administer their proposed programs.

One of the first and most notable attempts made by Puerto Rican students to influence the creation of a Puerto Rican curriculum occurred at Northeastern Illinois University — a teachers college until 1966 when the school's curriculum and scope were expanded to form a university program. In the fall of 1971, when the enrollment of Spanish-surnamed students totalled 79 (Torres, 1983:2), a small group of Puerto Rican students (less than 15) formed the Union for Puerto Rican Students. The organization was established to influence change commensurate with the desired wants and needs of Puerto Rican students on this campus. In his insightful account of the formation and implementation of a particular program which members of the Union helped to develop, Professor Max Torres provides a thorough description of the members of this newly formed organization: "The students who were active on behalf of the small Latino population on campus were primarily freshmen and sophomores. But their familiarity with their experiences of the harsh environment they had endured in their community may have been the sustaining force that guided them to recognize, perhaps instinctively, the prevalent needs Hispanic American students face in higher education and to articulate recommendations to address such needs" (1983:38).

Puerto Rican students at Northeastern Illinois University were convinced that a Puerto Rican curriculum was significantly related to their progress at the university as well as to their professional pursuits. This link is articulated by Miguel Del Valle, one of the founding members of the Union for Puerto Rican Students, in an interview with Professor Torres (1983:332–33, 343):

> It was at this time I found out I didn't have to be alone at the school. There were a handful of students who had the same concerns as myself. So I became involved in the Union. And it was at that time we saw the need for counseling geared towards us. We were standing alone with little direction. We were struggling with our own feelings of inadequacy, and at that time we needed to band together in order to deal with the monstrous institution. We felt we needed some one person at the school who was acquainted with our community, who understood the culture, someone who we could go to with our problems. . . . We not only wanted someone to listen to our problems, we wanted someone who would come in as an authority figure, someone we knew would be respected by the administration, that would be considered a colleague by the professors. . . . We [also] wanted to look at our roots, find things out about where we came from. We didn't know much

about Puerto Rico; sure, we retained the language and grew up in a Puerto Rican community, but still we wanted to learn more. We wanted to feel more comfortable in school, to develop the kind of pride we needed to survive. We felt if we were going to make it through this experience, we're going to have to feel strength and where do we derive that strength from? There are many different sources and one definite source was our own culture, that gave us a feeling of self-worth, made us feel we counted, that we were just as important as anyone.

The Union for Puerto Rican Students set out to change the course the university had taken in responding to the presence of Puerto Ricans and other Spanish-surnamed students. Following a pattern adapted by other schools in the Midwest, and perhaps in other parts of the country, Northeastern Illinois University's central administrators argued that the needs of Spanish-speaking students were being serviced by Project Success—a "minority"-oriented university program established initially for and by blacks. Conversely, members of the Union argued that the needs of Puerto Ricans and other Spanish-speaking students were culturally, ethnically, and socially distinct from other student populations. Puerto Rican students were very critical of Project Success since "the program's Latino recruitment was so low that the Latinos it had recruited appeared to [have been] more an act of sheer expediency as to give the impression that it was recruiting Latinos, rather than a needed commitment to the city's Latino community" (Torres 1983:46). Puerto Rican students also recognized that it was unfair to demand that Project Success provide them with necessary services at a time when the black community itself was just beginning to receive a few concessions from the power structure. After many long years of suffering, as indicated by Professor Torres (1983:49–50): "it was not a case of Project Success . . . walking away from the child [metaphorically, a Spanish-surnamed child] it had brought into the world of the university, . . . a more fitting analogy would be that the mother simply miscarried the child, for she had been abandoned for over two centuries, she had been neglected, beaten, unclothed, and unnourished—she could hardly bear her own child, let alone now care for the Latino child, too."

Rather than be pitted against another "oppressed population," for a period of almost a year Puerto Rican students organized and became involved in efforts to force the university's central administrators to acknowledge and respond to their special needs and demands. There were negotiations, demonstrations, and sit-ins. Finally, in the winter of 1972 the organization submitted to the President of Northeastern Illinois University a proposal calling for the establishment of a program by the name of "Proyecto Pa'Lante." Three leading demands were highlighted in the proposal

A—Staff: Proyecto Pa'Lante will be under the direction of the Puerto Rican Counselor—who will receive the support from the University Administration, Admissions and Financial Aid Offices. He will have the final decision in admitting students in the program. As necessary, the University will hire additional staff to assist the Puerto Rican Counselor in the operation of Proyecto Pa'Lante.

B—Financial Aid: All financial aid at the University will be made available to these students.

C—Retention: Northeastern Illinois University—through Proyecto Pa'Lante—promises these students a unique opportunity to academic progress, thereby working with them in the program to assist them to develop their academic potentials. Each student will be given the first two years to work toward academic achievement and prove his academic abilities. (quoted in Torres 1983:252–3)

The creation of Proyecto Pa'Lante soon followed. In late winter of 1972 this program became an official student service and academic unit of Northeastern Illinois University.

At the University of Illinois—Chicago Circle Campus, the merging efforts of Puerto Rican and Mexican students led to the creation of the Department of Latin American Studies as well as a student recruitment and studies program under the name of Latin American Recruitment Education System (LARES) in 1975. The establishment of these two programs had been preceded by student activism, demonstrations, and protest. Similar efforts were made at the Urbana-Champaign campus of the University of Illinois. The Latin American Student Organization (LASO) formed at Loyola University of Chicago and the Organization of Latin American

Students (OLAS) of Northern Illinois University are examples of other student groups which were formed to make the university environment and curriculum reflect the cultural and ethnic backgrounds as well as social needs of Puerto Ricans and other Spanish-surnamed students.

The quest for ethnic study programs coupled with a demand for increased enrollment and retention of Puerto Rican students were facilitated by two interrelated factors. First, the activism of Puerto Rican students coincided with a stiffened affirmative action policy by the federal government. In 1971, the Department of Health, Education, and Welfare (HEW) and the Department of Labor (DOL) intensified their enforcement of the Civil Rights Acts' employment provisions, which the academic world had appeared to assume were intended primarily for business, industry, and the trade unions (Glazer, 1975). The vigor and determination of the federal government were personified by J. Stanley Pottinger, who then headed HEW's Office for Civil Rights and was strongly supported by Elliot Richardson, then Secretary at HEW. At a press conference in late 1971 Pottinger, in referring to enforcement of nondiscriminatory hiring practices in academe declared: "we have a lot of power, and we are prepared to use it" (quoted in Glazer, 1975:107).

Persistent federal muscle forced an often painful reassessment of both stated and actual academic hiring policies. Pleas for more time and piecemeal steps which in the past had seemed to satisfy federal demands were declared unacceptable. Threatened by loss of federal funds, universities began to establish affirmative action committees, appoint affirmative action officers, and widely publicize their status as "affirmative action employers." As equality of opportunity gave way to equality of result as the immediate target, numbers became the currency of equalitarianism and quotas began to dominate the national dialogue. Thus did bureaucratic instrumentation set affirmative action somewhat at odds with its ideological roots.

The other major factor which contributed to the activism of Puerto Rican students on various campuses in Illinois was that in many cases students were able to make common cause with HEW or DOL enforcement agents. Puerto Rican students would threaten to file complaints, launch protests, and publicize noncompliance or evasion of affirmative action and quotas when the university refused to give in to their demands. These policies served as weapons used by the students to justify their grievances and activities.

Overall, the Union for Puerto Rican Students and similar organizations were very important for they organized a large pool of manpower for social movement participation in el barrio. These organizations served as reinforcing and channeling mechanisms for young Puerto Ricans whose unease with American society had not formed into specific career choices and political ideologies. When the students at Northeastern and several other campuses committed themselves to action in the early 1970s, they became the triggers that released a growing surge of young and local Spanish-speaking energy. They gave impetus, direction, and a base of identification to the new and growing force of this second-generation Spanish-speaking population.

Higher education for second-generation Puerto Ricans was of utmost significance for it not only provided training and developed skills, it inculcated values, commitments, and modes of behavior. As a group those with college education would be more concerned with public affairs, better informed, more active in community organizations, more concerned with interpersonal relations, more geared toward reasoning and problem-solving in the resolution of conflict, more tolerant of nonconformity, more protective of civil rights, more optimistic, and more aspiring than the less well-educated. As college-educated persons, Puerto Ricans have the competence and motivation to seek not only material rewards of success but also the assurance of a respected position in the community. They find racial barriers placed so that much of the achievement they desire (and have come to demand of themselves) is barely out of reach. Puerto Rican college-trained persons who see disparity between goals and their attainments can reasonably attribute it to institutional arrangements rather than personal inadequacies. Higher education afforded some members of this generation not only skills, but a grasp of institutional dynamics in American society — a grasp unavailable to the underclass.

To better illustrate this point, I will use a poem written in the mid-1970s by Julio Noboa, a second-generation Puerto Rican from Chicago. In it, the writer provides a very concise definition of the educated Puerto Rican person (1974:51):

From the seed of Intelligence
Could emerge and develop
The plant of wisdom
Only when the roots are
Firmly embedded in the
Rich soil of Knowledge,
The leaves are lit by the
Radiant sunlight of Truth
And both are bathed in the
Cleansing rainwaters of Experience.

Many good seeds not nurtured in rich soil
Nor blessed with sunlight and rain
Never develop into mature, healthy plants,
But when knowledge nourishes,
Truth illuminates and Experience
Invigorates, the growing plant of
Wisdom blossoms into full maturity,

Capable of procreation and expression.
Only by this ultimate achievement,
The ability to create, to spill its
Own seed, with the spirit within
The plant of Wisdom forms a link
In the cosmic chain of life
And stakes a claim for immortality.

THE PROFESSIONALIZATION OF
COMMUNITY ORGANIZATION

The continuous growth of a segregated Puerto Rican population during the 1970s encouraged further institutional developments
among barrio residents which, in turn, created occupational and
leadership opportunities and thus, contributed directly to the distributive changes operative during this period. As in earlier periods,
Puerto Rican community organizations or social service agencies
were the leading structures developed to meet the needs of this
rapidly expanding urban group. In a study entitled, *The Political*

Organization of Chicago's Latino Communities published in 1977, Walton and Salces counted a total of 130 community organizations and social service agencies operating in the various Spanish-speaking communities of the city. Of these, 40 (30.8 percent) were classified by the two authors as pure Puerto Rican (1977:49–50).

The expanding Puerto Rican organizations or social service agencies were one of the leading avenues to white-collar employment for a certain sector of the Puerto Rican population. According to the 1980 Census, 1,894 Spanish-speaking individuals, residents of the Division Street Area (Westtown/Humboldt Park communities), Logan Square, and Lakeview communities, were employed in "Professional Specialty Occupations." Of these, 344 were social, recreation, or religious workers. The largest number of these white collar workers (161) lived in the Division Street Area. The Logan Square community had the second largest number, a total of 138.

This emerging group of community organization workers represented what is referred to in the social movement literature as "paid functionaries" — full-time employees whose professional careers are defined in terms or community organization participation (Zald and Ash, 1966). While the regular activities of social service organizations of an earlier period, such as Los Caballeros, were performed by a small staff of paid employees with the general membership making up their governing boards, performing some of the committees' work, and even paying expenses or dues; during the 1970s this began to change. The newly developed Puerto Rican community organizations were headed by a professional leadership which devoted full time to the organization. Wilensky (1964) has referred to this group of white-collar employees as "program professionals," highly competent experts in a particular social policy such as public assistance or race relations. These professionals move in and out of government agencies, private agencies, community organizations, foundations, and universities. According to Wilensky, these program professionals have been able to pursue such careers successfully for some time.

A combination of factors contributed directly to the professionalization of community organization in el barrio. Puerto Ricans were committed to return to the "community" after completing their formal university training. In most cases, formal schooling for this group meant acquisition of special skills necessary to combat the oppression and inequality experienced by residents of Chicago's Puerto Rican communities. Other Puerto Rican university graduates were simply excluded from participation in the wider institutional life of the larger American society. There were severe limitations even for Puerto Rican professsionals in the areas in which they could in fact advance. As a consequence of institutional racism and discrimination, this group also became part of the programs and structures created to serve the needs of this growing urban population.

The rise of external funding for community or social service work was another major contributor to the professionalization of community organization in el barrio. Several foundations, churches, and donors external to the Puerto Rican community began to fund community service programs in substantial numbers. According to the records of the Donor's Forum, a regional association of grant makers which annually lists the names of formal organizations in the city of Chicago receiving external funding, the number of Spanish-speaking organizations receiving external funding increased from 4 to 18 during a five year period beginning in 1974. Groups such as Aspira, Inc. of Illinois, Association House, Latino Institute, Allies for a Better Community were now recipients of grants from funding sources such as the Chicago Community Trust, People's Gas, Illinois Bell, Continental Bank, United Methodist Church, the Wieboldt's Foundation, and the Joyce Foundation.

As Puerto Rican community organizations began to rely more and more on a base comprised of external foundations and donors, leaders, in lieu of goal transformation, were now obligated to renew their moral credentials in the "eyes" of their financial supporters. In other words, Puerto Rican organizations and agencies using outside funds had to insure their credibility in the eyes of the donors. As a result, these organizations became more dependent on the donors than on their membership base for support.[2]

Outside financial support for Puerto Rican community organizations resulted in the dispensability of membership in the classic sense. Outside funding allowed Puerto Rican leaders to replace volunteer manpower drawn from the community with paid staff members chosen upon criteria of skills and experience. The traditional sociological view has been that social movement organizations are dependent upon their members for movement operations. Members provide all of the resources for the infrastructure of social movements; organizations depend upon members for money, work (time and energy), sacrifice, and leaders. They are also dependent upon their members to demonstrate to elites that society must change to accommodate the movement. Conversely, membership in some of el barrio's burgeoning community organizations of the 1970s became "inclusive," implying little more than support for the founders' stated aims.

Community organizing for Puerto Ricans now came to mean more than just activism and protest, it also included working through the system or using the system's institutions as mechanisms of social change. The contribution made by leaders of newly established community organizations to the Puerto Rican "struggle" or "cause" resulted from their skill at manipulating images of relevance and support primarily through communication media. The leadership of Aspira Inc. of Illinois, a local branch of a national organization primarily involved in education issues as they pertain to Puerto Rican high school students, is one example of an organization which has relied heavily upon the media and published reports to mobilize sentiment bases in order to directly and indirectly influence elite decision makers. Since the official establishment of Aspira in the state of Illinois in 1969, the basic method of the organization has been to publicize their own investigations or those of other agencies and individuals. Beginning in 1974, Aspira started publishing a newsletter in which it described the educational conditions of Puerto Rican youth as discovered by certain investigations and the views of some individuals pertaining to these circumstances. The organization's newsletter would also feature a particular education proposal or policy calling for a specific piece of legislation.

These externally funded community organizations did not replace those traditional or classic organizations in el barrio. The latter continued to rely quite extensively on a mass membership for support. There were even times when some of these organizations secured external funding and used it to further politicize their efforts. However, the existence of externally funded structures in the Puerto Rican community added another dimension to the efforts of community workers and organizations/agencies.

STRATEGIES FOR OVERCOMING INEQUALITY

Machine Politics

As the Puerto Rican community began to accumulate a larger and more visible number of formally trained professionals active in the institutional life of their community, a wider range of options and strategies became available for overcoming inequality. One major pattern of Puerto Rican political adaptation to Chicago's urban life during the 1970s was "machine politics." This attempt toward the systematic inclusion of the Puerto Rican community in the dominant pattern of "machine or boss" rule assumed that the unprecedented concentration of Puerto Ricans in the Division Street Area would permit the entire community to take a more active role in electoral politics. It was expected, in return, that elected politicians would make the city's political organization accessible to barrio residents; patronage could contribute substantially to the uplifting of the Puerto Rican community. Since the political arena had worked for other ethnic groups in the past, Puerto Ricans anticipated similar results. Like many other ethnics before them, Puerto Ricans began to regard politics as a "service industry" capable of allocating material benefits rather than as a mechanism for resolving ideological and policy issues. Hence, a growing number of Puerto Ricans were determined to harness the political power their numbers seemed to make possible, and to use it, in turn, to acquire social and economic power. Puerto Ricans were convinced that the American political system would enable them to force their way into what they uniformly refer to as the "city's power structure," that vague and shadowy coalition of government officials, politicians, businessmen, and civic leaders who in legend, if not always in fact, make the crucial decisions in society.

The arrival of this Spanish-speaking population had almost coincided with the reign of Richard J. Daley as "boss" of the city's Democratic Political Organization. Although the political machine had dominated in Chicago since 1931, it was under the hegemonic leadership of Richard J. Daley, who became Cook County party chairman in 1953 and mayor of the city two years later, that the organization became a successful and powerful political instrument known the world over (Rakove, 1975). In the words of Masotti and Gove (1982:x): "Having combined the two most powerful offices in the city, Daley spent the next twenty-two years presiding over the strongest urban political organization in America. The Daley machine not only dominated Chicago and Cook County government, but it also had considerable influence in Springfield and a major voice in presidential politics."

Since its inception, the primary concern of the Chicago political machine had been to maintain its white and largely ethnic power base, while accommodating and neutralizing the city's black vote. Well into the 1960s, black wards represented "controlled wards"—turning out only modestly but solidly in the corner of the Democratic organization (Kemp and Lineberry, 1982:7; Preston, 1982:88). Beginning in the early years of the 1970s the machine began to experience an erosion in its popular base. The migration of a large proportion of the city's white electorate to the suburbs, corresponding with the rise of the Sunbelt and the "decline of the Frostbelt," contributed significantly to a decrease in the machine's major constituency. The hegemony of the machine was also being challenged by former Democratic and newly emerged independent politicians as they competed for the support of a significant proportion of the organization's coalition. Last, and perhaps more importantly, during the 1970s the machine also started to lose the political loyalty of the black population—at that time the city's fastest growing population with upwards of one million residents. While their numbers grew, urban blacks, who had been loyal Democrats for several decades, began to defect, signaling the failure of the municipal political machinery in responding to their needs. When writing about the political mood of blacks during the 1970s, Preston (1982:88–89) concludes that "by losing black voters, the machine [was] losing some of its most loyal supporters. . . . The trend seems clear: blacks [were] seeking alternatives to machine candidates and policies. Black voters are no longer the loyal, predictable, controllable, deliverable voters they once were; since 1975 they have become increasingly more unloyal, unpredictable, uncontrollable, and undeliverable."

Attempts by Puerto Ricans aspiring to win elective office to integrate their community into the city's political system came at a time when the city's democratic political organization was losing the support of white electorates and experiencing an increasing disloyalty among black voters. Thus, "maintaining white ethnic support—holding white exodus from the city—while simultaneously nurturing the city's fastest growing constituency [blacks] were the prime items for the agenda of the Chicago machine" (Kemp and Lineberry, 1982:2). In this context, very little effort was geared toward the absorption of the Puerto Rican community as the Puerto Rican vote was dispensable as far as white politicians were concerned. For over two decades, Puerto Rican voters had been taken for granted by the Democratic Political Organization of the city of Chicago. Understanding the electoral power they could potentially yield in Chicago, the Puerto Rican leadership, on the other hand, became involved in a fascinating attempt to forge an activist political bloc and realize that potential. Puerto Rican leaders struggled to mobilize its barrio constituency effectively, to organize and hold Puerto Ricans together in order to deal in the political power which was (and continues to be) the currency of this midwest metropolis.

In 1975, three independent candidates from el barrio Miguel A. Velázquez, José "Cha-Cha" Jiménez, and Frank Díaz, challenged incumbents backed by Mayor Daley's Democratic Organization for the aldermanic seat in Wards 31, 46, and 26, respectively.[3] Both Velázquez and Jiménez were second-generation Puerto Ricans; the former was an attorney and the latter was the former leader and one of the founders of the Young Lords. Frank Díaz was a first-generation migrant and one of the founders of the Spanish Action Committee of Chicago (SACC). The 31st and 26th wards formed the heart of the Puerto Rican Westtown/Humboldt Park community, the 46th ward was located in the community of Lakeview. For these men, winning elective office became a means of gaining esteem within el barrio, but more importantly, it was a way to provide barrio residents with real political representation. The three Puerto Rican candidates tried to draw this Spanish-speaking population into the political arena on the basis of ethnic ties, believing that the bond between themselves and the Puerto Rican rank and file was more than a functional relationship, it was a bond of common identity.

Velázquez, Jiménez, and Díaz failed to win a seat in the city council. Both Jiménez and Velázquez received 27 percent of the votes in their respective wards. Only 7 percent of the electorate from the 26th ward supported Díaz's candidacy (Salces, 1978a:177–78).

That Puerto Ricans did not succeed in gaining elective office in 1975 was hardly surprising (nor were they successful four years later). Their challenge was made against candidates backed by the Democratic Political Organization of the city of Chicago. During the Daley years, few republicans or independent candidates ever won aldermanic seats in the city council. In 1971 independent and republican aldermen combined controlled 13 of the 50 seats in the City Council; four years later this number dropped to 6; and by 1978 there was a reduction of another seat (Salces, 1978a:104). In a real sense, winning office as independents was very unlikely for Puerto Ricans or any other aspiring political candidates during this time.

Another explanation for the unsuccessful efforts made by Velázquez, Jiménez, and Díaz to win elected office was that the Puerto Rican population and registered-voter concentration did not coincide. In the 31st and 26th wards less than half of the Puerto Rican eligible voters were registered. Salces (1978a:178) shows that in the 31st ward, while 76 percent of Spanish-speaking residents were Puerto Ricans, only 33 percent were registered voters. Puerto Ricans constituted 62 percent of the Spanish-surnamed population of the 26th ward but only 25 percent of the registered voters. A very small percent of registered voters, 8 percent, were Puerto Ricans in the 46th ward where Puerto Ricans represented 38 percent of the Spanish-speaking residents.

Another common explanation of the underutilization of the Puerto Rican vote is to link it to socioeconomic factors. The fact that lower class individuals are less likely to participate in politics has been amply documented by numerous studies in the United States and in cross-cultural research.[4] Thus, the high degree of poverty in the Puerto Rican barrios of Chicago can be said to act as a depressant on Puerto Rican electoral participation. In accordance with this argument, the high incidence of poverty leaves a large segment of this Spanish-speaking population vulnerable to control by machine politics; those who receive welfare benefits, CETA jobs, and other low-level patronage jobs form the hard core of voters who would rather not register to vote than to go against candidates the machine runs for office.

On the contrary, the existence of the small proportion of registered voters has more to do with the particular tactics employed by the machine to keep the Puerto Rican vote unregistered. As long as the Puerto Rican vote in the 31st and 26th wards remained underutilized, incumbent aldermen of newly emerged machine candidates in these political areas were guaranteed continuous victory and control. On several occasions Puerto Rican community groups sought financial support from the city's political organization to fund registration campaigns in el barrio, but each time the requests were denied. In the fall, 1971, an article in *El Puertorriqueño* indicated: "Although the Commissioner of the Board of Elections, Stanley Kusper, has directed a call to all the city's residents to register to vote, little or no official activity has been seen in the wards populated by Spanish-speaking residents as a way to make contact and register the Spanish-speaking element. The traditional 'canvassing' is totally absent in every Spanish-speaking ward of the city" (October 28, 1971:8). From this point of view, it can be seen that the so-called "voters' apathy" among Puerto Ricans is actually regarded or considered to be "functional" for systematic stability.

One demographic factor which also limited the political participation of Puerto Ricans in the 1970s, but which became the major force in the 1980s, was their relative youthfulness. "The youthfulness of the Spanish American population," concludes Salces (1978:48), "reduces their level of electoral political participation in two ways. First, it reduces the number of eligible voters. Secondly, the Spanish American collectivity has a greater proportion of its population in the age bracket (20–35 years) which traditionally has been less politically active." The 31st and 26th wards contained a large proportion of children. According to the 1970 Census, the median age of the city's Spanish-speaking population was only 20.3 percent (compared to 30.5 years for the non-Spanish-speaking population). Moreover, 46 percent of the Spanish-speaking population was under 18 years of age compared with 31 percent for the non-Spanish-speaking groups.

But, perhaps, more importantly it was the limited relationship developed over the years between Puerto Ricans and the white-controlled city machine which really deprived the Puerto Rican leadership from utilizing Puerto Rican ethnicity as an instrument for political efficacy in both el barrio and the city. The Puerto Rican community in Chicago had been prevented from taking on the attributes of an "ethnic political subsystem," that is, an articulate and politically cohesive group within the structure of the city machine.

Lacking elected representation barrio residents easily fell victim to the whims and caprice of Chicago's political machine. The largest proportion of the Puerto Rican vote was geographically divided into two political wards, the 31st and 26th. The separation of the Puerto Rican community into two distinct wards severely limited their political power. This situation was exacerbated by a pattern of gerrymandering individual wards every ten years or so by the City Council. In an article to the *Chicago Sun-Times*, Watson and Wheeler (Sept 12-20, 1971) reported how the 31st ward was gerrymandered in 1970. The two correspondents point out that under the control of Mayor Daley's right arm in City Hall, Alderman Keane, the western boundary of the 31st ward was moved from Pulaski Road to the Chicago and North Western Rail tracks, incorporating an area not yet populated by Puerto Ricans. On the other hand, a twenty-five block area heavily populated by Puerto Ricans was shifted to the 26th ward.

The gerrymandering hindered attempts by Puerto Ricans to elect their ethnic candidate as it did not leave sufficient numbers of Puerto Ricans to form majorities in wards located in el barrio. In 1976, the 31st ward contained the highest concentration of Spanish-speaking voters with 9,269 registrants, which represented 39 percent of the total number of voters in the ward. In the 26th ward, the number of registered Spanish-speaking voters totalled 6,185 or 26.3 percent of all voters for the same year.

Despite the difficulties encountered in this political progress in mid-1970, there obviously was greater advance in this sphere of community activity than in the past. Several major lessons were learned from the 1975 local elections. Independent Puerto Rican candidates discovered that Puerto Rican voters indeed showed a preference for their ethnic candidate. Salces (1978a: 183) concludes that "the ethnic factor played a positive role on the turnout of Velázquez in ward 31 and Jiménez in ward 46. In the case of the 26th ward, the effect of ethnicity was positive but rather weak." The candidates also discovered that ethnic identification alone did not siphon off many votes from the Democrats. Puerto Rican candidates needed to mobilize the Puerto Rican vote, but also to register all residents of the community to vote and to get them to the polls on election day. Puerto Rican candidates came to realize that they needed the support of other ethnics with whom they shared several geographical-political communities in the city.

The election of 1975 also demonstrated that the Puerto Rican vote counts in local aldermanic elections. According to estimates by Salces (1978a:60), "Velázquez . . . needed about 6,400 votes to win. But in order to achieve this goal Velázquez had to get 82% of the 7,696 Spanish-surnamed registrants to vote for him. This was obviously a very difficult although not impossible task to accomplish in a ward which had an overall turnout of 60.8%." Just as important, there was an increasing recognition that Puerto Ricans together with other Spanish-surnamed groups in Chicago could represent a significant voting bloc in citywide politics in future years. It was expected that as "*one* Spanish-speaking population," these groups could become the city's next political ethnic power.

The Puerto Rican leadership became more convinced that if politics were to play an important part in the urban life of barrio residents, it was urgent to combat institutional barriers that stood in their way. In particular, the gerrymandering of the Puerto Rican vote represented the leading impediment. Puerto Ricans awaited the 1980s with a great deal of anxiety and enthusiasm. When it was learned that the re-mapping of the city political wards, which followed the Census population count for the new decade, resulted in further disadvantage for this and other oppressed communities in the city, legal action was taken. Puerto Ricans collaborated with the Mexican and black communities and filed a legal suit against the City of Chicago. They won the suit and forced a new re-mapping of certain wards. For Puerto Ricans this meant the creation of two Puerto Rican wards and the subsequent election of two Puerto Ricans to the City Council.

Clientele Politics

Another leading strategy adapted by some Puerto Ricans during the 1970s which still continues today was "clientele politics." Clientele politics entailed a process by which a small group of Puerto Ricans fashioned personalized links with influential city politicians, becoming "clients" for a variety of sociopolitical purposes. More specifically, clientele politics was a political arrangement which made appointive political and civic posts the main means of exchange from political patrons to Puerto Rican clients.

Chicago's Democratic Political Organization felt it expedient to employ as go-betweens individuals who spoke the language of the community and who knew the customs, prejudices, and best means of molding opinions and winning votes, if and when necessary. From the beginning, the clientele appointments have involved jobs in specific city departments and sitting on commissions and special interest groups concerning issues such as bilingual education, affirmative action, etc.

Officials of the political machine tended to use these traditional clientalistic structures as instruments for mediating and legitimizing their rule. Conversely, this means that the clientele political technique, critical in "accommodation politics," has given the mass of Puerto Rican residents only the appearance of inclusion in the existing political organization. In other words, clientele politics was a means of providing evidence that the city's political organization had honored the group and taken account of its accumulated grievances by symbolic leadership incorporation into the governmental process. As Wolfinger (1966:52) aptly concludes: "ethnic appointments are often made because it is expected that voters will be happy with the recognition and will not make substantive demands as well. The appointees owe their positions to outside selection, often with implicit understanding that they will dissuade their fellow ethnics from main policy demands."

Puerto Rican political appointments were and continue to be a largely middle-class affair. From the early 1970s on to the present these appointed political figures have been mainly middle-class, those most socialized in the forms and style of "pluralistic politics." The clientele-type of politics, which the neglect of the city's Democratic machine caused some of the Puerto Rican elites to adopt, had a class bias clearly reflected in Belenchia's (1982:130) discussion of "Latinos" political appointments made during the Jane Byrne administration from 1979–1982:

> None of the previous appointments and none of those presently being considered can be said to have strong ties to the mostly working- or lower-class Latino communities in the city. Charges of tokenism are the usual response of community-based organizations to city hall's attempts to provide for Latino representation. Those Latinos who come to the notice of the Anglo power structure are typically highly educated Cubans and Puerto Ricans living in the upper-income neighborhoods in the city.

One concern commonly shared in the Puerto Rican community is that the politics pursued by a segment of the Puerto Rican elite in Chicago has not produced a vertical integratiqn of the elites with the Puerto Rican underclass: those who obtained political power were resented by their constituents. While these community leaders, supposedly representing a deprived or aggrieved group, are given specific recognition in the form of political appointments, jobs, and other benefits, the working class poor are granted symbolic participation through the recognition of this leadership. Litt (1970:64) makes a similar point in his discussion of what he refers to as "recognition politics:"

> At the same time that recognition politics limited mass participation and concern with public policies, its organizational consequence was to maintain the dominance for its leadership. Despite lip service to the contrary, no successful organization wishes to engage in extensive intraparty competition. Thus, there are numerous historical examples in which assertive ethnic leadership has been bought off by the dominant political group and, in return, has managed to suppress members of its own group who wished to act more aggressively within the party. Symbolic recognition and the judicious use of divisible benefits are cheaper coins than intense primary fights and challenges to the party ticket.

Puerto Ricans have not taken this selection process of their political representatives sitting down. Time and time again, Puerto Ricans have demanded that the "city's power structure" recognize them and negotiate with them—that public officials, businesses, and civic leaders come to the bargaining table not as patrons but as equals. They have insisted that city officials recognize the leaders selected by the Puerto Rican community itself, however distasteful they are found to be. It's not a question of how many Puerto Ricans are selected for public office, but rather, who and how are they selected. The interest in how Puerto Ricans are selected for office reflects considerably more than just a play for personal power. The demand of Puerto Ricans for a voice in selecting Puerto Rican officials reflects one of the most profound Puerto Rican concerns, a concern which city officials must recognize if there is to be any peace or agreement on the part of the Puerto Rican leaders. Nothing rankles Puerto Ricans quite so much as the city power structure's habit of choosing the "Puerto Rican leaders" whom it wants to reward or with whom it wants to deal. And the city officials naturally enough have chosen only Puerto Ricans willing to accommodate themselves to city interests.

There always has been a strain between the Puerto Rican community and its ostensible leaders. A great many Puerto Ricans believe their appointed political representatives have been too responsible to the interests of the city's power structure and insufficiently attentive to Puerto Rican needs; they believe that only leaders who are in no way beholden to the city's political machine are free to represent them without fear or favor. A crucial part of the Puerto Rican struggle of liberation, therefore, is the attempt to replace the "ethnic diplomats" with a new breed of "ethnic conscious men and women."

As often as not, some of the accusations proved true; some of the Puerto Rican appointed politicians were a venal lot. Even when the Puerto Rican political leadership appointed by city officials was honest and sincere, it tended to be highly ineffective. Some leaders were reluctant to take the risks that "activism" might involve; other leaders were so flattered at being appointed by the city's political organization that any thought of activism they might have harbored simply melted away.

Of course there have been instances when Puerto Ricans have had no choice but to recognize the leaders whom the city power structure selected. In Chicago, Puerto Ricans have needed representatives who could establish contact with influential city officials, who could gain favors, or perhaps, by winning favors and confidence, could persuade politicians to meet some of their more urgent needs. Thus, despite the limitations of clientage politics or, in Litt's terms, the suppressive role played by this leadership, it is also the case that the efforts of these appointed leaders have been terribly important to the development and growth of the Puerto Rican community. These appointive positions permitted some Puerto Ricans to influence some part of the political process that allocates services to barrio residents, especially social services. In addition, these political jobs have facilitated strategic contacts and communication with individuals holding direct access to political resources. As Puerto Ricans began to enter politically appointed positions, they also continued to produce ethnic peer associations that encourage both personal advancement and a usually diffuse sense of obligation to other Puerto Ricans. Clientele politics represent a moderate strategy that, according to some members of the Puerto Rican community, has a better chance of realization in current circumstances. The dreams of ethnic uplift are not dead, but they have often been channeled into the practicality of developing careers, making a particular school or organization work, or maintaining funding for a manpower program necessary for both the unemployed barrio worker and the middle-class persons who administer the program.

Puerto Rican appointed leaders believe that if Puerto Ricans are to be elected or appointed to "high office" — if they are, in fact, to enter the "power structure" and help shape the decisions that count — they will have to give up a good deal of their freedom to criticize and protest. This is the price of power. No member of a city, state, or federal administration can expect to keep any influence over that administration if he/she is always denouncing it: to be an effective advocate of Puerto Rican interests within the power structure, one must abandon the social activist role. This individual cannot have it both ways. There are, therefore, strong pressures to work within the system.

The Emergence of Latino Solidarity

Another major strategy used by Puerto Ricans during the 1970s to overcome inequality in Chicago was the formation of a "Latino ethnic unit." Latino solidarity and cleavage is a form of ethnic innovation which entails a relationship of cooperation and mobilization among two or more Spanish-speaking groups to pursue and protect the common good. Beginning in the early 1970s, Puerto Ricans and Mexicans became engaged in a process of interaction, transcending their individual ethnic boundaries and leading to the formation of a wider Latino ethnic unit.

The idea of a Latino bond represented an identity separate and distinct from their respective national and cultural identities. This form of solidarity needed to be created as part of the process of interaction and mobilization. The "taking-on" of a Latino identity involved the assertion that this wide-scale frame was more significant, for certain purposes, than individual affiliations or national origin, while at the same time maintaining that the Puerto Rican and Mexican ethnic ties would not be lost or replaced in the process. Latino affinity represented a form of "situational ethnicity" — certain situational contexts influenced the creation and expression of Latino-related behavior and mobilization.

As I have discussed the process by which the Latino ethnic unit comes into being somewhere else (Padilla, 1985), I only intend to present in this discussion several cases of the organizational expression of the Latino identity and behavior among Puerto Ricans and Mexicans in Chicago.

For the most part, the daily life of Puerto Ricans and Mexicans in Chicago had been demarcated by individual ethnic boundaries. Having arrived in Chicago during the period of World War I, Mexicans established communities of settlement in areas of the city where Puerto Rican barrios were later built in the 1950s and 1960s (see Map 5). Official policies of "repatriation" during the depression years and "Operation Wetback" in the 1950s, which returned thousands of Mexicans to their native land, made the size of the Mexican population in 1970 only slightly larger than that of Puerto Ricans. The Census for that year listed 107,652 persons who were born in Mexico or who had at least one parent born in Mexico. It listed 80,482 persons of Puerto Rican birth or parentage. While Puerto Ricans and Mexicans were in constant physical contact and were tolerant of one another, their individual ethnicity circumscribed social interaction in the churches, social agencies and clubs, taverns, and recreational areas of each neighborhood during the 1950s and 1960s. In other words, an ethnicity based on national ties formed the basis for personal trust for individual Puerto Rican and Mexican American residents. As these personal bonds were vital to social interaction and mobilization in the separate Spanish-speaking communities, the residents had little reason for crossing their respective ethnic boundaries.

This began to change in the 1970s as significant similarities in the experiences of Puerto Ricans and Mexicans, particularly their employment/labor conditions, were being attributed to the language or cultural commonality of these two Spanish-speaking groups. The hardening dimensions of urban-based inequality, the continued shrinking of the industrial job base coupled with the relegation of Puerto Rican and Mexican workers to common economically less

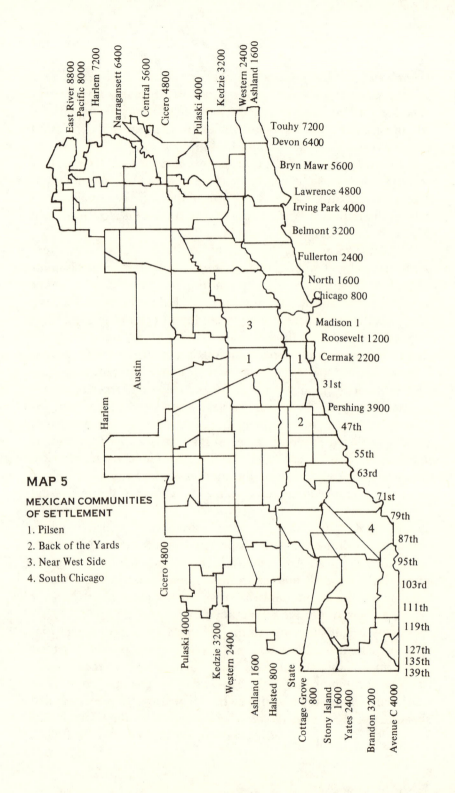

East River 8800
Pacific 8000
Harlem 7200
Narragansett 6400
Central 5600
Cicero 4800
Pulaski 4000
Kedzie 3200
Western 2400
Ashland 1600

Touhy 7200
Devon 6400
Bryn Mawr 5600
Lawrence 4800
Irving Park 4000
Belmont 3200
Fullerton 2400
North 1600
Chicago 800

3

Madison 1
Roosevelt 1200
Cermak 2200

1   1

31st

Austin

Pershing 3900

2   47th

Harlem

55th
63rd
71st
79th

4   87th
95th
103rd
111th
119th
127th
135th
139th

MAP 5

**MEXICAN COMMUNITIES
OF SETTLEMENT**

1. Pilsen
2. Back of the Yards
3. Near West Side
4. South Chicago

Cicero 4800

Pulaski 4000
Kedzie 3200
Western 2400
Ashland 1600
Halsted 800
State
Cottage Grove 800
Stony Island 1600
Yates 2400
Brandon 3200
Avenue C 4000

productive and increasingly marginal positions in the urban labor force, caused both groups to reexamine these circumstances within the context of their shared commonalities. The two populations finally accepted the idea that their shared circumstances of inequality were a consequence of language or cultural discrimination, thus developing a generalized belief or ideological justification concerning their disadvantaged social and economic position. As a result, these two groups began to cross the boundaries of their individual ethnic communities and interact as one Latino unit to seek redress of their disadvantaged situation.

One of the first Latino responses to the overall situation of both Mexican and Puerto Rican working class came through the efforts of the Spanish Coalition for Jobs. Established as a coalition of 19 community organizations from these Spanish-speaking communities in 1971, the Coalition for Jobs forced firms like Illinois Bell, Jewel Tea, and Sears to open up employment opportunities for the Spanish-speaking working class of the city. Using protests, demonstrations, and other similar tactics for a period of four years, the Spanish Coalition for Jobs successfully fought against these and other firms to implement the affirmative action policy and hire Puerto Rican and Mexican workers. The successes of the Spanish Coalition for Jobs demonstrated that adoption of a "Latino ethnic identity" could indeed alter institutional racist practices, and thus contribute to the development of feelings of political effectiveness as one "Latino group."

Another important attempt on the part of Puerto Ricans and Mexicans in Chicago to build a Latino frame came through the establishment of the Latino Institute. The Latino Institute, founded in 1974, represented an organizational attempt to provide Spanish-surnamed community organizations with, in the words of one of the persons most responsible for this idea, "a communication network for Spanish-speaking residents of the city." The Latino Institute was viewed as the creation of a highly systematic and orchestrated effort to eliminate the obstacles which had frustrated the attempts of Spanish-speaking groupings in improving the quality of their shared collective life in the city ("Latino Institute: History and Philosophy," mimeographed). The organization was formed to seek self-determination and economic and social progress, and to impact those institutions and agencies that stood in the way of the progress of these multi-ethnic communities. The founders of the organization hoped to accomplish this by the "legitimation of Latino ethnicity." This meant that the Latino Institute strove for recognition of the collective Spanish-speaking groups' viability in the polity of the larger society. In order to create a successful, all-embracing Latino community of interest, the founders saw a critical need to devise techniques to establish credibility with various "outsiders" — groups whose behavior the organization was trying to influence or with those who might otherwise be indifferent or hostile to the Spanish-speaking communities in the city.

This new organization offered to deliver the support of an "ever-growing Latino community," destined to be of significant importance to the political and economic life of society. The founders and members of the organization claimed there was no longer a need to fear "Latino radicalism" as long as the Latino Institute was the mouthpiece of the populations. They perceived the essence of coercion (e.g., the threat of harm) as being more costly in arousing suspicion and resistance in the long run; the "traditional integrationist" program of the organization eschewed protest or coercion as unacceptable and/or ineffective. Overall it was assumed that the more tough-minded and pragmatic business and governmental leaders would be responsive to the bargaining appeals and approaches of the Latino Institute.

Latino ethnic solidarity provided both Puerto Ricans and Mexicans with a large-scale unit from which certain of the groups' needs and wants were negotiated and even attained. Puerto Ricans and Mexicans became involved in a "formation or developmental process" which preserved the individual and separate ethnic foundations of each group while it transformed them into a wider, politically mobilized population. For these two groups of Spanish-speaking, the Latino unit came to represent a highly conscious cleavage and a new mode of interest-articulation.

THE SALIENCE OF PUERTO RICAN ETHNICITY

As long as participation in a Latino bond was aimed at addressing "city-wide" concerns and issues shared in common by two or more Spanish-speaking ethnics, the Puerto Rican ethnic boundary would continue to play a significant part in the urban life of Puerto Rican residents. Coinciding with the expression of Latino-related behavior and mobilization, a host of local community interests and issues appeared, reinforcing the salience and affinity of Puerto Rican ethnicity during the 1970s.

The Problem of the "Dropout"

A concern about the education of Puerto Rican youth became one of the major local issues responsible for the acceleration and growth of Puerto Rican ethnic-conscious behavior during the 1970s. Puerto Rican students attending barrio schools were simply not continuing as far in school as middle-class students who attended middle-class schools. Puerto Rican people had been led to believe that education was the "key to success"—they had also accepted the view that schools were the "great equalizers" in American society. They found, however, that for Puerto Rican students the benefits of education had never been realized. *Barrio* schools were singled out as the cause of this failure. The dropout rate was the main level of failure used by parents and community leaders to measure the effect of schools in the Puerto Rican community.

According to figures that appeared in a Board of Education survey in September 30, 1971, "Student Racial Survey Recapitulation," there were 574,495 pupils enrolled in the city's regular elementary schools, of whom 59,778 or 10.4 pecent spoke Spanish as a first language. This represents, noted the report, an increase of 3,404 pupils or 0.7 percent over the 1970 figure. The greatest number of these youngsters, 27,303, listed Puerto Rico as their country of family origin, and the greatest number of Spanish-speaking students (2,327) attended Von Humboldt School located in the heart of the Division Street Area. The "Teacher Racial Survey Recapitulation- Elementary Schools" for September 22, 1971 showed that of a total of 17,738 teachers, 10,774 (60.7 percent) were white; 6,632 (37.4 percent) were black; 8 (0.1 percent) were American Indian; 106 (0.6) were Oriental; 79 (0.4 percent) were Mexican; 54 (0.3 percent) were Puerto Rican; 46 (0.3 percent) were Cuban; and 39 (0.2 percent) were other Spanish-speaking Americans. A comparison of statistics for pupils and teachers who are Spanish-speaking indicates that there were only 202 Spanish-speaking teachers for 59,778 children who spoke Spanish as a first language, that is, 1,758 students for each teacher.

A study conducted by Dr. Isidro Lucas of the United States Commission on Civil Rights in 1971 and data from the 1970 Census indicated very explicitly how the schools in Chicago were failing to educate Puerto Rican children. Dr. Lucas found that for each of the years 1969 and 1970, the cumulative drop-out, or more accurately, push-out rate for this Spanish-surnamed population was 71.2 percent (1974). The 1970 Census showed that the average schooling for Puerto Ricans was 7.9 years and only 15 percent had completed high school. In contrast, the Census pointed out an average schooling of 11 years for both black and all adults in Chicago, with 40 percent of black adults and 44 percent of all adults shown as having completed high school.

The massive failure of the schools to educate Puerto Ricans was also impressed on the consciousness of barrio residents by the local press. *El Puertorriqueño* featured no less than twelve editorials in a period of twelve months in 1972 denouncing public education for not helping to correct the disadvantaged situation of Puerto Ricans in Chicago. In a way similar to the "conservative" and "liberal" views of education (e.g., Coleman, et. al., 1966 and Fischer, 1966, respectively), the newspaper demanded that since education had been the route through which other disadvantaged groups had achieved social mobility, Puerto Rican students should be provided with the same opportunity. But how can the schools in el barrio accomplish their historical mission when the conditions there are so deplorable? was a question consistently raised in the editorials. In one instance *El Puertorriqueño* denounced all existing programs in one barrio school for their ineffectiveness: "It's because of these various irrelevant classes that the Puerto Rican child is often better off not attending school. Why should he go to school when there is nothing there to learn, to make a part of his human experience" (June 27, 1972:3). In another case the newspaper called for the dismissal of many of the teachers in barrio schools: "The teachers are the cause of the massive failure of our schools." The editorial continued, "These teachers do not understand how to make the school a place of learning, how to prepare our children for a better tomorrow" (August 2, 1972:5).

In "Tuley Products," a poem written in 1974 by Emma

Rodríguez, a second-generation Puerto Rican writer, the overall social circumstances faced by Puerto Rican high school students, in and out of school, are further elaborated:

> Little Spanish children
> Warm smiles, dark eyes
> Stare at whiteness
> of milk-faced teachers.
> Day in, day out
> Little funny kids,
> You know, the ones
> With the 'problem,'
> Speaking the odd tongue
> put in 'slow learner' classes
> Regardless of their abilities.
> Put there and forgotten.
> Year in, year out
> Spanish children grow
> INTO
> Gang bangers, drug pushers
> Street hangers, night walkers.
> Devoured by monstrous
> 8 til 4 factory jobs
> Haunted by eviction notices
> Chased by cockroach tribes
> Enclosed within Latin sounds,
> Bacardi, happy wine-filled dreams
> of
> 'I never go back to Georgia'
> Which means, never leave, always
> die
> And the only crib they will ever
> own
> In Puerto Rico is a death crypt.

The Puerto Rican community became restless and demanding about the problem of schooling in el barrio, proposing new programs and directions with a sophisticated sense of political and educational organization. Puerto Rican community leaders and parents agreed that the needs of Puerto Rican students could only be met through and by a bilingual-bicultural school curriculum and school environment. They were very critical of the traditional school approach, which had continuously shamed and ridiculed Puerto Rican students for speaking Spanish and for expressing their traditional cultural ways. The schools were seen as alien and hostile. The American education system as it had occurred in the Island during the first thirty years of American colonial domination aimed to destroy the Puerto Rican culture including, of course, the language. The Puerto Rican community saw the relevance of bilingual-bicultural instruction for barrio youth as the kind of instruction that could serve the needs and address the cultural values of Puerto Rican students.

Puerto Rican community leaders and parents were fully aware that Spanish-speaking communities in other cities of the United States had pressed for and won the right to provide their children with bilingual education instruction. They, too, saw the need to embark on such pursuits. The Puerto Rican community became involved in efforts to force the state of Illinois to sanction and allocate fundings for bilingual-bicultural instruction in the city of Chicago.

A summary of the history of bilingual education programs in American public schools for Spanish-speaking children shows this form of instruction starting in 1962. In that year, a completely bilingual education program was launched in the Coral Way School in the City of Miami with the support of public and private foundation funds. The program was implemented by the Dade County, Florida school system to meet the educational needs of the children of Cuban immigrants who were rapidly arriving in Miami. In 1964, two other noteworthy bilingual education programs were begun in Texas: one in the Nye School of the United Consolidated Independent School District in Webb County outside of Laredo, and the other in the San Antonio Independent School District.

A major effort in the growth of bilingual education and a commitment on the part of the federal government was the passage of the Bilingual Educational Act of 1968 which became Title VII of the Elementary and Secondary Education Act. This act recognized that the use of children's native language in school can have beneficial effects upon their education.

In December, 1971, Massachusetts became the first state to have mandatory bilingual education programs for non-English speaking pupils. A state law required every school system with twenty or more children of limited English-speaking ability to provide a "transitional" bilingual education program. The transitional education approach to bilingual education required that children be enrolled in classes in which all subjects were taught in their native language. After an unspecified time, as their proficiency in English increased, the children were transferred to classes taught in their second language.

Realizing that the Court decree for bilingual education was not readily enforced by either the state or city government, Chicago's Puerto Rican parents, community leaders, and residents took the issue to the streets of el barrio. Puerto Ricans met with representatives of the State of Illinois' Spanish-speaking Peoples Study Commission and pressured for the passing of the bilingual education bill in the state. In June, 1973, the Commission initiated a bill similar to Massachusetts', and the governor signed it in September, 1973 for implementation in 1974.

Puerto Rican residents of the Division Street Area also charged that an important element of a successful bilingual-bicultural program was its teachers. It was recognized that bilingual-bicultural teachers needed to comprise the ranks of these programs, otherwise the reform would result in little or no gains for the Puerto Rican community. The Puerto Rican community stressed that any attempt to delay the recruitment of bilingual-bicultural teachers would in effect delay communication to the Spanish-speaking child and the successful implementation of bilingual-bicultural education programs. Any official claim of improvements in the quality of teachers as well as in all segments of the institution and general society had not enhanced the Spanish-speaking child's education. It was argued that the bilingual-bicultural teachers, who in most cases came from el barrio, represented the new breed of educators who could begin the needed chain of changes.

In an interview, Mr. Zeferino Ochoa, director of the Archdiocesan Latin American Committee — an outgrowth organization of Los Caballeros de San Juan, informed me that while Spanish-speaking students in Chicago were falling behind in school each passing year there were hundreds of unemployed or underemployed teachers living in Chicago with college and university degrees from Puerto Rico, Mexico, or Cuba. He added:

In our work, we have found over 475 Spanish-speaking persons with teaching experience who were refused teaching certificates in the city of Chicago. Most were turned down because the schools they graduated from were not accredited or because they did not have basic U.S. education course credits. They are working in factories, putting screws on the back of television sets, or cooking and waiting on tables in restaurants.[5]

Puerto Rican parents argued that while Puerto Rican and other Spanish-speaking teachers were turned away because they did not meet minor educational requirements, the Board of Education was hiring English-speaking teachers who had taken every required course but who couldn't communicate with their students. Residents of the Puerto Rican community were not saying that only Spanish-speaking teachers could teach Spanish-speaking children. They were saying that the employment of bilingual-bicultural Puerto Rican personnel represented the required approach to educating and preparing their children for a humanizing and liberating way of life. It was not only that Puerto Rican children needed bilingual-bicultural "role models" in their classroom but, more importantly, that these teachers would teach courses geared to maintaining and encouraging the genuine Puerto Rican culture and history as well as acknowledging the oppressive conditions of Puerto Ricans and other ethnic minorities in American society.

After meeting and negotiating with residents and parents from the Division Street Area, the Board of Education agreed to employ the "underutilized" Spanish-speaking teacher labor which existed in Chicago. Through a program called the Transitional Teacher Program (TTP), the Board of Education was committed to recruit and train bilingual-bicultural persons with teaching degrees from Puerto Rico, Mexico, Cuba, or other Spanish-speaking countries. Also considered for the TTP recruitment and training were bilingual-bicultural persons who had earned 90 credit hours of undergraduate work from American universities as well as bilingual-bicultural persons with degrees from American universities who lacked courses in education and did not meet teaching certificate requirements.

"They're Burning El Barrio" and the Problem of Gentrification

Beginning in 1970, the sound of fire sirens became increasingly a part of the daily life in the Division Street Area. Like many other neighborhoods populated by poor people, the Puerto Rican barrio was the scene of a rash of fires during this period. In February, 1978 Eduardo Camacho, a graduate student at the University of Chicago, conducted a survey of the housing conditions in East Humboldt Park—a neighborhood in the Division Street Area. His findings revealed that since 1970 over one-third of the housing there had been destroyed by fires, demolition, and abandonment.

In his "Torches: Arson for Sale," an article in *Newsweek*, correspondent Terry Atlas stressed that "buildings are sometimes torched for revenge, sometimes to cover other crimes such as murder, and sometimes just for kicks. But a great many deliberate fires, perhaps the majority, are the work of the arson industry—a shadow world of property owners, mortgage men, corrupt fire officials, insurance adjusters and mobsters" (Sept. 12, 1977:89). The fires in the Division Street Area destroyed more than just property and anyone unlucky enough to be trapped inside. Large sections of the community collapsed into heaps of blackened debris. Just as important, local residents came to accept the premise that because of these fires their community was in danger of being "taken-over" by outsiders. Puerto Ricans were convinced that the fires in their community represented an organized plot to obtain land for development and subsequently, to provide quick and lucrative profits to redevelopers. They equated the fires with gentrification and feared that they would be moved out in order to make room for white, middle-class people. The threat of the transformation of the Division Street Area from el barrio Puertorriqueño to a white, middle-class area became another major factor which helped strengthen Puerto Rican ethnic solidarity during the 1970s.

The urban gentrification trend so common in other areas of Chicago and in many communities of America's larger cities during the early 1970s was also spreading into Wicker Park—the east boundary of the Division Street Area. This added further evidence to the residents' claim that el barrio was fast becoming a popular residential location for middle-class whites.

Urban gentrification has been referred to as the process of middle-class ecological "invasion" of lower-class, central-city neighborhoods in the 1970's. According to Clay (1979:6):

> Gentrification is derived from a British term used to denote the resettlement of professional and upper middle-class home owners in city neighborhoods. In this type of revitalization

population change is more important than physical change, although the physical improvements are also important. The 'gentry' create a neighborhood ambience and a style that reflect upper middle-class tastes and values; their tastes and values supplant those of the lower-income population that dominated the area before revitalization.

It's reasonable to suggest that interest in the Wicker Park neighborhood was sparked primarily by the same reasons given by residential location researchers for gentrification. Some social scientists have proposed a convergence of family, occupational, and status changes as the reason for the new interest in central-city residential locations. Such changes include a shrinking family size with a concomitant decline in the preoccupation with obtaining child-related residential amenities and an increase in spare time available for non-child-related activities (Gale, 1977); greater numbers of two journeys to work (Long, 1980); and the seeming devaluation of the status of suburban location by the generation raised in the suburbs (London, 1980).[6]

As the preeminence of Chicago's Loop was being reestablished during the 1970s, principally with corporate firms, service sector activities, and specialty retail opportunities, interest in areas such as Wicker Park grew substantially. The central city was becoming very convenient to work opportunities for the professional class, and in so doing, it was influencing residential decisions. By location and the quality of its housing stock, Wicker Park was a logical successor to the string of neighborhoods which were being rehabilitated and upscaled into the Yuppies' North Side beachhead. (The term "Yuppies" refers to young urban professionals, who are single individuals or couples without children, generally employed in white-collar professions in central-city firms.) In 1979, an article in the *Chicago Sun-Times* indicated:

> Until about five years ago, Wicker Park was home for an ethnically and economically mixed community of Poles, blacks, and Puerto Ricans. However, like many central neighborhoods, it has two mixed blessings: some sound mansion-like Victorian structures and a good location with good transportation. The blessings are mixed because while the Victorian mansions are nice to look at and the location is good for everybody, this

combination brings on the so-called "urban pioneers." They come to save the mansions and stay to destroy the fabric of the neighborhood, whether they intend to or not (November 30, 1979:56).

For Puerto Ricans, property fires and urban gentrification combined to predict that their days in the Division Steet Area were numbered. A forced dislocation would mean not only the loss of a residential environment but also a disruption in a significant component of their urban life. Barrio residents were fully aware that relocation would mean a fragmentation of routines, of relationships, and of expectations; that it would imply an alteration in the world of physically available objects and spatially oriented action. This is implicit in the strong, positive attachments to this area expressed by those who lost their homes to fires:

> My roots are in this community. I lived here for twenty years; I never lived in any other area of the city. I know the reputation of el barrio, but I tell you, only the fires was the only way to get me out of it. The hope of my family is to find another apartment nearby — all of our family and friends are here. We don't want to go anywhere else ("Los Fuegos Siguen," *Prensa Libre*, June 22, 1975:1).

> The fires finally did it. It happened to our friends and now to us. We are really going to have a difficult time establishing an environment similar to this one. I have been part of Division Street for as long as I can remember. Now we have to start all over again (*"El Barrio se Quema,"* *El Puertorriqueño*, June 27, 1975:2).

As these various statements clearly reflect, relocation was certain to undermine the established interpersonal relationships and group ties of the people involved and, in effect, destroy the sense of group identity of a great many individuals. Common to the various patterns of group identity operative in el barrio (i.e., belonging to organizations or interpersonal networks with which a person is directly involved; membership in social groups, as a group of people sharing a common ideology) is an integrated sense of shared human qualities, of some communality with other people which is essential for meaningful social functioning. And, as suggested in chapter two, the Division Street Area represented an important physical space and the locus for meaningful interpersonal ties. It was this sense of belonging to this community, to a particular place which was quite familiar and easily delineated, to an area which the residents considered "home," which influenced Puerto Rican residents to become actively involved in efforts to prevent the tide of housing destruction in their community and the possible development of the area into a middle-class community. The political and social problems involved in relocating Puerto Rican families from the Division Street Area were sufficiently formidable to make opposition to the perceived development very powerful.

Puerto Ricans displayed a deep sense of obligation toward their community. "We can't keep running from place to place all over the city," Miguel Del Valle, then director of the Barreto Boys Club, told two correspondents for *The Chicago Reporter* (Feb. 1979:1). He also added: "We know we have problems, but we are committed to this community, to staying here and holding on to what is left." This deep sense of obligation led those local residents who possessed a propensity for looking at and making policy for the community "as a whole" and who had a high sense of personal efficacy, a long-time perspective, a general familiarity and confidence in the community to participate with other not-so-active members in efforts to halt the trend.

Dramatic actions taken by local residents escalated during the summer of 1976. In particular, a coalition of thirty-three community organizations was formed to force the city to "do something" about the problem of fires. The office of the mayor and that of the alderman of the 31st ward were constant targets of protests and demonstrations as community residents demanded that these politicians assume the responsibility for ending the fires in the Division Street Area. On July 21, 1976 at a meeting attended by 500 community residents at St. Mark's Church, the crowd refused to discuss their concerns with a city official sent by Mayor Daley to represent him. A few days later, residents of the Division Street Area held a four-hour sit-in in the Mayor's office demanding and eventually winning a private meeting with the Mayor. *El Puertorriqueño's* editorial on July 29, 1976 suggested that the Puerto Rican community take a principal role in stopping the fires by forcing city officials to do their jobs:

What is the problem in Chicago's Hispanic barrios? We are being burned alive and no one is saying anything about it. People, you have the word. Another way to control or remedy these problems is for the entire Puerto Rican community to unite and demand from our so-called representatives that they do something so that we can live and sleep in peace. Our community has been burning for three barbarous and long years, particularly in the 31st ward, and yet, we don't even hear the voice of the alderman of this district address this problem. It is time for the Puerto Rican community to begin fighting for its own cause, otherwise, these fires may very well destroy that which belongs to you — protect yourself in light of the fact that no one wants to protect you.

The city decided to approach the problem of fires in the Division Street Area by the usual professional ritual of calling for the holding of local public hearings to explore different propositions as a way to arrive at an overall solution. For several weeks, local residents participated in the hearings with the largest held in the auditorium of the Roberto Clemente High School on August 5, 1976 when more than 800 persons were in attendance.

The public hearings stimulated public awareness of the necessity and practicality of change and gave people confidence that something could be done to save their neighborhood. Second, the hearings managed to create a climate of opinion in which the actual planning for the area was done. Although it is impossible to tell exactly what impact this climate had on city officials, it is likely that the general mood of the community as articulated by the neighborhood organizations influenced at least the most immediate actions to remedy the situation.

Following the various public hearings, representatives of the 33 community organizations met with city officials on September 1, 1976 to discuss a "plan of action" to prevent fires in the Division Street Area. The *Chicago Sun-Times* reported that "the meeting was called to co-ordinate efforts of community groups and the Special Arson Task Force, formed by the city to combat a wave of arson, especially on the Northwest Side, including a July 17 fire at 2313 W. Thomas that killed five children and two adults" (Sept. 2, 1976). An ordinance prohibiting persons from entering vacant or abandoned buildings was proposed at the meeting. Members of the various organizations agreed to put "no trespassing" signs on vacant or abandoned buildings. They also volunteered to distribute posters and bumper stickers bearing the city's arson "hot line" numbers as well as arson prevention instruction in schools and taking school children to see arson trials in progress as a warning.

Most importantly, a special arson investigation team was made up of police and fire officials and representatives of the criminal justice division and the Department of Human Resources. This task force was assigned to patrol the community each night to investigate vacant buildings and fires of suspicious origins.

As the fires began to decline in late 1976, residents of the community countered gentrification with a different type of revitalization: incumbent upgrading. The major feature of this process was physical improvement by incumbent residents at a substantial rate with no significant change in the socioeconomic status or characteristics of the population. The working-class ambience of the neighborhood was not to be changed, and the physical investments would reflect greater confidence on the part of owner-investors in the neighborhood.

Leading members of the community pressed city officials to provide special funds to remedy specific neighborhood housing problems. The Westtown Concerned Citizens Coalition, a community organization established in 1976 in the Division Street Area with the purpose of helping with its uplifting and betterment, received, initially, a small grant from the Community Development Block Grant to help organize the neighborhood to discuss renewal plans calling for rehabilitation, spot clearance, and the construction of lower-income housing. In turn, the leadership of the Westtown Concerned Citizens Coalition established a separate entity primarily for this purpose. The new group was named Community Housing Education Corporation (CHEC) and its primary function was to bring to an end the ever-increasing problem of housing deterioration by rehabilitating apartment buildings, which later would be sold or rented to low and moderate income families.

The programs of CHEC were filled with many controversies and problems; internal fighting between the organization's leadership and members of its board of directors, misuse of funds, poor planning of programs, and the like. There are some critics who argued that CHEC's programs accomplished very little for a community so desperately in need of housing rehabilitation and improvement (e.g., Cruz and Neff, 1983). Yet, the efforts of this newly created organization contributed significantly in discouraging the fires as well as gentrification in the Division Street Area.

Participation in these various community activities of the 1970s contributed significantly to maintaining Puerto Rican ethnic and cultural traditions. Certain aspects of el barrio-building process aroused Puerto Ricans to a high state of ethnic consciousness and behavior, continuing in a modified way the Puerto Rican way of life of the first generation migrants. Part of the Puerto Rican ethnic-conscious behavior crystallized under different conditions into growth of a deeper sense of the type of society desired by this Spanish-speaking population. For example, the demand for integrated education was replaced by a concern for bilingual education which would reflect the cultural heritage of the community. The implication of this and other similar demands is immense. They call for nothing less than adopting a new rationale for social organization in the continuous desire to create a society based on the Puerto Rican ethnic and cultural foundations.

6

Conclusion

The growth process of the Puerto Rican ethnic consciousness in Chicago with its several modifications in the course of the past four decades came primarily through institutional and ideological expressions regarding local community concerns. The community organization became, and continues to represent, the foremost institution in the developing Puerto Rican barrio. The Puerto Rican newcomers built a network of community organizations and agencies, social clubs, and newspapers which brought about a "we-feeling" or consciousness of ethnic solidarity and community. This form of group affinity absorbed many internal conflicts and developed ethnic leadership and an institutional network which the established American social system had to take into account. As Puerto Ricans built these institutions they endeavored to fit them into the American social landscape. This dual process—the struggle to maintain ethnic integrity and to achieve social recognition and equality—describes Puerto Rican life in Illinois' largest metropolis.

In the course of the first four decades of Puerto Rican life in Chicago, several major forces shaped the urban experience of this Spanish-speaking population. For over half a century before the arrival of thousands of Puerto Ricans in Chicago, racial lines were being more tightly drawn against blacks and later against Mexicans. With the large and rapid increase in the Puerto Rican population in the 1940s and 1950s, these newcomers also were subjected to the vicissitudes of American racism. Since arriving from the Island, Puerto Ricans in Chicago have lived in the constant shadow of racial discrimination.

Economic and social changes wrought by industrial expansion

and technological development after World War II made the migrant life of Puerto Ricans very different from that of other earlier immigrant groups. The economic expansion of the late nineteeth and early twentieth centuries with its need for an abundant supply of cheap, unskilled labor had provided the most obvious channel of upward mobility for European newcomers. By the time of the mass migration from the Island, industrial and technological growth and expansion had reduced the importance of these jobs in Chicago and other older cities of the Midwest and Northeast. As these metropolitan areas became America's centers of finance, trade, and service, Puerto Ricans and other populations were left to depend on marginal occupations—dead-end jobs in the declining blue-collar sector. Lacking options, Puerto Rican workers accepted whatever terms they were offered. As a class of "useless or underutilized workers," Puerto Rican migrants and their children have been increasingly irrelevant to the burgeoning economic order of post-World War II urban America.[1]

Economic and technological developments since World War II eliminated precisely those positions which Puerto Ricans might have utilized as leverage for subsequent mobility. Without these jobs, they could not even hope to climb the class ladder. Puerto Ricans had little chance of moving themselves from the lower class since employment in these occupations constitutes the barest minimum necessary for ethnic betterment and mobility.

In terms of politics, the Puerto Rican community was marginally linked to the city's political organization. For the first three decades, clientele politics represented the only connection between Chicago's political organization and the Puerto Rican community. The deprivation imposed by the white-controlled democratic machine upon Puerto Ricans jeopardized the latter's capacity for political adaptation to life in the city.

Reflecting on the economic and socio-political developments encountered by Puerto Ricans in Chicago, one must be impressed by their sheer drive to survive and build their own institutional community life. Puerto Ricans in Chicago are not losers. Despite the absence of meaningful occupational oppportunities and exclusion from traditional electoral politics, Puerto Ricans learned to create, to innovate, cultural and ethnic symbols and other forms of solidarity and cleavage in their extraordinarily difficult pursuit of self-determination and equality in a strange and otherwise hostile social environment. Puerto Ricans created an infrastructure from which the Puerto Rican community was established and has existed to the present. This infrastructure has been responsible for ensuring that changes going around them are directed to the good of the community or are halted if they appear to threaten the well-being of barrio residents. The evidence presented in this book indicates that Puerto Ricans in Chicago worked actively and positively to create a viable social and cultural life of their own—indeed, the institutional barrio stands as the creation of Puerto Rican leaders and entrepreneurs determined to make the Puerto Rican community a respectable and decent place to live.

Within the broad set of institutional practices and constraints imposed upon them since the early days of the migration period, the Puerto Ricans have written their own history and shaped their urban life. This is not to suggest that Puerto Ricans have asserted the glory of the human spirit to emerge victorious against all odds— they are far too practical and have been too preoccupied with survival to rely on such unproductive sentiment. Instead they have tapped their own resources as well as those external to the group by overcoming social constraints through the imaginative use of their skills and their intelligence. They have had to be flexible and adaptable in the face of American racism and discrimination. Through the employment of a collective conscience, Puerto Ricans have rarely prospered, but they have always survived.

In keeping with the preceding discussion, I would like to present the argument that the various manifestations of Puerto Rican politics of the 1960s and 1970s have been evidence of highly integrated and socially organized behavior. They do not represent alignments of "atomized" and "pathological" people but rather socially organized and politically aware people who have introduced a variety of new and original political tactics. A great deal of the literature on the process of Puerto Rican community formation in New York City (e.g., Glazer and Moynihan, 1970) distorts the picture by giving far too much emphasis to the impersonal and disorganizing aspects of the movement of rural *jibaros* (peasants) to the northeastern industrialized urban milieu. There are other features of this process that are equally deserving of attention and have contributed to social and politial organization and even to the eventual outbreak of collective protest. As increasing numbers of Puerto Rican migrants entered the city of Chicago, they congregated in relatively confined neighborhoods in certain communities in the city. Their choices were severely limited by the prevailing discrimination, both individual and institutional, which divided the city into distinctive black and white areas. Thus, geographic residential segregation became one of the most crucial and continuing social facts both for Puerto Rican residents and the areas in which they reside.

The social networks and organizations that emerged in the Puerto Rican community promoted a substantial degree of social cohesion, conventional social pathology theories notwithstanding. Moreover, as a result of the nature of their associations, and as a consequence of the omnipresent discrimination, Chicago's Puerto Ricans have tended to develop common perspectives. This dual base of social cohesion and a common sense of experience of discrimination has provided a potential nexus around which to advance the collective interests of the Puerto Rican community, or significant segments thereof.

Thus the great variety and strength of the Puerto Rican organizations can no longer be denied. They are so strong, visible, and organized that it would seem rather anachronistic to term them as organizational manifestations of atomized and alienated people who manifest social disorganization. Furthermore, the sophistication of political alternatives that the Puerto Rican community now possesses cannot be interpreted as simply reactions to the white society. The common themes of Puerto Rican consciousness and cultural pride are now mainstays in all Puerto Rican organizations. With these themes, generated through the religious base of Los Caballeros, the consciousness-raising of direct action organizations, and the struggles and failures of many civil rights organizations and groups, has come a more visible and more strongly articulate sense of ethnic identity and political organization.

PROSPECTS FOR THE FUTURE

What is the future of the Puerto Rican community in Chicago? Where is it going? What kinds of strategies must it adapt to achieve the wants and needs of its residents? These are some of the leading questions raised by the Puerto Rican leadership of Chicago today.

The fact that Puerto Ricans have made unquestionable gains in all areas since 1950 may lull observers into an unwarranted sense of accomplishment. Many of the gains are satisfying only by comparison with a dismal past. For example, can we expect Puerto Ricans to be very excited about the election of the first Puerto Rican politician to the city council in 1983, or that for the next four years there will be two Puerto Rican elected councilmen or women in City Hall? While elected political representation is an instrument of magnificent power, it hardly fills one's life. The day-to-day problems of inferior jobs, schools, and housing loom very large beside the gains of recent years.

Most of the Puerto Rican leaders today assume that the goal of the Puerto Rican struggle of liberation is full equality and participation in society's major insitutions, and that the means to this end will be found within the broad confines of the existing institutional structures of the larger society. More importantly, the dramatic struggle by Puerto Ricans for self-determination and equality has historically taken a variety of ethnic-related strategies and forms and will doubtlessly manifest itself in other guises in the future. Not the least of these have been ideas summed up by phrases such as "Puerto Rican power" and "Latino Power."

The present and future lifeways of the Puerto Rican community, or any other community, cannot be divorced from the encompassing political economy within which it is embedded and through which it manifests its particular functions and form. The rapid transition that Chicago's economy has undergone and is still experiencing is bound to continue shaping the course of action Puerto Ricans will follow in the remaining years of the 1980s and ensuing decades. Whatever else is done, it is clear that the "Puerto Rican problem" simply cannot be solved unless descent jobs are made available. For the Puerto Rican worker, unemployment, underemployment, and equally important, employment that is demeaning by its very nature all serve to compound the injuries that society has inflicted. Without a job Puerto Rican men and women cannot possibly be socially effective. No amount of economic relief can offset the social destruction of chronic unemployment in an industrial society.

The painful fact is that the city's economy continues to lose blue-collar manufacturing jobs to suburban areas, to other regions in the country, and to countries outside the United States. Moreover, manufacturing jobs continue under the threat of automation or obsolescence. Under these circumstances, it is inevitable that Puerto Rican organizations should use their power to try to increase job opportunities for Puerto Ricans *qua* Puerto Ricans. Indeed, Puerto Ricans should no longer be content with equal opportunity, the hallmark of the civil rights movement over the years. It's time to recognize that equality of opportunity provides "even access" in a social context that is basically "unequal." Under the rules of this game, Puerto Rican individuals start with a severe handicap, and will not be able to catch up under prevailing circumstances if they are merely given "improved chances." The accumulated disadvantages in economic resources, educational attainment, and political power conspire to freeze conditions of inequality.

Instead of equal opportunity, Puerto Ricans must demand a "positive discrimination" in their favor. They should want their investments in the city's economy, for example, to be reinvested in their community in the form of job development. They need to insist that industries and business firms create jobs for Puerto Rican workers. Further, they should demand intensive recruiting in the Puerto Rican community for qualified personnel, crash training and upgrading programs, and the allocation of given numbers of positions to be filled by qualified Puerto Rican members when they can be recruited or trained. This arrangement may entail a certain degree of favoritism, but the point to stress is that historical oppression and inequality can only be corrected by such means—this is not an end but rather a beginning by which Puerto Rican inequalities in the city can be corrected.

The job situation in Chicago is so depressing that Puerto Ricans are increasingly accepting the idea that their chances of penetrating the city's corporate service economy are very slim. They doubt the efficacy of corporate or entrepreneurial involvement as an avenue of mobility or that corporate employment will result in anything more than a symbolic number of Puerto Rican executives. They are turning more and more to the political arena as an agent of social change as well as a source of employment. The popular enthusiasm in the Puerto Rican community that attended the election of Miguel Santiago as alderman of the 31st ward in 1983 as the first Puerto

Rican to be elected to the city council, as well as the reapportionment victory, gave considerable heart to those who see the electoral process as the surest means of ethnic betterment.

However, the Puerto Rican bid for political power may be taking place at a time when the payoffs are being drastically reduced. For example, the traditional revenue source for the city government, the property tax, has been inadequate for some time. It has become almost a cliché to observe that this has gone hand in hand with an urban population whose claims on public services have increased dramatically. The relative decline in the property tax base as industry and the more affluent leave the city seems likely to continue at an even more rapid rate. Industry is following (sometimes leading) whites to the suburbs.

At present Chicago's municipal government structure is under the direction of Harold Washington, the first black ever to be elected mayor of this midwest metropolis. Mayor Washington, unlike his predecessors, has opened the door to City Hall for the city's Spanish-speaking population, having appointed a large number of Spanish-speaking individuals to his administration, including a Puerto Rican as Vice-Mayor. The Mayor continues to aggressively seek the support of Puerto Ricans and other Spanish-speaking groups. In spite of Mayor Washington's "good intentions," the political system has gone through a major transformation which may very well prevent large numbers of Puerto Ricans from making real gains. In the era of the "big city machine," Mayor Daley maintained the allegiance of diverse groups by distributing public goods in the form of private favors. Today public goods are distributed through the "service bureaucracy": and the process of dispensing public goods has become more formalized, the struggles between groups more public, and the language of city politics more professional. This changing style of urban politics has made concessions a very treacherous matter. The Mayor has found it hard to finesse even his black constituents, let alone his Spanish-speaking supporters, as the jobs, services, and contracts which fueled the Democratic political organization in the past are no longer dispensed covertly in the form of private favors but rather as matters of public policy. As a result, each concession is destined to become a subject of open political conflict.

Another development in city politics which is bound to limit Puerto Rican access to traditional politically related employment opportunities comes in the form of the establishment of large associations of public employees, teachers, policemen, firemen, sanitation workers, and the like. These groups have become numerous, organized, and independent enough to wield substantial control over most matters affecting their jobs and their agencies, i.e., entrance requirements, tenure guarantees, working conditions, job prerogatives, promotion criteria, retirement benefits. The city's "new" political organization has very little control over jobs which might have been given as concessions to Puerto Ricans and other political constituents.

Puerto Ricans are maneuvering themselves into Chicago's political life several generations after ethnic claims on sectors of municipal employment have become firmly established, with white ethnics dominating the police and fire departments, sanitation, education, and the park district. At present, blacks are aggressively challenging the white ethnics' hegemony over these government economic sectors. By the time this kind of Puerto Rican political consciousness is being realized, the only sector of municipal life left to monopolize is welfare—as recipients.

At present, it may be of little more than a psychological benefit to Puerto Ricans to have two of their own in the City Council. However, it is important that we do not discount completely benefits which may acrue as Puerto Ricans continue to elect their ethnic political representatives. Tangible service and status rewards seem more probable. Certain welfare services may be more humanized. Curriculum and other educational changes in the schools may offer some hope to Puerto Rican youngsters, even if educational budgets are tightened and more is spent on white suburban children. Again, the psychological value of having Puerto Ricans in authority positions may improve the self-images of many Puerto Ricans. These would be limited but real achievements. They would not fundamentally alter the life chances of Puerto Ricans, for that is simply not within the control of any municipal government. The years ahead are bound to be harsh and painful. It would be naive to pretend that any set of policies adopted by government or business can bring a cure to the Puerto Rican case in the next few years.

Puerto Ricans and other Spanish-speaking ethnics may not be able to achieve their wants and needs alone, and, like in most movements for social change, their future may very well depend on whether the contradictions of this society can be resolved by a coalition of progressive forces. In addition to the two ethnic dimensions adopted by Puerto Ricans (e.g., Puerto Rican and Latino ethnic ties), a more recent development should be noted. Efforts among Puerto Ricans and other Spanish-speaking groups to eliminate barriers to equality are beginning to lead to a merger with the aspirations of black Americans — historically the most exploited population in America.

The role of a Latino/black coalition in the reorganization of American political life is programmatic as well as strategic. The Puerto Rican and other Spanish-speaking communities in the city are challenged now to broaden their social vision, to develop functional programs with concrete objectives. The need is to propose an actual mobilized "minority" to call for public works and training, for local economic planning, for federal and state aid to education, for attractive low-income housing — all this on a sufficiently massive scale to make a difference. The major goal of a Latino/black coalition would be to enlarge the responsibility of federal, state, and local governments in the promotion of full employment, adequate housing, quality education, and equal opportunity.

The increasingly obvious confluences of class and race/ethnicity may set the spark and ignite this new movement, but there is little chance of such a movement effecting progressive social change without a profound alteration of views shared by each population. It may be well argued that a Latino/black coalition will force Spanish-speaking groups to surrender their political independence to the black political agenda — that they will be neutralized, deprived of their cutting edge, and absorbed into the Establishment. For Puerto Ricans and other Spanish-speaking ethnics for whom ingroup solidarity and self-determination are central objectives, this can be a vital forfeit. Thus, it is of great importance that the process which led to the establishment of a "Latino ethnic-conscious movement or agenda" be considered as one possible model to be used when constructing a Latino/black alternative to conditions in Chicago. Thus, several preconditions must be met before mobilization can occur: (1) mutual recognition of cultural/ethnic differences and respective self-interests, (2) attention to specific identifiable goals and proportional distribution of gains attained, and (3) the continuing existence of independent power bases within the units of the coalition. In other words, the trick in shaping a Latino/black coalition would be emphasizing those issues on which there is agreement and reasonable expectations of mutual benefit, while understanding, recognizing, and playing down divisive matters. The real hope is an imaginative politics based on a people connected to their sources; otherwise we are simply doomed to perpetuate a system that is in a permanent state of ethnic war.

The continuous and explicit communal-based, organized movements established by Puerto Ricans in their quest to achieve equality (whether in the form of Puerto Rican ethnic consciousness or Latino identity or hopefully the Latino/black coalition just described) can not overshadow the mass of despair found in the lives of so many Puerto Rican individuals today. A large number of people in the Puerto Rican community are increasingly losing hope. Every passing day, more and more Puerto Ricans are recognizing that they are, indeed, a colonized and conquered people. More and more are accepting the fact that they can not create a separate world of their own. The idea of developing an alternative economic structure also seems less likely today than four decades ago when the Puerto Rican presence in the city was just beginning. The idea of returning to Puerto Rico for second- and third-generation Puerto Ricans is another unrealistic alternative.

As a result, a large number of Puerto Ricans are resigning themselves to "economic assimilation." During an age of individual achievement and mobility, when an economic system based on individual competition is contributing to a social system based on relative income and status, Puerto Ricans desire economic success just like everyone else. But unlike everyone else, Puerto Ricans, especially high school- and college-age young people, wish to do it on their own ethnic/cultural terms. They seem to want to strike a deal with society: "We are willing to learn computer skills, we are willing to receive a college education whenever possible, etc., but we want to be able to be all of that and still retain pride in our traditional identity and cultural background."

This is not to be confused with reaching up to kiss the whip that lashes them. This view of the present and future society reflects the competitive character of the life of the poor as well as its cooperative spirit. The masses of Puerto Rican youth in Chicago, New York, and elsewhere are convinced that their present and future society must be built on and around the traditional Puerto Rican culture (or at least some of its elements). Despite the forces of American assimilation in both Puerto Rico and mainland cities of Puerto Rican settlement their cultural way of life has managed and will continue to survive.

Puerto Ricans are very conscious of the costs to be paid for social and cultural assimilation in a society where they continue to be victims of racial discrimination. They appear to be acutely aware of the inequalities operative in a system they perceive to be racist in nature—a society where the life chances of individuals are determined by their racial background. Puerto Ricans are very aware of gains made by European ethnics after assimilation, but they are just as much aware of how blacks, Mexicans, and other non-white groupings have come up against the reality of racism—invoked by law in the early years of contact and continuing to the present in both institutional and interpersonal relations.

Thus, the idea that Puerto Ricans, being inferior and despairing, have adopted a cooperative spirit, signaling their acceptance of present day American competitive doctrine, is belied by their enduring desire for the expression and survival of Puerto Rican ethnic/cultural determination. The salience of Puerto Rican ethnicity provides a very specific form of identity which enhances their sense of well-being, feelings of self-esteem, and efficacy, rather than self-blame and powerlessness. The increasing manifestation of ethnic-related behavior among the Puerto Rican youth and the emerging middle class is sparked by many different forms of cultural expressions. For some the Spanish language has become fused with English forming a distinctive "Spanglish" idiom and for others who do not speak Spanish at all, this language has come to be a particular cultural symbol. The graffiti art seen on the walls of barrio buildings displays the emergence and expression of a particular ingenious art under the most depressing of conditions. Puerto Rican art, theater, and literature are incredible accomplishments on the part of a population which, according to latest reports, has the highest drop-out rate (in excess of 70 percent) among high school students (e.g., Kyle, 1984). The love and respect among all the members of the family and a belief that there are other things in life is preferred over what is seen as a cold and calculating attempt by members of the larger American society to increase material wealth regardless of the consequences. All of these cultural forms have combined to preserve the Puerto Rican cultural tradition.

The leading expression of cultural determination among Puerto Ricans and several other Spanish-speaking groups, however, is music—in particular, a musical form called Salsa. (Roughly translated "Salsa" means "spice," literally it means "sauce.") Salsa music is an international artistic movement, mainly Puerto Rican, which came into the limelight in New York in the 1970s (Roberts, 1979).[2] Puerto Ricans, Cubans, Dominicans, Panamanians, Venezuelans, and others have come to make Salsa music part of their cultural heritage.

The musical or artistic component of the Puerto Rican culture is significant in several ways. First, it is one area in the Puerto Rican life that has not been stripped away or obliterated by American colonialism—these cultural traditions have an indisputable Puerto Rican and Latin American foundation. Unlike the European immigrant cultural traditions which were either diluted or dissolved almost completely in the American context, this important cultural legacy linking Puerto Ricans in the United States to their past heritage or homeland has not only survived but has thrived on adversity and grown stronger through the years. The musicians (and for that matter, artists and writers) are the ablest representatives of this long cultural tradition. These individuals can be said to be identity experts, cultural heroes, who are masters of sound, moment, timing, the spoken word, and the visual world. One can therefore find in their music, art, and stories the essentials and defining features—the very core in fact—of the Puerto Rican culture as a whole.

The variety of Salsa music songs is very wide. There are love songs, songs about music, unhappy love songs, nonsense songs, and others. There is, too, an ever increasing category which I will term political—that is, songs involving people in a powerful shared experience and thereby making them more aware of themselves and their responsibilities toward each other. In this way, Salsa music represents more than an art for passive enjoyment or an eminently danceable music, attuning the listeners to pure pleasure. Instead, Salsa music has come to represent a significant aspect of social reality and is an important means for the "information consciousness"— it is, as it were, a form of the "cognition of reality."

The productions of Salsa music groups and individual performers, such as El Gran Combo de Puerto Rico, Ruben Blades, Willie Colon, Ismael Miranda, Hector Lavoe, Celia Cruz, La Sonora Poncena, Ray Barreto, and others, like those of the protest singers of *La Nueva Canción* (the New Song) found in Puerto Rico and throughout Latin America, aim not only to raise the political consciousness of whole masses of people but they serve as interpreters or bridges to a way of life beyond the present circumstances commonly shared by many Spanish-speaking people in the United States. Above all, Salsa music performers seem to be in agreement that the untiring desire for social equality in the United States among Puerto Ricans and other Spanish-speaking groups should not negate the need to defend the originality of their way of life and the dignity of their culture.

In a series of recordings, Ruben Blades, a Panamanian lawyer-singer-composer who is fast becoming the personification of political Salsa music as well as the industry's most visible performer to the American public,[3] provides excellent examples of both the despair operative in el barrio and the increasing desire to make it in American society while retaining and expressing pride in the Spanish-speaking groups' cultural traditions. The message Ruben Blades conveys in "Buscando América," (In Search of America), is to the point. Though he sees America filled with ugly darkness and injustices, Ruben Blades shows an incredible patience and faith in the prospects for Spanish-speaking integration in the larger society. He is convinced that this integration will be realized only after Spanish-speaking people lend a hand in the liberation of America from "darkness" and unjust treatment of particular groups and individuals:

> Te han secuestrado, América, y amordazado tu boca
> y a nosotros nos toca ponerte en libertad
> Te estoy llamando, América, nuestra futuro espera
> Y antes que se nos muera, te vamos a encontrar.

> They have kidnapped you, America, and have gagged your
>   mouth.
> And it's up to us to set you free,
> I'm calling you, America, our culture awaits you
> And we will find you before it dies.
> (Blades, 1983)

In "Siembra," which in English means "to plant the seeds," (Blades, 1978) the cultural quality of the Spanish-speaking is once again highlighted. In this song, Ruben Blades assigns to the culture of the Spanish-speaking groups the highest degree of excellence. To be sure, he says, the future life of Spanish-speaking individuals in the United States must include participation in the life of that society; however, in planting the seeds for that future life it's necessary that the seeds of the Spanish-speaking culture—"the seeds of freedom, of faith, and of humility"—shine above all others.

But it is in the song "Plástico" (Plastic), recorded with Willie Colon, one of the most renowned Puerto Rican Salsa musicians in New York, that Ruben Blades' message pertaining to the future society of Spanish-speaking groups in the United States is the sharpest. The title of the song refers directly and negatively to an American society very different from the way of life of people whose roots are found in Latin America. The American society is shown as overwhelmingly polluted by people with false smiles (*falso reir, de gente de rostros de polyester*), lust for material possessions (*pensando siempre en dinero, donde en vez de un sol, amanece un dolar*), living in a world of illusion (*viviendo en un mundo de pura ilusión*), racist (*diciendole a su hijo de cinco años, no juegues con niños de color extraño*). These are the main elements of the American society that Spanish-speaking individuals must try to avoid. The cultural guidelines prescribed by Ruben Blades for this future world are well captured in the following stanza:

> Oye, Latino, oye hermano, oye amigo, nunca vendas tu destino por el oro, ni la comodidad;
> aprende, estudia, pues nos falta andar bastante, marcha siempre hacia adelante
> para juntos acabar
> con la ignorancia que nos trae sugestionados, con modelos importados que no son la solución.
> No te dejes confundir, busca el fondo y su razón,
> recuerda, se ven las caras, y jamás el corazón.

> Listen my Latino brother, my Latino friend, never sell your future for gold nor for comfort;
> learn, study, we still have quite a bit to walk yet, always

march to the front
to finish together
the ignorance that we are often suggested in addition to
imported models are not the solution.
Do not allow them to confuse you, look deep to the very
bottom for reasoning,
and remember, you may see their faces, but you'll never see
their hearts.
(Blades, 1978)

El Gran Combo de Puerto Rico, the Island's leading group for
over 30 years and which consistently has sung about the need to
preserve the culture and dignity of Puerto Rico, is another example of a Salsa group that emphasizes the importance of fighting to
make it. In "Prosigue" (Carry On), recorded in 1985, the struggle
leading toward a better future society, in spite of many constraints,
is clearly delineated:

Camina y camina sin hallar el rumbo
No encuentra en el mundo quien le dé la mano
El que dijo ser su hermano se vino y le dió la espalda
La soledad lo acompaña; ella vive su destino.

Prosigue
Parar sería ceder
y eso si no puede ser,
El que no anda no llega.
Si es condena lo que te toca vivir
tendrás que un día cumplir
Se romperán las cadenas

Hay que prosegir
El que no anda no llega

He walks and walks without finding direction
He doesn't have anyone in the world who will give him a hand
The one who said he was his brother came and turned his back
    on him
Loneliness accompanies him—she is his destiny.

Carry on,
to stop would be to give up

and that can't happen.
He who doesn't walk doesn't arrive
If what you're living is a prison sentence
one day you'll finish your term

You have to carry on
He who doesn't walk doesn't arrive.
(El Gran Combo, 1985)

Ray Barreto, a second-generation Puerto Rican band leader from New York, is another Salsa music performer who is well aware of his heritage and the intricate strategies developed by Puerto Ricans in an effort to cope with America. In his "Fuerza Gigante," (Giant Strength), we are reminded of Spanish-speaking people who have come together to create a wide base of great strength, and who are proud of belonging to *una raza de fuerza y valor* (a race of strength and courage), and who have continuously fought to retain their cultural heritage. Not only does the song strongly encourage Spanish-speaking people to follow the footsteps of this struggle, it also defines the struggle of the future as necessitating the use of one's intellectual, academic strength: "*Yo te lo dije, mi hermano, que te pongas a estudiar. Usa bien la cabeza, no te me quedes atrás.*" (I've told you, my brother, to study. Use your head well, do not stay behind) (Barreto, 1980).

The lyrics of these and many other Salsa music songs constitute a cultural refuge capable of protecting the personalities and self-worth of Puerto Ricans and other Spanish-speaking groups in a society which historically has repressed and rejected their cultural lifestyles. Through Salsa music, Puerto Ricans are seeking their own forms of cultural expression and identity as opposed to those imposed by the wider American society and demonstrating their resistance to American cultural assimilation. Despite so much despair, they have not given up their will to struggle against those structures and practices increasingly used to destroy their cultural identity and maintain them in the condition of exploited people or "lost souls." This musical form serves as further evidence that Puerto Ricans continue to reject the notion that they must subjugate their cultural tradition in order to rise within American society. Instead, they continue to present the American society with the alternative to accept them as equals.

The rejection of cultural assimilation is based on several grounds. In addition to the devastating effect of racism, there exists a strong belief in the value of the Puerto Rican culture and a desire to see it develop according to its internal logic. There is also distaste for cultural homogenization and a regard for human diversity. There is also a feeling that cultural assimilation for most Puerto Ricans would involve the trading of a genuine human culture for a bland, dehumanized, consumer-oriented, made-in-America mass culture. From this perspective, the assimilationist approach in America is not only an expression of cultural imperialism but in effect an instrument of dehumanization.

The foregoing analysis of the cultural content of the Puerto Rican ethnic identity leads, I feel, to some intriguing and fundamental questions concerning the future. Of primary importance is the following concern: Must Puerto Ricans assimilate to succeed, or must the American definition of success be reevaluated? This is not an either/or question that can be answered in simply Puerto Rican/white terms. It's clear that Puerto Ricans, Spanish-speaking groups in general, as well as other oppressed populations in the United States, all have a distinct culture to guard and protect. The crucial retention of Puerto Rican traditions, the history of oppression in the United States, and America's refusal to allow equal participation in its major institutions and structures—all have combined to give Puerto Ricans a different reality and have promoted the continuous growth of a different culture with which to master that reality.

Thus, a Puerto Rican ethnic/cultural tradition exists and will continue to exist—its existence ought to be recognized by all concerned, no matter what their policy or proposed solution to the American racial dilemma. The failure to recognize this culture and a reluctance to work with and within it accounts in large measure for the failures of the "warriors of poverty" who have not been able to reach the barrio majority, much less effect any basic changes in its way of life.

The special musical and artistic base of the Puerto Rican culture wherein Puerto Ricans have proved and preserved their humanity in the face of American colonialism cannot continue to be a neglected area in social science research concerning the Puerto Rican experience. This domain or sphere of interest may be broadly defined as "entertainment" from the public point of view but as "ritual" from the Puerto Rican or theoretical standpoint. Certain Puerto Rican cultural expressions such as art, music, and literature have an added and conscious ritual significance for Puerto Ricans. They help to reveal the intrinsic cultural ideals and lifeways of the Puerto Rican. An analysis of the situation of Puerto Ricans in America today, if it is to be thorough and constructive, must take the group's culture base into account.

If the American potential for a productive and meaningful cultural pluralism is to be realized, Puerto Ricans must continue to identify themselves in ethnic/cultural terms. They must struggle with their past and accept it—all of it; they must honor their heroes and prophets, past and present; they must define with greater care who they are now and what they want their children to become; they must consciously decide what they will continue to accept from the American tradition and what they will reject.

Notes

INTRODUCTION

1. Similarly, in the summer of 1980, *The Futurist* suggested that the "northward migration of Hispanics [was] changing the culture of the United States, which may be the hemisphere's third-largest Spanish-speaking nation by the end of the 1980s" (1980:1).

2. The only exception here may be Suttles' brief description of Puerto Rican youths (gang members) in the Near West Side (1968). Padilla (1947) also provides another short account of the lives of a small number of Puerto Rican migrants who arrived in the city in 1946.

3. First-generation respondents represent the large majority of Puerto Ricans who came to live in Chicago during the late 1940s and early 1950s. In terms of age, most of these early migrants are now in their 50s and 60s, in comparison to the second-generation Puerto Rican residents of the city (referred to in this study as second-generation respondents) whose median age is early to mid-30s.

4. As used in this study, Puerto Rican ethnic consciousness will follow Professor Jim Pitts' definition of race consciousness and will mean "behavior and attitudes oriented either to preserving or overcoming a system of racial stratification" (1982:141). I will also follow Ossowski's use of "social consciousness" to refer to concepts, images, beliefs, and evaluations that characterize certain millieus that are more or less common to people of a certain social environment, and that are reinforced in the consciousness of particular individuals by mutual suggestion and by the conviction that they are shared by other people in the same group (1963:6). The idea underlying the concept of Puerto Rican ethnic consciousness can not be confused with what has often been described as a search for identity. I'm convinced Puerto Ricans know their identity perfectly well. Rather they are constantly attacking the social definitions which

prevail in American society, and which rationalize their economic and political deprivation.

5. As will be shown in chapter one, during the 400 year history of colonization under the Spanish regime, Puerto Ricans had valued a minifundio or small farm tenure pattern of land use based on subsistence and local exchange of surplus farm products. The combined impact of San Ciriaco (the Island's worst hurricane which hit during the U.S. military occupation in 1899) and the arrival of carpetbaggers and big plantation growers from the U.S. meant the loss of land for the vast majority of Puerto Ricans. This changed their status from independent farm owners to hired farmhands in a system that resembled share-cropping and semi-indentured labor in the rural South following Reconstruction (1865–1877). So, as blacks became an internally colonized people marked by a system of exploitation that made it almost impossible to succeed except by migration to the city, so, too, did the Puerto Rican common people find that they had to work the soil for the conquerors on the conqueror's terms.

6. In 1985 one Puerto Rican had been elected to the city council and, after many years of community activism, a Puerto Rican was finally named principal of a barrio high school.

7. There are several similar examples to this approach. For instance, Bell (1975:158–159) claims that people choose a level of ethnic consciousness "in relation to an adversary." Referring to shifting levels of ethnicity, Van den Berghe (1971:512) has called attention to the propensity of people to activate the level most favorable to themselves. The result is a "continuous process of fission and fusion . . . with ever shifting patterns of alliance between groups and subgroups."

8. A similar case is presented by Warner and Srole (1945) in their detailed description of the process of ethnic succession, defined by the authors as a process through which "the workers of the newly arrived groups started at the very bottom of the occupational hierarchy and through the generations climbed out of it and moved to jobs with higher pay and increased prestige. Each new ethnic group tended to repeat the occupational history of the preceding ones" (1945:63). From this point of view, Warner and Srole concluded that the ethnics moved into "occupations abandoned by middle-class natives." The natives did not leave "because the ethnics with their lower wage demands had forced them out [rather] ethnics replaced natives" (1945:65).

Another familiar example is the labor migration of blacks in the 1930s and 1940s. In the depression years, northerly migration of southern blacks slowed to a trickle. There were few jobs in the depressed North, and every opening had numerous white claimants. But in 1942 war production produced a labor shortage. Whites grabbed the best jobs. Blacks then moved northward in great numbers to fill lower ranking vacant positions—and the newcomers encountered no opposition (Thernstrom, 1973: 195; Handlin, 1959:48–49).

9. The mechanisms of exclusion/retardation are basically ones Bonacich (1972 and 1976) describes in her victory-for-expensive labor theory in a split labor market. When this victory is total (and it hardly ever is) high-priced, old-ethnic labor is totally successful in its self-interested effort to forestall and frustrate an invasion of their industries or occupations by newcomers. The exclusionary mechanisms include, first of all, political exclusion of the newcomers from the territory, and therefore, from the labor market. When territorial exclusion fails, exclusion from the labor market is attempted, and often with protective barriers to prevent penetration of high-wage sectors already occupied by old-ethnic labor. Devices to assure labor market exclusion include: child and woman labor restrictions, mandatory education provisions, minimum wage and working standards legislation, and public welfare programs to care for the unemployed. Welfare makes it possible to survive without working; the other restrictions make working at subsistence wages impossible and unemployment more common. Together the measures create a survival program for the permanently unemployed. Devices to protect high-priced, old-ethnic industries include: caste segregation of occupation and industries, nepostic or racially exclusive hiring practices, educational credentialism, civil service tenure, seniority systems, occupational licensure requirements, and "fair trade" laws. These measures neutralize the chief advantage of newcomer ethnics: a desperate willingness to work long hours for low wages under inferior working conditions. Unable to penetrate these defensive perimeters, newcomers in the labor market cannot displace incumbents in violation of rank sequence. The overall result is a dual labor market in which old-ethnics work in regulated sectors while substandard working conditions, low wages, and laissez-faire prevails in newcomer-dominated industries and occupations (for a similar discussion, see Hechter, 1978).

10. It is important to recognize that most ethnic minorities in the United States have found the internal colonial concept interesting and provocative. This does not mean, however, that the term has the same meaning for each of these groups as their experiences of oppression have been widely varied. Thus, in cases where I lump the groups together this will be for illustrative purposes rather than to suggest commonalities of experiences.

11. The way it will be used in this study, the Puerto Rican struggle of liberation in Chicago does not represent attempts demanding a separate

nation-state as in the case of Quebec, or a desire to return to the homeland. Instead this is a struggle towards community control and establishing cultural pride and self-determination.

1. THE BEGINNINGS OF MARGINALIZATION: THE MIGRATION PERIOD

1. The term "mainland" will be used here to simply designate "stateside."

2. Although seen for the first time in 1492 by Columbus, initial Spanish occupation of the Island did not begin until 1508.

3. Similarly, Crist adds that "because the island Spaniards were blinded by the gold beyond, fertile regions, which, by modern standards, were richly endowed with natural resources, for centuries, were not made to produce enough to pay the expenses of government. The result was that the Philippines, Cuba, and Puerto Rico, and at times even Venezuela, Florida, and Louisiana, were subsidized from the treasury of New Spain [Mexico] in amounts varying from three to four million dollars a year" (1958:180).

4. It is important to note that earlier efforts to turn Puerto Rico into a productive colony were started by the beginning of the nineteenth century. Quintero-Rivera (1974:92–93) makes this point in his discussion of the hacienda plantation in the Island:

In the first two decades of the nineteenth century a large number of Spanish families from the emancipated colonies on the Spanish American mainland arrived in Puerto Rico. So did French families from Louisiana and Haiti. Many of them brought their slaves and working tools (or some agricultural machinery) with them. The Spanish government gave them land and facilities to start cultivation. It did away with a whole set of impediments to trade that had been imposed on the island in favor of traders from Seville and, later, Cadiz. As a result, agricultural production for export increased rapidly.

5. Although *hacienda* will be used here as representing another form of plantation system, it is important to note that scholars make a clear distinction between the two systems. For instance, Mintz (1953:227) writes: "the most important distinction between the family-type *hacienda* and the slave-and-*agregado* plantation which preceded it was its use of free, rather than slave and forced labor."

6. Under the Foraker Act of 1900, "The United States allowed Puerto Rico only token representation in Washington. At the time of the

American invasion the Spanish had appointed the island 16 representatives and three senators in the *Cortes*, the Spanish equivalent to the U.S. Congress. The Foraker Act provided nothing more than a figurehead 'resident commissioner,' elected in Puerto Rico and allowed to speak but not vote in the House of Representatives. . . . The Foraker Act significantly reduced Puerto Rican control over local affairs" (Christopulos, 1974: 125–126).

7. Not surprisingly, American educators undoubtedly believed that the establishment of an American education system in the Island would serve as a panacea for Puerto Rico's problems:

> American officials did little to dispel the image of cultural imperialism. They clearly considered education and Americanization synonymous cures for all of Puerto Rico's ills. Within a few years, the island was flooded with American teachers drilling students in the English language, assigning them work from American textbooks, and instructing them in the values of American business society (Christopulos, 1974:133).

8. Even Puerto Rico's upper classes opposed the introduction of English instruction in the insular education system. "Elitist Puerto Ricans," writes Christopulos, "argued that the United States were trying to destroy essential social distinctions and obliterate Hispanic culture while creating a better investment climate for American corporations" (1974:133).

9. The idea of independence for the Island had been exprressed much earlier in the program of another insular political party. According to Professor Gordon Lewis, "The creation of the Unionist Party on 1904 . . . marked the turning point, for its endorsement in its program of that year of political independence as one feasible status, among others, for the island was the first declaration by a political group that a separatist status could be viewed as a possible solution to the problem" (1963:104).

10. In the 1940 elections, El Partido Popular captured ten of the nineteen Senate seats and shared equally thirty-six of the thirty-nine House seats with another party; the other three were won by the third competing party.

2. GROWTH OF THE PUERTO RICAN BARRIO AND INTENSIFICATION OF ETHNIC SUBORDINATION

1. Similarly, Moor (1976) argues that interracial relations in the Southwest between Mexicans and whites were to a certain extent supported, justified, and determined by the stereotypes whites held about Native Americans, blacks, and Asians.

2. Professor Gordon Lewis' summary interpretation of the Puerto Rican migrants' quest to establish their own community in New York reflects sentiments commonly expressed by respondents of this study: "Only too often the Puerto Rican who regards himself at home as 'white' rapidly discovers to his horror that the American scheme of ethnic identification classifies him as Negro; and his own fatal ambiguity in relation to the color problem receives a new emphasis by the shame and degradation that he experiences" (1963:2).

3. In *Benjy Lopez: A Picaresque Tale of Emigration and Return*, Barry Levine (1980:xviii) makes the point that "once the Puerto Rican migration to New York gained momentum, and the Puerto Rican population in the city became more visible, Anglos reacted by classifying individual Puerto Ricans as members of an undesirable group. The latter's differences in language and life style were taken as proof of both homogeneity and inferiority. . . . Moreover, the Americans did not approve of what they saw. Puerto Ricans, as the newest and poorest group to immigrate to New York, were viewed as intruders in the normal life of the city and were looked down on as people unable to understand what life in New York was supposed to be about."

4. This letter was made available from the archives of Los Caballeros de San Juan, a community organization developed in the mid-1950s to render a wide range of services to Puerto Rican residents of the city of Chicago. A fuller discussion of Los Caballeros appears in chapter five.

5. Tumin makes a similar observation in his discussion of how blacks absorb stereotypes about themselves: "The rise of Black African consciousness in America today, with its deliberate effort to create a belief that 'Black is Beautiful,' must be seen as a reaction to the extent to which American society has managed to make many Blacks ashamed of being Black and of having the other physical traits that identify them, even if only stereotypically" (1969:20).

6. All data for this section were taken from the 1960 Census.

3. ORGANIZATION RESPONSE TO ETHNIC OPPRESSION

1. Gordon's (1977:19) definition of a dual labor market is applicable here:

> In the primary labor market, workers enjoy stable jobs, secure and sheltered incomes, higher wages, and more favorable working conditions. In the secondary labor market, workers are fated to insecure

jobs, lower wages, almost no promotion or training opportunities, the recurrent threat of dismissal, and the prevailing reality of miserable working conditions.

2. "A racial dual market," writes Baron and Hymer (1977:190), "means that there exists a primary metropolitan labor market in which firms recruit white workers and in which white workers look for jobs; side by side with the major market there exists a smaller labor sector in which blacks are recruited and in which blacks look for employment. For each sector there are separate demand and supply forces determining the allocation of jobs to workers and workers to jobs."

3. The role of accessibility in location has to be revised. Business and service institutions are now much less restricted in their economic locational decisions. They can locate part of their operations in the city, another part in the suburbs, and still another part in a different state. The opportunities provided by electronic communications, a well developed transportation system, and other communication techniques now free corporations to split their operations. The city, in other words, continues to represent a very profitable location for owners of firms.

4. Professor Clara Rodríguez reports similar findings for Puerto Ricans in New York during the 1950s. She writes that the arrival of Puerto Ricans after World War II in New York paralleled a decreasing demand for low-skilled jobs, as many were being eliminated by automation, others were protected by unions, and yet others were being moved to suburban areas. Puerto Ricans became concentrated, concludes Professor Rodríguez, "in low-wage work in the service sector as waiters, kitchen help, porters, hospital orderlies, and workers in light manufacturing as sewing machine operators" (1980:40).

5. I'm deeply indebted to Los Caballeros de San Juan for allowing me access to their organization's records and the use of this letter. The correspondence was sent to Father Mahon, then Executive Director of the organization, and signed by R. J. Lechven of Zengeler Cleaners on December 19, 1957.

6. This theme has been the view of Litt in referring to the importance of organizations generally in American politics (1970:42).

7. The following is an example of the emphasis given to religious participation in the Catholic Church. This was a letter sent by Father Mahon to managers or coaches of the various teams sponsored by Los Caballeros instructing them to make their players participate in one particular religious activity:

July 14, 1961
Mr. Manuel González
1305 S. California Avenue
Chicago, Illinois
Dear Manuel:

    I congratulate you on the fine work you have been doing with the young men of your neighborhood. It's very important to give them an opportunity to exercise a chance to associate with other decent men. But, Manuel, we must do more. Many of the ballplayers on your team, and on all the teams, are far from being good Catholics. Many times this condition doesn't result from viciousness but from ignorance, the problems of youth, and inadequate religious background.

    It is not your duty to force them to Mass and the Sacraments. Force is generally the wrong tactic to use. But still, you have a responsibility for their spiritual welfare. The coming retreat will be an excellent opportunity for us to help them. The occasion will be a wonderful weekend in the country with many great guys. While on retreat these young men will have the chance and maybe the courage and grace to straighten themselves out spiritually. However, no one will force them. They will be on their own.

    There is no one in the entire city that I would rather see on the retreat than your peloteros [baseball players]. I ask you, in the name of Christ and His Mother, to do everything in your power to get them all out there. Many years from now when you see these young men leading good lives you can look back proudly and say, "Thank God, I helped him when he needed help the most."

    It goes without saying that you as the manager should make the retreat. I expect you to lead your men on the right road and I can hardly think of a reason that would excuse you from making the retreat.

    Please let me know if there is any way in which I can help you in this matter. Asking God to bless you in your important work, I remain,

                                        Sincerely yours in Crist Rey,
                                        Padre Mahon

    8. I am deeply indebted to Mrs. Regina F. Marin of the University of Puerto Rico at Rio Píedras for producing an additional micro-filmed copy of *El Centinela* in its entirety. This newspaper is part of the univer-

sity library's collection. I am also grateful to Mr. Alfredo Torres de Jesús for letting me use his personal collection of *El Puertorriqueño*. Although this collection was not complete, that is, editions for certain weeks were missing, it served as the major source of data presented in this section. I was informed by one of my respondents that a monthly newspaper by the name of *El Sol* was indeed the first Puerto Rican newspaper in Chicago. I was unable to find copies of *El Sol* or another paper by the name of *La Gaseta*, which is believed to have been among the earliest newspapers published in the community. Not able to locate either paper, this examination does not include a discussion of their content.

4. EVOLUTION AND RESOLUTION OF CONFLICT

1. In their *Ghetto Revolt: The Politics of Violence in American Cities*, Feagin and Hahn, after reviewing several examinations of major rioting in the 1960s, conclude that with only a few exceptions, every major incident of urban violence was triggered by the police. Using a study which focused solely on 14 major ghetto riots for the 1964–1967 period, Feagin and Harlan (1973:145) indicate the resulting distribution of final precipitating events being as follows:

Killings or interference with blacks by policemen	50%
Civil liberties, police facilities, demonstrations	22%
Miscellaneous altercations	14%
Interracial fights	7%

Feagin and Hahn also cite the findings of the often used *Report of the National Advisory Commission on Civil Disorders* to illustrate further the impact caused by police-resident encounters as the precipitating incident for numerous riots in 1967 (1973:146):

	ALL RIOTS (N=24)	MAJOR RIOTS (N=6)	SERIOUS RIOTS (N=10)	MINOR RIOTS (N=8)
Police Action	50%	67%	60%	25%
Black Protest	21%	33%	20%	13%
Previous Disorders in Other Cities	21%	0%	10%	50%
Other	8%	0%	10%	13%

2. This argument derives support from other analyses of urban riots among blacks. Feagin and Hahn (1973:157), as one example, write:

Perhaps most important, police officers represent accessible agents of government that directly link the black public to the highest levels of governmental decision-making. Policemen are the extended arm of the government, and blacks probably have more contact with law enforcement officers than with any other political representatives. For many, therefore, abstract concepts of governance are personified more by the cop in the police car or on the street than by elected leaders.

3. This approach is in line with that of some scholars of civil violence. Arguing that the riots cannot be adequately explained simply as pathology or a symptom of social change, sociologists Kurt and Gladys Lang examined the developmental stages in the dynamics of civil disorders from face-to-face confrontations through epidemic spread of disruptive behavior and the acceptance of violence as a "technique of protest." The Langs focused on riots as a form of collective political protest, the evidence of which they found in the pattern of riots throughout the nation: "However spontaneous the elements that underlie any incident and its particular pattern of expansion, the riots reflect at the same time the stirrings of a major social political movement" (1968:126). The resort to violence, they feel, is indicative of social, and not individual, pathology.

4. In 1974, SACC filed a class action lawsuit against Chicago's Police Department for violation of the organization's constitutional rights. The case was finally brought to trial June 18, 1984, with SACC emerging victorious. Most of the material in this section is from the various police reports dating back to the summer of 1966 presented in the trial as well as from the testimonies of witnesses.

5. INSTITUTIONALIZATION OF THE ETHNIC MINORITY CLASSIFICATION

1. The first official survey of students by race or national origin by the State of Illinois was conducted in 1973.

2. Similarly, Tullock (1966) argues that the growth and maintenance of organizations whose formal goals are aimed at helping one population but who depend on a different population for funding are ultimately more dependent upon the funding group.

3. In 1971, Graciano López ran for alderman in the 26th ward, making him the first Puerto Rican candidate to run for political office in the city. Lack of sufficient empirical data on this election makes it more suitable to rely on the 1975 race.

4. See, for example, the work of Gabriel A. Almond and Sidney Verba (1965) *The Civic Culture: Political Attitudes and Democracy in Five Nations* (Boston: Little Brown).

5. As early as 1967, an editorial in *El Puertorriqueño* presented a similar call. The editorial forcefully recommended to the superintendent

of the Board of Education that it initiate a teacher's exchange program to recuit teachers from Puerto Rico (1967:3). It was also recommended that the school system develop specific programs to train teachers and other staff in the culture and language of the Puerto Rican child.

6. Surveys of Yuppies in several cities have supported these speculations (Fichter, 1977; Laska and Spain, 1979). In Gale's (1977:6) study of people buying homes in Washington's Mount Pleasant neighborhood between August 1974 and October 1975, respondents were asked to rank the three major reasons for selecting their home. Economic reasons were the most frequently mentioned. Other factors such as convenience to place of work, physical character of the neighborhood, and the appeal of an integrated neighborhood were also ranked highly.

6. CONCLUSION

1. Wilhelm and Powell advanced a similar argument after examining the economic integration of blacks during the 1970s. According to the two writers, "The tremendous historical change for the Negro is taking place in these terms: he is not needed. He is not so much oppressed as unwanted; not so much unwanted as unnecessary; not so much abused as ignored. The dominant whites no longer need to exploit him. If he disappeared tomorrow he would hardly be missed. As automation proceeds, it is easier and easier to disregard him" (1973:225).

2. This brief discussion is based on information I am presently gathering for the preparation of a larger study on Salsa music and its relationship to the ethnic and cultural expressions of Spanish-speaking groups in the United States.

3. Ruben Blades has appeared as a guest on several major television talk shows, including Johnny Carson. He has also appeared on the cover of *New York* magazine and was featured in such prominent national magazines as *Newsweek*. Further national exposure came via a movie, "Crossover Dreams," written, produced, and performed by Ruben Blades.

References

Alba, Richard D. 1976. Social Assimilation Among American Catholic National-Origin Groups. *American Sociological Review* 41 (Dec.): 1030–1046.

Allen, Robert L. 1969. *Black Awakening in Capitalist America: An Analytic History*. Garden City, N.Y.: Doubleday.

Almond, Gabriel A., and Sidney Verba. 1965. *The Civil Culture: Political Attitudes and Democracy in Five Nations*: Boston: Little, Brown.

Ashton, Patrick J. 1978. The Political Economy of Suburban Development in *Marxism and the Metropolis: New Perspectives in Urban Political Economics*. ed. William K. Tabb and Larry Sawers, 64–89. New York: Oxford University Press.

Baron, Harold M. 1975. Racial Discrimination in Advanced Capitalism: A Theory of Nationalism and Division in the Labor Market. In *Labor Market Segmentation*, ed. Richard C. Edwards, 48–63. Cambridge, Mass.: Harvard University Press.

Baron, Harold M, and Bennett Hymer. 1977. Racial Dualism in an Urban Labor Market. In *Problems in Political Economy: An Urban Perspective*. 2d. ed., ed. David M. Gordon, 188–195. Lexington, Mass.: D.C. Heath.

Barrera, Mario. 1979. *Race and Class in the Southwest: A Theory of Racial Inequality*. Notre Dame, In.: University of Notre Dame Press.

Barreto, Ray. Fuerza Gigante. New York: Fania Records.

Barth, Fredrik. 1969. Introduction. In *Ethnic Groups and Boundaries: The Social Organization of Cultural Differences*, ed. Fredrik Barth, 1–12. London: George Allen and Unwin.

Belenchia, Joanne. 1982. Latinos and Chicago Politics. In *After Daley: Chicago Politics in Transition*, ed. Samuel K. Gove and Louis H. Masotti, 118–145. Urbana-Champaign, IL.: University of Illinois Press.

Bell, Daniel. 1975. Ethnicity and Social Change. In *Ethnicity: Theory and Experience*, ed. Nathan Glazer and Daniel P. Moynihan, 141–174. Cambridge, Mass.: Harvard University Press.

Berkowitz, Leonard. 1968. The Study of Urban Violence: Some Implications of Laboratory Studies in Frustration and Aggression. In *Riots and Rebellion: Civil Violence in the Urban Community*. ed. Louis H. Masotti and Don R. Bowen, 39–49. Beverly Hills, Calif.: Sage.

Berry, Brian J., et al. 1976. *Chicago Transformations of an Urban System.* Cambridge, Mass.: Ballinger.

Betances, Samuel. 1971. Puerto Rican Youth. *The Rican: A Journal of Contemporary Puerto Rican Thought*, (Fall): 4–13.

Biddle, Ellen H. 1976. The American Catholic Irish Family. In *Ethnic Families in America: Patterns and Variations*, ed. Charles H. Mindel and Robert W. Haberstein, 89–123. New York: Elsevier Scientific Publishing Co.

Blades, Ruben. Buscando America. New York: Elektra/Asylum Records. 1983.

_____. Plastico. New York: Fania Recordings. 1978.

_____. Siembra. New York: Fania Records.

Blanco, Tomas. 1935. *Prontuario Histórico de Puerto Rico*. San Juan: Biblioteca de Autores Puertorriqueños.

Blauner, Robert. 1966. Whitewash over Watts. *Trans-Action*, 3 (Mar.-Apr.): 3–9.

_____. 1969. *Racial Oppression in America*. New York: Harper & Row.

_____. 1972. "Colonized and Immigrant Minorities." In *Nation of Nations: The Ethnic Experience and the Racial Crisis*, ed. Peter I. Rose, 243–258. New York: Random House.

Blumer, Herbert. 1958. Race Prejudice as a Sense of Group Position. *Pacific Sociological Review* (Spring): 3–7.

Bonacich, Edna. 1972. A Theory of Ethnic Antagonism: The Split Labor Market. *American Sociological Review*, (37): 547–559.

_____. 1976. Advanced Capitalism and Black-White Race Relations in the United States: A Split Labor Market Interpretation. *American Sociological Review* (41): 34–51.

Bonilla, Frank. 1974. Beyond Survival: Por que Seguiremos Siendo Puertorriqueños. In *Puerto Rico and Puerto Ricans: Studies in History and Society*, ed. Adalberto López and James Petras, 438–451. New York: John Wiley & Sons.

Bowen, Don R., and Louis H. Masotti. 1968. Civil Violence: A Theoretical Overview. In *Riots and Rebellion: Civil Violence in the Urban Community*, ed. Louis H. Masotti and Don R. Bowen, 11–31. Beverly Hills, Calif.: Sage.

Bowles, Samuel. 1973. Understanding Unequal Economic Opportunity. *American Economic Review Proceedings* (May): 346–356.

Burgess, Ernest, 1923. "The Growth of the City: An Introduction to Research Project. In *Proceedings of the American Sociological Society*, vol 18: 57–85. Chicago: University of Chicago Press.

Cabral, Amilcar. 1970. *National Liberation and Culture*. Program of East African Studies, Occasional Paper No. 57. Syracuse, N.Y.: Syracuse University.

Camacho, Eduardo. 1978. Housing Abandonment in East Humboldt Park. School of Social Work, University of Chicago, Chicago.

Camus, Albert. 1967. Metaphysical Revolt and Historical Action. *Modern Language Review* 62 (April): 248–255.

Castell, Manuel. 1975. Immigrant Workers and Class Struggles in Advanced Capitalism: The Western European Experience. *Politics and Society* 5 (1): 33–66.

_____. 1976a. Is There an Urban Sociology? In *Urban Sociology: Critical Essays*, ed. C. G. Pickvance, 33–59. New York: St. Martin.

_____. 1976b. Urban Sociology and Urban Politics: From a Critique to New Trends of Research. In *The City in Comparative Perspective*, ed. John Walton and Louis H. Masotti, 291–300. Beverly Hills, Calif.: Sage.

Chicago Daily News. Aug. 11, 1959. Puerto Ricans Are Eager to Work, Want No Handouts, by Sam King.

_____. August 2, 1965. Cops Brutal in Arrest, Latin Group, by Phillip O'Conner.

_____. June 13, 1966. NW Side Riot Probe Ordered; Judge's Warning: Respect Police; Aftermath of NW Side Battle: Wilson Orders Riot Probe.

_____. June 14, 1966. How Mistrust Triggered Explosion on NW Side.

_____. June 15, 1966. Behind the Rioting, a Ghetto: Puerto Ricans in Chicago.

_____. June 18, 1966. Defendants in Riot Causing Court Jam.

_____. July 31, 1970. A New Group Seeks the American Dream, by Larry Green.

Chicago Reporter. February, 1978. Vol 8, no. 2. Aloof City, Scared Investors, and Divided Community Watch as Housing Destruction Devastates East Humboldt Park, by Tom Brune and Alfredo S. Lanier.

_____. November, 1983. Vol. 12, no. 11. Latino Group's Collapse Shatters Rehab Plans in Humboldt Park, by Wilfredo Cruz and Alan Neff.

Chicago Sun-Times. June 13, 1966. Fight Area Residents Tell of Police-Puerto Rican relations.

_____. June 14. 1966. 7 Shot, 5 Hurt in New Division Street Violence.

_____. June 15, 1966. West Side Story: Daley Issues Peace Appeal.

_____. May 16, 1969. 3 Protest Groups Occupy Seminary.

_____. June 23, 1969. Federal Program Approved for Lincoln Park Area.

_____. September 12-20, 1971. The Latins, series by J. Watson and C. N. Wheeler III.

_____. September 30, 1971. Debt Trap: Some Can't Spring it.

_____. September 2, 1976. NW Side Groups, City Officials Meet on Arson.

_____. November 30, 1979. The Middle Class Revives Inner-City But Displaces Poor.

Chicago Sun-Times, Midwest Magazine. September, 1969. For Carlos, Marcelino, and Cayetano: An American Dream Come True.

Chicago Tribune. September 17, 1961. Los Medinas, A Model Puerto Rican Family.

_____. January 24, 1968. The Puerto Rican Families in Chicago, by Thomas Hall.

_____. December 14, 1969. Council Chairman Calls Housing Biggest Need.

_____. February 12, 1970. Assail Lincoln Park Decision.

Christopulos, Diane. 1974. Puerto Rico in the Twentieth Century: A Historical Survey. In *Puerto Rico and Puerto Ricans: Studies in History and Society*, ed. Adalberto López and James Petras, 123–163. New York: John Wiley & Sons.

City of Chicago:

Board of Education. 1972. Teacher Racial Survey Recapitulation.

_____. 1972. Student Racial Survey Recapitulation.

Commission on Human Relations. The Puerto Rican Residents of Chicago: A Report on an Open Hearing, July 15 and 16, 1966.

Dept. of City Planning. 1958. Development Plan for the Central Area of Chicago.

_____. 1964. Basic Policies for the Comprehensive Plan of Chicago.

_____. (Dept. of Development and Planning). 1966. Basic Policies for the Comprehensive Plan of Chicago.

_____. 1967. The Comprehensive Plan of Chicago.

Dept. of Human Resources. 1973. Chicago's Spanish-speaking Population.

Mayor's Committee for Economic and Cultural Development. 1966. Mid-Chicago Economic Development Study, 3 vol.

Clark, Victor S., et al. 1930. *Porto Rico and Its Problems.* Washington, D.C.: Brookings Institution.

Clay, Phillip L. 1979. *Neighborhood Renewal: Trends and Strategies* Lexington, Mass.: Lexington Books.

Cohen, David, and Marvin Lazerrson. 1972. Education and the Industrial Order. *Socialist Revolution* (Mar.-Apr.): 47–72.

Coleman, James S., et al. 1966. *Equality of Educational Opportunity.* Washington, D.C.: Doc. FS5.

Colon, Elizabeth. 1983. Predators Dash. In *The Other Chicago Poets*, 10–11. Chicago: Chicago Council on Fine Arts.

Commerce. 1978. Overall View of Chicago Space. Dale A. Dreischarf. 64 (6 November).

Cressey, Paul F. 1938. Population Succession in Chicago: 1898–1930. *American Journal of Sociology* 44 (July): 59–69.

Crist, Raymond E. 1948. Sugar Cane and Coffee in Puerto Rico. Parts 1, 2. *American Journal of Economics and Sociology* 7 (2): 173–184; 7 (3): 321–336.

Devise, Pierre. 1980. Social Change. In *Chicago's Future: An Agenda for Change*, ed. Dick Simpson, 56–69. Champaign, Il.: Stipes.

Diffie, Bailey W., and Justine W. Diffie. 1931. *Porto Rico: A Broken Pledge.* New York: Vanguard.

Dillard, Dudley. 1979. Capitalism. In *The Political Economy of Development and Underdevelopment* 2d. ed., ed. Charles K. Wilber, 69–76. New York: Random House.

Donner, Frank. 1982. Age of Surveillance, Manuscript.

Drake, St. Clair, and Horace Cayton (1945) 1962. *Black Metropolis*, 2 vol. New York: Harper & Row.

Drucker, Peter F. 1969. *The Age of Discontinuity.* New York: Harper & Row. *El Centinela.* January 8, 1959. El Padre Mahon Dice.

————. February 1, 1959. El Padre Mahon Dice.

————. February 9, 1959. El Padre Mahon Dice.

————. April, 1959. Necesitamos La Participacíon del Pueblo.

El Centro de Estudios Puertorriqueños. 1979. *Labor Migration Under Capitalism: The Puerto Rican Experience.* New York: Monthly Review Press.

El Gran Combo de Puerto Rico. Prosigue. Puerto Rico: Rico Records.

El Puertorriqueño. August 11, 1965. Enérgica Protesta de Caballeros de San Juan y Comunidad Puertorriqueña.

————. June 1, 1966. Editorial; Los Puertorriqueños Heredamos Los Problemas, by Alfredo Torres de Jesús.

————. June 6, 1966. Editorial; El Instituto de Cultura Puertorriqueña, by Trina Davilla.

————. September 9, 1966. SACC es Nido de Comunistas.

————. December 7, 1966. Huelga Puertorriqueña.

————. December 7, 1966. Millares de Obreros Hispanos son Desocupados por Zenith Radio, By Claudio Flores.

————. October 28, 1971. El Voto Puertorriqueño en Chicago.

————. June 27, 1972. El Problema Educativo de Nuestras Escuelas.

————. August 2, 1972. Continuan Los Problemas en las Escuelas del Barrio.

————. June 27, 1975. El Barrio se Quema.

————. July 29, 1976. Editorial; La Linea Caliente del Departamento de Bombas e Incendios, Muy Ineficiente.

Estades, Rosa. 1980. Symbolic Unity: The Puerto Rican Day Parade. In *The Puerto Rican Struggle: Essays on Survival in the U.S.*, ed. Clara Rodríguez, et al., 82–89. New York: Puerto Rican Migration Research Consortium.

Fanon, Frantz. 1963. *Wretched of the Earth*, tr. Constance Farrington. New York: Grove.

Feagin, Joe R. 1974. Community Disorganization: Some Critical Notes. In *The Community: Approach and Application*, ed. Marcia P. Effrat, 1234–1246. Glencoe, Il.: Free Press.

Feagin, Joe R., and Harlan Hahn. 1973. *Ghetto Revolt: The Politics of Violence in American Cities*. New York: Macmillan.

Femminella, Francis, and Jill S. Quadagno. 1976. The Italian American Family. In *Ethnic Families in America: Patterns and Variations*, ed. Charles H. Mindel and Robert W. Haberstein, 61–88. New York: Elsevier Scientific Publishing Co.

Fichter, Robert. 1977. *Young Professionals and City Neighborhoods*. Boston: Parkman Center for Urban Affairs.

Fischer, John H. 1966. Race and Reconciliation: The Role of the School *Daedalus* 95 (1 Winter): 24–43.

Fitzpatrick, Joseph. 1966. The Importance of "Community" in the Process of Immigrant Assimilation. *International Migration Review* 1 (Fall): 5–16.

————. 1971. *Puerto Rican Americans: The Meaning of Migration to the Mainland*. Englewood, N.J.: Prentice Hall.

Fogelson, Robert M., and Robert B. Hill. 1968. Who Riots? A Study of Participation in the 1967 Riots. *Supplemental Studies for the National Advisory Commission on Civil Disorders*, 217–244. Washington, D.C.: Government Printing Office.

Forni, Floreal. 1971. *The Situation of the Puerto Rican Population in Chicago and Its Viewpoints about Racial Relations*. Community and Family Study Center, University of Chicago, Chicago.

Fortune. October, 1968. O Say Can You See? The Crisis in our National Perception, by Max Ways.

Fried, Marc. 1973. *The World of the Urban Working Class.* Cambridge, Mass.: Harvard University Press.

Fusfield, Daniel R., and Timothy Bates. 1984. *The Political Economy of the Urban Ghetto.* Carbondale, Il.; Southern Illinois University Press.

Futurist. August 1980. Hispanics in the U.S.: Yesterday, Today, and Tomorrow.

Gale, Dennis. 1977. The Back-to-the-City Movement—Or Is It? A Survey of Recent Homebuyers in the Mt. Pleasant Neighborhood of Washington, D.C. Washington, D.C.: George Washington University. Mimeo.

Gans, Herbert, 1963. *The Urban Villagers.* Glencoe, Il.: Free Press.

García, Richard. 1974. America, You Lied to Us. *The Rican, a Journal of Contemporary Puerto Rican Thought* 2 (1) 15–17.

Glazer, Nathan, 1975. *Affirmative Discrimination: Ethnic Inequality and Public Policy.* New York: Basic Books.

Glazer, Nathan, and David P. Moynihan. 1963. *Beyond the Melting Pot.: The Negroes, Puerto Ricans, Jews, Italians, and Irish of New York City.* Rev. ed. 1970. Cambridge, Mass.: MIT Press.

Goldstein, Robert J. 1978. *Political Repression in Modern America, from 1870 to Present.* Cambridge, Mass.: Schenkman.

González-Casanova, Pablo. 1965. Internal Colonialism and National Development. *Studies in Comparative International Development* 1 (4): 27–37.

Gordon, David M. 1977. Digging Up the Roots: The Economic Determinants of Social Problems. In *Problems in Political Economy: An Urban Perspective*, ed. David M. Gordon, 16–20. Lexington, Mass.: D.C. Heath.

———. 1978. Capitalist Development and the History of American Cities. In *Marxism and the Metropolis: New Perspectives in Urban Political Economics*, ed. William K. Tabb and Larry Sawers, 25–63. New York: Oxford University Press.

Greenstone, J. David, and Paul E. Peterson. 1973. *Race and Authority in Urban Politics: Community Participation and the War.* Chicago: University of Chicago Press.

Grier, George, and Eunice Grier. 1977. *Movers to the City: New Data on the Housing Market for Washington, D.C.* Washington, D.C.: Washington Center for Metropolitan Studies.

Guest, Avery. 1977. Residential Segregation in Urban Areas. In *Contemporary Topics in Urban Sociology*, ed. Kent P. Schwirian, et al., 268–336. Morristown, N.J.: General Learning Press.

Gurr, Ted. 1968. Urban Disorder: Perspectives from the Comparative Study of Civil Strife. In *Riots and Rebellion: Civil Violence in the Urban Community*, ed. Louis H. Masotti and Don R. Bowen, 51–67. Beverly Hills, Calif.: Sage.

Handlin, Oscar. 1959. *The Newcomers: Negroes and Puerto Ricans in a Changing Metropolis*. Cambridge, Mass.: M.I.T. Press.

Harvey, David. 1978. The Urban Process Under Capitalism: A Framework for Analysis. In *Urbanization and Urban Planning in a Capitalist Society*, ed. Michael Dear and Allen J. Scott, 91–122. London: Methuen.

Herberg, Will. 1955. *Protestant-Catholic-Jew: An Essay in Religious Sociology*. Garden City, N.Y.: Doubleday.

Hechter, Michael. 1975. *Internal Colonialism: The Celtic Fringe in British National Development, 1536–1966*. Berkeley, Calif.: University of California Press.

_____. 1978. Group Formation and the Cultural Division of Labor. *American Journal of Sociology* 84 (2): 293–318.

Hernández-Álverez, José. 1967. *Return Migration to Puerto Rico*. Population Monograph Series, No. 1. Berkeley, Calif.: University of California.

_____. 1968. The Movement and Settlement of Puerto Rican Migrants Within the United States, 1950–1960. *International Migration Review*, 2 (2 Spring): 40–52.

_____. 1980. Social Science and the Puerto Rican Community. In *The Puerto Rican Struggle: Essays on Survival in the U.S.*, ed. Clara Rodríguez, et al., 11–19. New York: Puerto Rican Migration Research Consortium.

Hernández, David, and Pedro Vales. 1973. Methodological Considerations Underlying the Definition of the Puerto Rican Syndrome. Río Piedras, Puerto Rico: University of Puerto Rico. Mimeo.

Hill, Richard C. 1976. State Capitalism and the Urban Fiscal Crisis in The United States. Paper presented at the International Conference on Social Problems and Urban and Regional Development, Calabra, Sicily.

Hunt, Lester, 1957, The Meanings of Democracy: Puerto Rican Organizations in Chicago, *Etcetera* (13): 182–192.

Illinois: Board of Higher Education. 1980. Data Book on Illinois Higher Education, Springfield, Il.

Janowitz, Morris. 1952. *The Community Press in an Urban Setting*. Glencoe, Il.: Free Press.

Kemp, Kathleen A., and Robert L. Lineberry. 1982. The Last of the Great Urban Machines and the Last of the Great Urban Mayors? Chicago

Politics, 1955–77. In *After Daley: Chicago Politics in Transition*, ed. Samuel K. Gove and Louis H. Masotti, 1–26. Urbana-Champaign, Il.: University of Illinois Press.

Kitagawa, Evelyn M., and Karl E. Taeuber. 1963. *Local Community Fact Book: Chicago Metropolitan Area, 1960.* Chicago: University of Chicago Press.

Kuper, Leo. 1975. *Race, Class, and Power: Ideology and Revolutionary Change in Plural Society.* Chicago: Aldine.

Kyle, Charles. 1984. The Magnitude of and Reasons for the Hispanic Drop Out Problems in Chicago: of Two Chicago Public High Schools. Ph.D. diss. Department of Sociology, Northwestern University, Chicago.

Lang, Kurt, and Gladys Engel Lang. 1968. Racial Disturbances as Collective Protest. In *Riots and Rebellion: Civil Violence in the Urban Community*, ed. Louis H. Masotti and Don R. Bowen, 121–130. Beverly Hills, Calif.: Sage.

Latino Institute. Latino Institute: History and Philosophy. Mimeo.

Levine, Barry B. 1980. *Benjy Lopez, A Picaresque Tale of Emigration and Return.* New York: Basic Books.

Levitan, Sar A. 1969. The Community Action Program: A Strategy to Fight Poverty. *Annals of the American Academy of Political and Social Science* (Sept.): 63–75.

Lewis, Gordon K. 1963. *Puerto Rico: Freedom and Power in the Caribbean.* New York: Monthly Review Press.

———. 1973. Puerto Rico: Toward a New Consciousness. *Latin American Review of Books* 1 (1): 147–158.

———. 1974. *Notes on the Puerto Rican Revolution: An Essay on American Dominance and Caribbean Resistance.* New York: Monthly Review Press.

Lewis, Oscar. 1965. *La Vida: A Puerto Rican Family in the Culture of Poverty—San Juan and New York.* New York: Random House.

Liebow, Elliot. 1967. *Tally's Corner.* Boston, Little, Brown.

Life. 1969. Special Report, by Betty E. Shiflett.

Litt, Edgar. 1970. *Ethnic Politics in America.* Glenview, Il.: Scott, Foresman.

Lojkine, James. 1977. Big Firms' Strategies, Urban Policy, and Urban Social Movements. In *Captive Cities: Studies in the Political Economy of Cities and Regions*, ed. Michael Harloe. London: John Wiley & Sons.

Long, Larry H. 1980. Back to the Countryside and Back to the City in the Same Decade. In *Back to the City: The Making of a Movement?* ed. Shirley B. Laska and Daphne Spain, 61–76. New York: Pergamon Press.

Longres, John F. 1974. Racism and Its Effects on Puerto Rican Continentals. *Social Casework* (Winter): 67–75.

London, Bruce. 1980. Gentrification as Urban Reinvasion: Some Preliminary Definitional and Theoretical Considerations. In *Back to the City: The Making of a Movement?* ed. Shirley B. Laska and Daphne Spain, 77–92. New York: Pergamon Press.

Lopata, Helena Z. 1876. The Polish American Family. In *Ethnic Families in America: Patterns and Variations*, ed. Charles H. Mindel and Robert W. Haberstein, 15–40. New York: Elsevier Scientific Publishing Co.

López, Adalberto. 1974. The Puerto Rican Diaspora: A Survey. In *Puerto Rico and Puerto Ricans: Studies in History and Society*, ed. Adalberto López and James Petras, 316–346. New York: John Wiley & Sons.

López, Adalberto, James Petras. 1974. Introduction. In *Puerto Rico and Puerto Ricans: Studies in History and Society*, ed. Adalberto López and James Petras: 313–315. New York: John Wiley & Sons.

Lucas, Isidro. 1974. El Problema Educativo del "Dropout." *The Rican: A Journal of Contemporary Puerto Rican Thought* (1): 5–18.

Lugo-Silva, Enrique. 1955. *The Tugwell Administration in Puerto Rico, 1941–1946*. Río Piedras, Puerto Rico: Editorial Cultural.

Maldonado-Denis, Manuel. 1972. *Puerto Rico: An Historic-Social Interpretation*. New York: Vintage Books.

_____. 1980. *The Emigration Dialectic: Puerto Rico and the USA*. New York: International Publishers.

Mann, Seymour Z. 1966. *Chicago's War on Poverty*. Chicago: Center for Research in Urban Government, Loyola University.

Masotti, Louis H., and Samuel K. Gove. 1982. Introduction. In *After Daley: Chicago Politics in Transition*, ed. Samuel K. Gove and Louis H. Masotti, ix–xvii. Urbana-Champaign, Il.: University of Illinois Press.

Memmi, Albert. 1967. *The Colonizer and the Colonized*. Boston: Beacon.

Merrill, Francis E. 1965. *Society and Culture, An Introduction to Sociology* 3d. ed. Englewood Cliffs, N.J.: Prentice Hall.

Mintz, Sidney. 1951. The Role of Forced Labor in Nineteenth-Century Puerto Rico. *Caribbean Historical Review* (2): 134–141.

_____. 1953. The Cultural History of Puerto Rican Sugar Cane Plantation: 1876–1949. *Hispanic American Historical Review* (1): 224–251.

Mirande, Alfredo. 1982. Sociology of Chicano or Chicano Sociology? A Critical Assessment of Emergent Paradigm. *Pacific Sociological Review* 4 (25): 495–508.

_____. 1985. *The Chicano Experience: An Alternative Perspective.* Notre Dame, In.: University of Notre Dame Press.

Mogey, John M. 1957. *Family and Neighborhood: Two Studies in Oxford.* London: Oxford University Press.

Mogulof, Melvin. 1969. Coalition to Adversary: Citizen Participation in Three Federal Programs. *Journal of the American Institute of Planners* 15 (4 July): 225–232.

Mollenkopf, John. 1976. The Crisis of the Public Sector in America's Cities. In *The Fiscal Crisis of American Cities*, ed. Roger E. Alcaly and David Mermelstein, 113–131. New York: Vintage Books.

_____. 1978. The Postwar Politics of Urban Development. In *Marxism and the Metropolis: New Perspectives In Urban Political Economics*, ed. William K. Tabb and Larry Sawers, 117–152. New York: Oxford University Press.

_____. 1981. Community and Accumulation. In *Urbanization and Urban Planning in a Capitalist Society*, ed. Michael Dear and Allen J. Scott, 319–337. New York: Methven.

Moore, Joan W. 1970. Colonialism: The Case of Mexican Americans. *Social Problems* (Spring): 463–472.

_____. 1976. *Mexican Americans.* Englewood Cliffs, N.J.: Prentice Hall.

Morley, Morriz. 1974. Dependence and Development in Puerto Rico. In *Puerto Rico and Puerto Ricans: Studies in History and Society*, ed. Adalberto López and James Petras, 214–254. New York: John Wiley & Sons.

Moynihan, Daniel P. 1965. *The Negro Family: The Case for National Action.* Washington, D.C.: U.S. Department of Labor.

Mumford, Lewis. 1961. *The City in History: Its Origins, Its Transformations, and Its Prospects*, New York: Harcourt, Brace & World.

Nelli, Humbert S. 1970. *Italians in Chicago: 1880–1930: A Study in Ethnic Mobility.* New York: Oxford University Press.

Newsweek. September 12, 1977. Torches: Arson for Sale, by Terry Atlas.

New York Times. February 23, 1953. Flow of Puerto Ricans Here Fills Jobs, Poses Problems, by Peter Kihss.

_____. June 4, 1961. Chicago Good City to Puerto Ricans, by Donald Janson.

_____. June 14, 1966. 7 Shot in Chicago in New Outbreak.

Noboa, Julio, Jr. 1974. Survival of the Species. *The Rican: A Journal of Contemporary Puerto Rican Thought* 1 (4 May):51.

Ossowski, Stanislaw. 1963. *Class Structure in the Social Consciousness*, tr. Sheila Patterson. New York, Free Press.

Padilla, Elena. 1947. Puerto Rican Immigrants in New York and Chicago:

A Study in Comparative Assimilation. Ph.D. diss., Department of Anthropology, University of Chicago, Chicago.

———. 1970. Race Relations: A Puerto Rican View. In *Agenda for a City: Issues Confronting New York*, ed. Lyle C. Fitch, et al., 557–562. New York: Sage.

Padilla, Felix. 1985. *Latino Ethnic Consciousness: The Case of Mexican Americans and Puerto Ricans in Chicago*. Notre Dame, In.: University of Notre Dame Press.

Park, Robert, Ernest Burgess, and R.D. MacKenzie. 1967. *The City*. 4th ed. Chicago: University of Chicago Press.

———. 1967. *On Social and Collective Behavior*. Chicago: University of Chicago Press.

Pedreira, Antonio S. 1942. *Insularismo*. 2d ed. San Juan Biblioteca de Autores Puertorriqueños.

Perloff, Harvey S. 1950. *Puerto Rico's Economic Future: A Study in Planned Development*. Chicago: University of Chicago Press.

Pitts, James P. 1982. The Afro-American Experience: Changing Modes of Integration and Race Consciousness. In *The Minority Report*, ed. Anthony G. Dworking and Rosalind Dworking, 141–167. New York: Rhinehart and Winston.

Prensa Libre. June 22, 1975. Los Fuegos Continuan.

Preston, Michael B. 1982. Black Politics in the Post-Daley Era. In *After Daley: Chicago Politics in Transition*, ed. Samuel K. Gove and Louis H. Masotti, 88–117. Urbana-Champaign, Il.: University of Illinois Press.

Puerto Rico. Department of Labor. 1960. Employment and Unemployment in Puerto Rico: Quarterly Reports, 1950–1959. Bureau of Labor Statistics.

———. Puerto Rican Planning Board. 1962. Annual Statistical Report of the Economic Development Administration Manufacturing Plants, 1960–61.

Quintero-Rivera, Angel G. 1974. Background to the Emergence of Imperialist Capitalism in Puerto Rico. In *Puerto Rico and Puerto Ricans: Studies in History and Society*. ed. Adalberto López and James Petras, 87–117. New York: John Wiley and Sons.

Rakove, Milton L. 1975. *Don't Make No Waves, Don't Back No Losers: An Insider's Analysis of the Daley Machine*. Bloomington. In.: Indiana University Press.

Reich, Michael, David M. Gordon, and Richard C. Edwards. 1977. Theory of Labor Market Segmentation. In *Problems in Political Economy: An Urban Prospective*, ed. David M. Gordon, 108–113. Lexington, Mass.: Heath.

_____. 1977. The Economics of Racism. In *Problems in Political Economy: An Urban Prospective*, ed. David M. Gordon, 183–188. Lexington, Mass.: Heath.

Reynolds, Lloyd G., and Peter Gregory. 1965. *Wages, Productivity, and Industrialization in Puerto Rico*. Homewood, Il.: Richard D. Irwin.

Rivera, Jaime. 1974. Children of the Damned. *The Rican: A Journal of Contemporary Puerto Rican Thought* 1 (4 May): 61–62.

Roberts, John S. 1979. *The Latin Tinge: The Impact of Latin American Music on the United States*. New York: Oxford University Press.

Rodríguez, Carmelo. 1973. Bembe at Humboldt Park. *The Rican: A Journal of Contemporary Puerto Rican Thought* (3 Spring): 13.

Rodríguez, Clara E. 1980. Puerto Ricans: Between Black and White. In *The Puerto Rican Struggle: Essays on Survival in the U.S.*, ed. Clara E. Rodríguez, et al., 1–10. New York: Puerto Rican Research Consortium.

Rodríguez, Clara E., Virginia Sánchez-Korral, and José O. Algers. 1980. The Puerto Rican Struggle To Survive in the United States. In *The Puerto Rican Struggle: Essays on Survival in the U.S.*, ed. Clara E. Rodríguez, et al., 1–10. New York: Puerto Rican Research Consortium.

Rodríguez, Emma I. 1974. Tuley Products. *The Rican: A Journal of Contemporary Puerto Rican Thought* 2 (1 Oct.): 62.

Ross, David F. 1969. *The Long Uphill Path: A Historical Study of Puerto Rico's Program of Economic Development*. San Juan: Editorial Edil.

Salces, Luis M. 1978. Spanish American Politics in Chicago. Ph.D diss. Department of Sociology, Northwestern University, Chicago.

_____. 1978a. Spanish Americans' Search for Political Representation: The 1975 Aldermanic Election in Chicago. *Journal of Political and Military Sociology* 6 (Fall): 175–187.

Sánchez-Korral, Virginia. 1980. Survival of Puerto Rican Women in New York before World War II. In *The Puerto Rican Struggle: Essays on Survival in the U.S.*, ed Clara E. Rodríguez, et al., 47–57. New York: Puerto Rican Research Consortium.

_____. 1983. *From Colonia to Community: The History of Puerto Ricans in New York City, 1917–1948*. Westport, Conn.: Greenwood Press.

Saturday Evening Post. November 5, 1960. Crime Without Reason, by John B. Martin.

Senior, Clarence. 1947. *Puerto Rican Emigration*. Río Piedras, Puerto Rico: Social Science Research Center, University of Puerto Rico.

Senior, Clarence, and Donald O. Watkins. 1966. Toward a Balance Sheet of Puerto Rican Migration. In *Status of Puerto Rico: U.S.-Puerto*

Rico Commission on the Status of Puerto Rico. Washington, D.C.:
Senate Document No. 108.

Smelser, Neil J. 1962. *Theory of Collective Behavior*. New York: Free
Press.

Smith, Richard A. 1968. The Progressive Movement: A Sociological Interpretation. Center for Social Organization Studies, Working Paper
No. 121, University of Chicago, Chicago.

Spanish Action Committee of Chicago. n.d. Proposal to Develop an Urban Service Training Center.

_____. n.d. Summary Report—1967–1969.

Spear, Allan H. 1967. *Black Chicago: The Making of a Negro Ghetto,
1890–1920*. Chicago: University of Chicago Press.

Suttles, Gerald D. 1968. Chicago: University of Chicago Press.

Taeuber, Karl E., and Alma F. Taeuber, 1964. The Negro as an Immigrant
Group: Recent Trends in Racial and Ethnic Segregation in Chicago.
American Journal of Sociology 69:374–383.

Thernstrom, Stephen. 1973. *The Other Bostonians: Poverty and Progress
in the American Metropolis, 1880–1970*. Cambridge, Mass.: Harvard University Press.

Time. October, 1978. It's Your Turn in the Sun. Vol. 112, no. 16.

Torres, Maximino. 1983. An Attempt to Provide Higher Educational Op-
portunities to Hispanics: The Evolution of Proyecto Pa'lante at
Northeastern Illinois—1971–1976. Ph.D. diss. Loyola University,
Chicago.

Tullock, Gordon. 1966. Information Without Profit. In *Papers on Non-
Market Decision Making*, vol. 1, ed. Gordon Tullock, 141–159.
Charlottesville, Va.: Thomas Jefferson for Political Economy,
University of Virginia.

U.S. News and World Report. July, 1974. The Newest Americans: A Second Spanish Invasion.

_____. December, 1959. 900,000 Puerto Ricans in the U.S.—Their Prob-
lems and Progress.

United States:
    Bureau of the Census. 1960 Economic Characteristics of Persons of
        Puerto Rican Birth and Parentage, by Age, for Selected Stan-
        dard Metropolitan Statistical Areas, Table 13. Final Report.
        Washington D.C.
        _____. 1960. Occupation of the Experienced Civilian Labor Force
        by Color, of the Employed by Race and Class of Worker, Chi-
        cago, Il., Table 12. Final Report. Washington, D.C.
        _____. 1960. Subject Reports. Puerto Ricans in the United States.
        Final Report. Washington, D.C.

Commission on Civil Rights. 1976. Puerto Ricans in the Continental United States: An Uncertain Future. A Report of the U.S. Commission on Civil Rights. Washington, D.C.

Urban American, Inc. and the Urban Coalition, 1969. *One Year Later.* New York: Praeger.

Valentine, Charles A. 1968. *Culture and Poverty: Critique and Counter-Proposals.* Chicago: University of Chicago Press.

Van den Berghe. 1971. Ethnicity, the African Experience. *International Social Science Journal.* 23 (4): 507–518.

_____. 1972. Neo-Racism in America. *Transition* (41): 15–18.

Verba, Sidney, and Norman Nie. 1972. *Participation in America: Political Democracy and Social Equality.* New York: Harper & Row.

Walton, John, and Luis Salces. 1977. *The Political Organization of Chicago's Latino Communities.* Evanston, Il.: Center for Urban Affairs, Northwestern University.

Ward, David. 1971. *Cities and Immigrants: A Geography of Change in Nineteenth-Century America.* New York: Oxford University Press.

Warner, William L., and Leo Srole. 1945. *The Social System of American Ethnic Groups.* New Haven, Conn.: Yale University Press.

Wells, Henry. 1969. *The Modernization of Puerto Rico: A Political Study of Changing Values and Institutions.* Cambridge, Mass.: Harvard University Press.

Wilensky, Harold L. 1964. The Professionalism of Everyone? *The American Journal of Sociology* 70 (2): 137–158.

Wilhelm, Sidney, and Elwin Powell. 1973. Marginality: Black and White. In *Modernization, Urbanization, and the Urban Crisis*, ed. Gino Germani, 224–321. Boston: Little, Brown.

Williams, Robin M. 1965. Social Change and Social Conflict: Race Relations in the United States, 1944–1964. *Sociological Inquiry* 35 (Winter): 8–25.

Wilson, James Q., ed. 1966. *Urban Renewal: The Record and the Controversy.* Cambridge, Mass.: MIT Press.

Wilson, William J. 1980. *The Declining Significance of Race: Blacks and Changing American Institutions.* Chicago: University of Chicago Press.

Wolfinger, Raymond E. 1966. Some Consequences of Ethnic Politics. In *The Electoral Process*, ed. M. Kent Jennings and L.H. Zeigler, 42–54. Englewood Cliffs, N.J.: Prentice Hall.

Young, Michael, and Peter Willmot, 1957. *Family and Kinship in East London,* Glencoe, Il.: Free Press.

Zald, Mayer N., and Roberta Ash. 1966. Social Movement Organizations: Growth, Decay, and Change. *Social Forces* 44 (3): 327–340.

Zimmerman, Erich W. 1940. Staff Report to the Interdepartmental Committee on Puerto Rico. Washington. D.C. Mimeo.

Zorbaugh, Harvey W. 1929. *The Gold Coast and the Slum: A Sociological Study of Chicago's Near Northside.* Chicago: University of Chicago Press.

Index

Activism: advisory council,
    165–168; staff, 162–165
Affirmative Action, 11, 188
Agrarian capitalism: under Spain,
    25–28; under U.S., 29, 32–38,
    45
Agregados, 27, 28
Agricultural economy of Puerto Rico,
    6
Aid to Education Act (Title I), 160
Alinsky, Saul, 130, 164
Allen, Robert, 16, 42
Allies for a Better Community
    (A.B.C.), 164, 165, 192
American Spanish Speaking Peoples
    Association (ASSPA), 176–177
"America You Lied to Us," 68
Anti-poverty programs, 157–165
Archdiocesan Latin American Com-
    mittee, 213
Armitage Avenue, 119
Armitage Avenue Methodist Church,
    120, 121
Arson, 214–221
Ashton, Patrick J., 100, 101
Aspira, Inc., 173, 192, 193
Assimilation: and the Catholic
    Church, 129–130; cultural,
    14–15, 21, 32, 157, 232,
    238–239; "El Padre Mahon Dice,"
    138–139; resistance to, 65–66,
    232

Association House, 192
Atlas, Terry, 215

Barrera, Mario, 18
Barreto, Ray, 234, 237
Barreto Boys Club, 218
Barrios, 6–7, 21, 78–83, 91–98; and
    sense of solidarity, 95–98, 143
Baron, Harold M., 102, 103
Barth, Frederik, 8
Bates, Timothy, 108
Belenchia, Joanne, 201
Benitez, Jaime, 139
Berkowitz, Leonard, 147, 153
Berry, Brian J., 84, 108, 109
Betances, Samuel, 86
Biddle, Ellen H., 75
Bilingual education, 15, 93,
    212–214, 221
Bilingual Education Act of 1968,
    212
Blacks, 82–87, 95–96, 110, 232;
    black/Latino coalition, 230, 231;
    in labor force, 102–103, 112,
    113; riots, 145; as voters, 195,
    200, 229
Blades, Ruben, 234–235
Blanco, Tomas, 43
Blauner, Robert, 4, 5, 153
Blumer, Herbert, 8
Bonacich, Edna, 9

269

Bonilla, Frank, 59, 64, 65
Borinquen, 24
Bowen, Don R., 153
Bowles, Samuel, 103
Braham, Thomas, 173
Brookings Institution Report, 39
Brooks, Dayton, 166
Burgess, Ernest, 2, 88
Burgos, Silvano, 124, 146
"Buscando America," 234
Byrne, Jane, 201

Cabral, Amilcar, 7
Camacho, Eduardo, 215
Campesinos, 6, 40, 73
Campos, Pedro Albizu, 43
Campos, 76, 143
Camus, Albert, 152
Castell, Manuel, 11, 116
Catholic Church, 127–129,
  135–137, 138
Cayton, Horace, 95
Celler, Emanuel, 115
Central Aguirre Association, 42
Central Business District, 108
Centrales, 33, 37
Central Intelligence Agency (CIA),
  172
Chicago: economic conditions,
  99–110; politics in, 194–208;
  social conditions, 99–110
Chicago American, 170
Chicago City Council, 199
Chicago Committee on Urban Op-
  portunities, 166
Chicago Community Trust, 192
Chicago Daily News, 60, 115, 124,
  147, 149, 150, 156
Chicago Department of Development
  and Planning, 105, 107, 109
"Chicago School," 88
Chicago Sun-Times, 115, 119, 121,
  134, 135, 146, 147, 149, 199,
  216, 219
Chicago Today, 199, 120

Chicago Tribune, 74, 76, 120, 122,
  170, 177–179
"Children of the Damned," 63
Christopulos, Diane, 33, 36, 38, 42,
  53
City of Chicago Commission on
  Human Relations, 141
Clark, Victor S., 39, 40
Clark Street, 84
Clientele politics, 200–204
Coalition for Jobs, 207
Coffee, 28, 34, 40
Coleman, James S., 210
Collective identity, 95–96. *See also*
  solidarity
Colón, Elizabeth, 93
Colón, Willie, 235
Colonía, 91
Colonial domination of Puerto Rico:
  under Spain, 23–28; under U.S.,
  4–8, 12–14, 29–45; anti-colonial
  movement, 42–45, 54
Colonialism: classic, 4–6, 12,
  17–18; internal, 4, 6, 7, 12, 14,
  17–19
Colonizer and the Colonized, 62
Commerce magazine, 108
Community, Puerto Rican: in
  politics, 202–204; sense of com-
  munity, 96–98. *See also* solidarity
Community Action Programs (CAP),
  157–162, 168
Community Development Block
  Grant, 220
Community Housing Education
  Corporation (CHEC), 220
Community organizations: on arson,
  219; on betterment of housing,
  220–221, 222; professional,
  190–194
Compadres, 73
"Comprehensive Plan," 107, 109
Concilios, 132
Continental Bank, 192
Coral Way High School, 212
Credit Squad, 135

Credit victimization, 133–135
Cressey, Paul F., 88
Cruz, Arcelis, 221
Cruz, Celia, 234
Cubans, 201, 212
Cultural alienation, 62–64
Cultural determinism, 13
Cultural imperialism, 31
Cultural, Puerto Rican, and Salsa, 237
"Culture of poverty" thesis, 13
Currency: change under U.S. colonization, 34; *vales*, 27
Cycle of poverty, 109

Daley, Richard, J., 108, 122, 124, 150, 159, 160, 194, 195, 197, 199, 218, 228
Decolonization, 4, 65
Defense Department, 172
Del Valle, Miguel, 185, 218
Democratic Political Organization, 194–197, 200
Department of Development and Planning, 105, 107, 109
Department of Health, Education, and Welfare (HEW), 188
Department of Human Resources, 220
Department of Labor (DOL), 188
Department of Urban Renewal (DUR), 122
DePaul University, 119, 181
Despierta Boricua defiende lo tuyo, 63
DeVise, Pierre, 106
Díaz, Frank, 196, 197
Díaz, Juan, 118, 165, 174, 176, 177
Diffie, Bailey W., 38
Dillard, Dudley, 29
Discrimination: anger and frustration about, 116, 151–155; housing, 60, 117–123; job, 102–103, 110–116; wage, 102–103

Division Street, 142, 145–155, 156, 157, 213–221; area characteristics, 83–98
Division Street Riots, 21, 91, 144–155, 156, 168, 172
Division Street Urban Progress Center, 160–163, 166, 167
Division Street Urban Progress Center Advisory Council, 167
Division Street YMCA, 91
Donner, Frank, 170
Donor's Forum, 192
Drake, St. Clair, 95
Drop-out rate, high school, 209–214
Drucker, Peter F., 183
Dual labor force, 101–103

Economic determinism, 13
Economic Development Administration, 45
Economic Opportunity Act (Title II), 158–159
Economy, Puerto Rico: under Spain, 23–28; under U.S., 45–55
Education: barrio schools, 209; enrollment in universities, 181–190; high-school drop-out rate, 209–214; investigation by Aspira, Inc., 193; level of education of barrio residents, 181; level of education of recent emigrants, 131; "Puerto Rican curriculum," 184, 189; in Puerto Rico under U.S. colonization, 31
El Centinela, 137–140
El Centro de Estudios Puertorriqueños, 25, 52
El Día de San Juan, 132
Elementary and Secondary Education Act (Title III), 212
El Gran Combo de Puerto Rico, 234, 236
El Instituto de Cultura Puertorriqueña, 141

Elite, Puerto Rican, 180–190; in politics, 201, 202
"El Padre Mahon Dice," 138
El Partido Popular Democrático, 44–46, 52
El Puertorriqueñismo, 8, 99
El Puertorriqueño, 125, 137, 140, 142, 178, 179, 198, 210, 218
El Puertorriqueños, 140–143
El Teatro San Juan, 91
Emigrants: characteristics of, 76–78; resistance to assimilation, 66–70; return ideology, 66–70
Employment: future prospects, 226–227; in industrial-technological jobs, 10–12, 45–55; in Puerto Rico, 45–55; in white-collar jobs, 191, 192; of women, 26, 49, 112–114; working class, 110–116
Estrades, Rosa, 132
Ethnic Consciousness, 8, 19, 21, 65, 99, 136, 203–209; "awakening," 155; Division Street Riot, 144; organizational response, 125
Ethnicity, Puerto Rican, 2, 65, 98, 204–221, 232; and politics, 198, 203–209
Ethnic solidarity. *See* solidarity
Ethnic studies program, 184–189
Exploitation: cultural, 7; of labor, 11–12, 16, 115; under U.S. colonization, 5–8, 35

Fair Play for Cuban Investigation, 177, 178
Fajardo Sugar Co., 42
Family, 72–78, 112, 232
Fanon, Frantz, 151
Feagin, Joe R., 97, 150, 169
Federal Bureau of Investigation (FBI), 145, 172
Federal Housing and Home Finance Agency (HHFA), 119
Federal Housing Authority, 122

Femminella, Francis, 75
Fischer, John H., 210
Fitzpatrick, Joseph, 13, 70, 73
Fogelson, Robert M., 150
Fomento, 45–50
Foraker Act, 30
Forni, Florneal, 70
Franco, Hector, 163–165
Fried, Marc, 95, 97
Friendship, among Puerto Ricans, 72–78
"Fuerza Gigante," 237
Fusfeld, Daniel R., 108
Future prospects for Puerto Ricans, 225–239

Gale, Dennis, 216
Gans, Herbert, 95
Garfield Park Community Center, 160
Garfield Park East, 83–87
Garfield Park West, 83–87
Garro, Guido, 61
General Neighborhood Renewal Plan (GNRP), 120
Gentrification, of el barrio, 214–221
Gerrymandering, 199
Glazer, Nathan, 224
Gold Coast and the Slum, 84
Goldstein, Robert J., 169
Gonzalez, Celestino A., 123, 146
Gonzalez-Casanova, Pablo, 4
Gordon, David M., 100
Gove, Samuel K., 195
Green, Larry, 115
Greenstone, J. David, 158, 159
Gregory, Peter, 46, 47, 49
Group solidarity, 73–75
Guest, Avery, 97
Gurr, Ted, 153
Gutman, Richard, 175, 179

Hacendados, 26, 28, 33–37
Hacienda economy, 23–28, 32, 35, 45

Hahn, Harlan, 150, 169
Hall, Thomas, 76
Handlin, Oscar, 70
Harvey, David, 11, 12
Head Start, 160
Hechter, Michael, 4, 18
Hernández, David, 64
Hernández, José, 17
Hernández-Álvarez, José, 58, 68, 91
Hijos de crianza, 73
Hill, Richard C., 100, 150
Home Ownership Bill, 118
House Committee on Un-American
    Activities, 177
Housing and Urban Affairs Subcom-
    mittee, 118
Housing discrimination, 60, 117–123
Humboldt Park, 88, 118, 155, 166,
    191, 196
Humboldt Park Recreation Commit-
    tee, 166
Hunt, Lester, 130
Hymer, Bennett, 102

Illinois Bell, 192
Independent Radio Workers of
    America (IRWA), 141
Industrial Incentives Act, 47
Industrial relocation, 106
Industial-technological industry,
    10–11, 45–52, 100–103
Institutionalization, of ethnic minor-
    ity classification, 180–221
Insularismo, 43
Intergroup relations, 9, 116; with
    blacks, 84–87, 230, 231; with
    Italians, 84; with Mexicans, 84,
    204–208; with whites, 9–12, 97,
    116–119, 123, 128
Internal organizational approach, 17
Intrametropolitan migration, 108

Janson, Donald, 60
Jibaros, 6, 37, 73, 75, 130, 224

Jiménez, José "Cha-Cha," 196, 197,
    199
Job Corps, 160
JOBS, 160
Johnson, Bruce, 120, 121
Jones Act, 30–31
José de Diego Academy, 93
Joyce Foundation, 192

Keane, Alderman, 199
Kemp, Kathleen A., 195, 196
Kihss, Peter, 115
King, Sam S., 60
Kitagawa, Evelyn M., 85
Kusper, Stanley, 198

Labor, 102, 114–116, 141, 205–207
Labor force, lack of opportunities in,
    10–12, 19, 104, 116
Labor market, 101–104, 115–116
La Casa del El Puertorriqueño, 141
La Gaseta, 137, 140
Lakeview, 79, 88, 118, 123, 191,
    196
La Nueva Cancíon, 234
La Parada Puertorriqueña, 132
La pieza de los pobres, 27
La Prensa, 91
LaSalle Street, 84
Latin American Boys' Club, 155,
    177
Latin American Defense Organiza-
    tion, 173
Latin American Recruitment Educa-
    tion System (LARES), 187
Latin American Student Organization
    (LASO), 187
Latin Boys' Club, 173
Latino Awakening, 1, 155
Latino/black coalition, 230, 231
Latino ethnic solidarity, 204–208
Lavoe, Hector, 234
Leadership, Puerto Rican, 225; in
    politics, 200–204

Leavitt Street, 90
Levitan, Sar A., 159
Lewis, Gordon, 24, 31, 34, 35, 37,
    38, 44, 54
Liebow, Elliott, 72
Lincoln Park, 79, 118–122, 132
Lincoln Park Conservation Associa-
    tion (LPCA), 119
Lincoln Park Conservation Commu-
    nity Council (LPCCC), 122–123
Lineberry, Robert L., 195–196
Litt, Edgar, 202
Logan Square, 88, 123, 191
Lojkine, James, 11
London, Bruce, 216
Long, Larry, H., 216
Loop, Chicago, 108, 109, 119, 216
Lopata, Helena Z., 75
López, Adalberto, 23, 24, 28, 29,
    38
López, Obed, 172
Los Caballeros de San Juan, 21,
    126–136, 138–139, 143–144,
    154–157, 165–166, 191, 213
Loyola University, 181, 187
Lucas, Isidro, 210
Lugo-Silva, Enrique, 45

McCormick Theological Seminary,
    119
Machine politics, 194–200, 201, 203
Mahon, Father Leo T., 128, 130,
    138
Maldonado-Denis, Manuel, 29, 30,
    42, 66
Mann, Seymour Z., 160
Manpower Development and Train-
    ing Act (MDTA), 160
Marín, Luis Munoz, 44
Masotti, Louis H., 153, 194
Massacre of Ponce, 43
Mayordomo, 26
Memmi, Albert, 62, 151
Merchant class, 26
Merrill, Francis E., 25

Mexicans, 16, 58, 59, 82, 84, 205,
    232; in Latino solidarity,
    204–208; as voters, 200
Mi gente, 96
Middle class, Puerto Rican, 11, 12,
    22
Migrant press, 137–143
Migration: to Chicago, 56, 78–83;
    external to U.S., 40–41, 53–55,
    57; internal, 39–40; López and
    Petras thesis, 23; mass, 52; return
    ideology, 66–70; temporary
    aspect, 66–67
Mintz, Sidney, 25, 26, 27, 37
Miranda, Ismael, 14, 234
Mogey, John M., 95
Mogulof, Melvin, 159
Mollenkopf, John, 102, 106, 107
Monopoly capitalism, 101–103
Morley, Morriz, 35
Moynihan, Daniel P., 161, 224
Mumford, Lewis, 100

National bourgeoisie, 41, 44
National Labor Journal, 115
National Liberation and Culture, 7
Nationalist Movement, 54
Nationalist Party, 43–44
Near North Side, 79, 84, 120
Near West Side, 74, 83, 84, 132
*Negro Family: The Case for Na-
    tional Action*, 161
Neighborhood Health Center, 161
Neighborhood Youth Corps (NYC),
    160
Nelli, Humbert S., 104
New Deal, 41
Newsweek magazine, 215
New York, migration to, 54
New York Times, 115
Noboa, Julio, 189
Nolan, Janet, 147, 148
Northeastern Illinois University, 181,
    184–187
Northern Illinois University, 188

Northwest Spanish Community Committee, 173
Nye School, 212

Ochoa, Zeferino, 213
Office of Economic Opportunity, 159
Office of the Commonwealth of Puerto Rico, 79, 126
Oliva, Sergio, 91
Olivieri, Edwin, 173
Operation Bootstrap, 46
Operation Wetback, 205
Organization for Latin Americans, 173
Organization for Latin American Students (OLAS), 187
Organizations, Puerto Rican: community, 71–72, 125–137, 143; ethnic, 71–72; political, 71–72

Padilla, Elena, 58, 62, 79, 110
Padilla, Felix, 3, 205
Paleros, 26
Park, Robert, 2, 88, 97
Pedreira, Antonio, 43
People's Gas, 192
Perales, Alfredo, 173
Peterson, Paul E., 158, 159
Petras, 23, 29
Pietrantonio, Thomas, 115
Pitts, James, 110
"Plástico," 235
Police Department, Chicago, 171–179
Police: injustices, 117, 123–125, 145–147; harassment, 168, 171–179; surveillance, 168, 171–179
Political Organization of Chicago's Latino Communities, 191
Political repression, 168–179
Politics, in Chicago, 194–208
Politicized ethnic consciousness, 155–179

Populares, 44–46, 52
Population: in Chicago, 56–58, 78–91, 106, 108, 109; in Puerto Rico, 32, 38–41, 52–54; in New York, 41
Pottinger, Stanley J., 188
"Predators Dash," 94
Presa Libre, 137
Press, migrant, 137–143
Preston, Michael B., 195
Project Success, 186
Prontuario Historico de Puerto Rico, 43
"Prosigue," 236
Protective tariff system, 34
Protest, 168; repression of, 168–169
Proyecto Pa'Lante, 187
Puerto Rican Congress, 126
"Puerto Rican curriculum," 184–189
Puerto Rican Department of Labor, 53
Puerto Rican independence movement, 20
Puerto Rican Reconstruction Administration (PRRA), 41
Puerto Rican Riot of 1966 (Division Street Riot), 144–155, 165
Puerto Rican Studies Movement, 15

Quadagno, Jill S., 75
Quie Amendment, 159
Quintero-Rivera, Angel G., 26, 27, 33, 45

Racial discrimination: housing, 117–123; jobs, 102–104
Racial minority stereotyping, 56–72
Racism, 15, 16, 58, 59, 60–65, 86– 87, 96–97, 102–103, 116, 232
Ramírez, Myrta, 175, 177
Ramírez, Ted, 175, 177
Red Squad, 175
Reich, Michael, 102, 103

Religious groups, 135
Repression, anger at, 116, 151–153, 155
Return emigration, 67–68
Return ideology, 66–70
Reynolds, Lloyd G., 46, 47, 49
Richardson, Elliot, 188
Riggs, Colonel Francis, 43
Rivera, Jaime, 63
Roberts, John S., 233
Roberto Clemente High School, 93, 219
Rodríguez, Clara, 19, 86
Rodríguez, Emma, 210, 211
Rodríguez, William, 134, 135
Ross, David F., 46

Salces, Luis M., 78, 191, 196, 197, 199
Salsa, 233–239
Sánchez-Korrol, Virginia, 40, 41, 112
Saturday Evening Post, 61
Senate Banking and Currency Committee, 118
Senate Committee on Territories and Insular Affairs, 43
"Siembra," 235
Smelser, Neil J., 146, 152
Social service agencies, 190–192, 203
Solidarity, Puerto Rican, 12, 95–98; and community organizations, 143; and Division Street Riot, 151; and El Día de San Juan, 132; and neighborhood, 95–96; university student groups, 185–189
"Spanglish," 94, 232
Spanish Action Committee of Chicago (SACC), 118, 165–168, 173–179
Spanish American War, 5, 29
Spanish Coalition for Jobs, 207
Spanish-speaking Peoples Study Commission, 213

Spear, Allan H., 100
Special Arson Task Force, 219
Split labor market theory, 9
State Street, 84, 108
Stereotypes, 58–65
Strategies for Overcoming Inequality, 194–208
Sugar industry: under Spain, 25–28; under U.S., 33–38, 42, 46
Suttles, Gerald D., 74, 117

Taeuber, Alma F., 82–83
Taeuber, Karl E., 82–83
Teachers Corps, 160
Time magazine, 1
Title I, Aid to Education Act, 160
Title II, Economic Opportunity Act of 1964, 158
Title VII, Elementary and Secondary Education Act, 212
Tobacco, 28
Torres, Max, 185, 186
Torres de Jesús, Alfredo, 140, 178
Transitional Teacher Program (TIP), 214
Tugwell, Governor Rexford B., 44
"Tuley Products," 210–211
Tydings Bill, 43–44
Tydings, Senator Millar E., 43

Underclass, Puerto Rican, 11, 21; in politics, 201, 202
Underemployment, 51, 52
Unemployment, 49–52
Union for Puerto Rican Students, 185–189
United Consolidated Independent School District, 212
United Methodist Church, 192
Universities: Chicago area universities, 181–190; student organizations, 185–189
University of Illinois-Chicago Circle, 181, 187

University of Illinois-Urbana-Champaign, 187
Urban America and Urban Coalition, 162
Urban Institution for Community Organization, 164
Urban Progress Center, 166
U.S. Commission on Civil Rights, 210
U.S. Department of Houing and Urban Development, 122
U.S. News and World Report, 1, 115

Valentine, Charles, 161
Valez, Pedro, 64
Van y ven, 69, 70
Velázquez, Miguel A., 196, 197, 199, 200
Vélez, Ted, 174
Vice President's Task Force on Youth Opportunity, 145
Von Hoffman, Nicholas, 130
Von Humboldt School, 167
Voting Wards: 16th, 196–199; 31st, 196–199; 46th, 196–199

Walton John, 78, 191
Ward, David, 82
Warner, William L., 59
War on Poverty, 19, 157, 160–162
Washington, Harold, 133, 229
Watson, J., 199
Weidrich, Bob, 177, 178
Wells Street, 84
West Side Organization (WSO), 85

Westtown, 88, 90, 118, 145, 191, 196
Westtown Concerned Citizens Coalition, 220
Wheeler, C. N., 199
Wicker Park, 215–216
Wieboldt's Foundation, 192
Wilensky, Harold L., 191
Williams, Robin, 154
Wilmott, Peter, 95
Wilson, James Q., 104, 105, 116
Wilson, Orlando, W., 149
Wilson, William, 9, 10
Wolfinger, Raymond E., 201
Women, Puerto Rican: in Chicago labor force, 112, 114; emigrants, 76, 77; in hacienda labor force, 26; in industrial labor force, 49, 112–114; and religion, 135
Woodlawn, 79, 80, 83–86, 117
Woodlawn Organization, 85
Work Incentive Programs (WIP), 160
Working class, Puerto Rican, 110–116; in politics, 201–202

Young, Michael, 95
Young Communist League of California, 178
Young Lords, 120–123, 157, 173
"Yuppies," 216

Zenith Radio Corporation, 141
Zimmerman Report, 39
Zorbaugh, Harvey W., 84
Zorno, James, 173